# PIANO ZEN

## Where Reality and Dreams Converge

THOMAS RHEINGANS

For more information, contact: thomas@pianozen.com.
ISBN Paperback: 979-8-9918756-0-8
ISBN Electronic: 979-8-9918756-1-5

Library of Congress Control Number: 2024923772



Printed in the United States of America.

Thomas Rheingans
PianoZen.com

# Contents

# Earth

Greetings to you, dwellers of the physical universe. My name is Nasim. There is a story I must share, one that begins with William Longfellow Emerson… when he was still a boy.

I encountered William when he wandered into our world, deep in the Whispering Woods of the Tall Pines. Alongside my companions, I journeyed with him through many dream realms—those strange, luminous places you too sometimes visit while asleep, only to forget upon waking… though some memories persist.

Henry David Thoreau, one of your own, once wrote: "Our truest life is when we are in our dreams awake."

And, my dear humans, few words have ever rung more true—in your world and mine.

You must understand, I do not usually speak through the written word. Such things lie beyond the ways of Wind Spirits. But this story… well, its truth must reach more of your kind. And so, I crossed into your realm of words, entrusting the author to shape what I could only whisper—stories he heard while wandering the dreamlands.

As for what lies beyond this telling, some journeys reveal themselves only when we are ready, for certain dreams wait patiently beyond the reach of time.

But for now, I invite you to listen. To truly listen. For music is more than sound… It is a bridge between worlds. And if you listen closely, perhaps you too will hear the wind… calling you to remember.

Musica Universalis
~ Nasim

# Chapter One

## *The Wildwood Trail*

The wooden door creaked behind them as Miss Rosa and William stepped onto the porch of the Gate Lodge, high above the city of Nightingale. Just up the drive, behind the black iron gates marked with an ornate gold P, the Prescott Mansion stood in its usual quiet grandeur, its red tile roof catching the morning light.

William had come here for piano lessons every week for the past year. But today felt different. Rosa had never invited him to do anything outside the familiar rhythm of their lessons. Now, here they were, preparing to venture deep into Prescott Forest on some mysterious pilgrimage.

He followed her down the steps, adjusting his backpack. His fingers brushed against the outline of his father's Master Samaritan Ring, which hung on a chain underneath his shirt.

Just beyond the lodge's stone path, Miss Rosa pushed aside a section of tangled laurel branches, revealing a small, black, iron gate hidden beneath the overgrowth. William's face lit up. A secret path. He and his mother, Aimée, had driven past this stretch of laurel hedge countless times on the way to his lessons, but he had never noticed anything unusual.

"Very few people know about the Wildwood Trail," Miss Rosa said. "It's one of the best-kept secrets of Prescott Forest." She pushed open the gate and motioned for him to follow.

As the iron gate clicked shut behind them, a birdcall rang out somewhere in the distance—sharp, clear, almost melodic. A tingling sensation ran through him as he followed her down the narrow, winding path of this secret trail.

The air smelled rich with pine and damp earth. Beneath his feet, the path was soft with fallen needles. Now and then, the faint sound of a trickling stream reached his ears, blending with the rustle of the trees. William thought about how much had changed since he first met Miss Rosa a year ago. He had just turned eleven, but he could still remember that first lesson as though it had happened yesterday. Her full name was Rosa María Garcia Carreño, but everyone simply called her Miss Rosa. Even now, as he followed her down the trail, he marveled at how different she was from other teachers. Once, in the sheet music room of Shelley's bookstore, William had overheard a pair of piano teachers muttering about Rosa's methods, smirking as they made little finger quotes around the words "Piano Zen." Indeed, the way she always rang a Tibetan bowl at the start of his lessons took some getting used to.

William had been drawn to the piano for as long as he could remember. There was something mysterious and irresistible about the instrument—the way it sounded, its shape, its history, and the music that seemed to live inside it. He often found himself thinking about Bartolomeo Cristofori di Francesco, trying to imagine how anyone could dream up an instrument like the piano in the first place.

He remembered when his mother had first mentioned lessons. They were barely getting by—she was always juggling jobs, always tired—and piano lessons felt like something they simply couldn't afford. Still, she always reassured him.

Once, brushing a lock of hair from his forehead, she'd said, "Music isn't just notes on a page, *mon chéri*. It's the language of the heart." She had paused, gazing out the kitchen window before adding softly, "Your father used to say that music is like the wind—you can't see it, but you can feel it, and it changes everything it touches."

Miss Rosa paused to breathe in the delicate fragrance of a blossoming Persian silk tree along the trail. William slowed beside her, taking in the hush of the forest, the filtered light... and the stillness.

Rosa's voice drew him back. "I never shared this with you, but Eleanor Prescott once took me on a tour of the mansion when I was a little girl."

"You've been inside?" William's eyes widened in surprise.

"Yes, but that was many years ago," Rosa said. "It was abandoned for a long time, but the McFarland Sisters Restoration Company is almost done with its renovations. Soon, the mansion will return to its former grandeur." She grinned. "Who knows, maybe when it opens as a museum, you'll get a chance to step inside. Maybe even play Madeleine Monnier's concert grand piano."

William's heart skipped a beat at the thought of playing Monnier's piano. He had spent hours at Shelley's bookstore, poring over books and articles about the estate of Randolf Cornelius Prescott. The sight of the mansion behind its black gates, week after week, had only deepened his enchantment—most of all with Prescott's wife, the world-renowned concert pianist Madeleine Monnier.

Something about her life haunted him—a mystery that refused to let go.

# Chapter Two

## *The Little Prince*

William's first piano teacher was Cecil Winwood, a man with an impeccable piano pedigree and a formidable reputation in the Nightingale music circles. He came from the old European tradition of strict, structured instruction—unyielding in its discipline and exacting in its standards.

His students regularly won local competitions and went on to music conservatories, but such results came at a price. His lessons demanded excellence, his expectations never wavered. Like his teachers before him, Winwood had no patience for students who lacked discipline or failed to progress quickly.

It was this reputation that had convinced Giselle, William's grandmother, to urge his mother to call Winwood. In her view, there was no substitute for rigorous discipline and elite instruction. He represented precisely the kind of influence she believed her grandson needed—something to temper the dreamy tendencies she had always associated with Phillip's free-spirited ways.

Giselle had never approved of Aimée's choice to marry Phillip Emerson, a man she saw as lacking ambition—content with a blue-collar lifestyle and rustic adventures that, in her mind, fell far short of her family's pedigree. William, with his wandering imagination and frequent daydreams, reminded her far too much of his father. Enrolling him with Winwood, she believed, was an act of course correction.

"*Je ne sais pas…*" his mother had said at the time, her hesitation to call Winwood revealing the deep rift between herself and her mother. For as long as Aimée could remember, Giselle had pulled the strings—dictating choices that often felt more like decrees. Even her youth had been shaped by her mother's will, split between summer holidays with her grandmother in the French town of Sarlat-la-Canéda and time at an exclusive boarding school in Nightingale, paid for by a biological father she barely knew. Distance hadn't been enough to sever the influence; Giselle's expectations reached all the way from Paris, like invisible threads tugging her back into line.

Despite her doubts, she conceded and reached out to Winwood.

His response was cool at first—he didn't seem eager to take on a new student, especially one just starting out. Though she kept her tone polite, a strain crept into her voice as she tried to convince him. She spoke of William's love for piano music, especially the works of Maurice Ravel, and his eagerness to learn how to play.

"It's wonderful that he loves the piano," Winwood said, his tone still measured. "But loving music and dedicating yourself to mastering it are entirely different things. And, frankly, I seldom accept beginners into my studio."

Aimée hesitated, then reluctantly dropped the name into the conversation. "Giselle Dubois is my mother. She suggested I call you."

There was a pause. "Ah, so this is Giselle's grandson, William? You must be Aimée Dubois, her daughter."

"That's my maiden name. I go by Aimée Emerson now."

"I see. How old is your boy again?"

"He's eleven."

"Hmm… loves Ravel, does he?" A soft chuckle. "Well, he has impeccable taste for someone so young. I don't usually take beginners, Madame Emerson, but let's see how things go. I'll accept him—but only on a trial basis."

William had been both excited and nervous about studying with such a famous pianist. When the first lesson finally came, Aimée watched her son walk into Winwood's studio with a flicker of hope—hope that would soon be tested.

After a few months, Winwood's composure had begun to fray, and things were starting to unravel. William's mind tended to wander, drifting into daydreams during his piano lessons—a tendency that pressed Winwood's patience.

It wasn't intentional, of course. It happened all the time when he read his favorite fantasy books too. His daydreaming would take unexpected detours, and sometimes he would close his eyes mid-story, letting his imagination spin out new adventures—bringing characters and places to life in ways the author had never written.

One evening, William found himself waiting a very long time for his piano lesson. He sat in the studio's reception area, his fingers drumming lightly on the arm of the chair. Winwood was running overtime again with Simon Penrose's lesson. Simon, a year older than William, was one of Winwood's star students—a technical prodigy with a disciplined work ethic.

While he waited, William's eyes wandered to the wide bookcases tucked against the wall. Books always called to him—gateways into other worlds. He felt an urge to browse, his fingers brushing along the spines of neatly shelved volumes. He thought of the ones he loved most—*The Lord of the Rings, The Golden Compass, Dune, Artemis Fowl,* and *Harry Potter.*

Winwood's study, with its rows of books, reminded him of his favorite place—M.W. Shelley's bookstore. On Saturday mornings, his mother would drop him off there, and he would spend hours exploring. Shelley's was the largest privately owned bookstore in the country, nicknamed the Metropolis of Manuscripts. Its maze-like aisles stretched across multiple floors, each section like its own literary kingdom. It was his sanctuary—a world of wonder, where the staff knew him by name. As he wandered through the aisles, familiar voices greeted him.

Tucked away in a remote corner of the store was The Modern Prometheus Room, a secluded wing dedicated to rare books. The main chamber looked as if it had been plucked from a Dickens novel. Rich, carved wood paneling lined the walls, and an old fireplace flickered with warm, golden light. Above, a narrow mezzanine held marble busts of famous authors, their stern gazes surveying the room from lofty pedestals. The stained-glass ceiling, an elaborate floral mosaic, bathed the space in shifting patterns of color. Compared to the bustling aisles of the main bookstore, the rare book room felt like stepping into an ancient forest, each book etched with stories of people and places from another era.

William loved the rare book room: the hushed reverence, the scent of aged paper, the soft hum of history surrounding him. Ordinarily, children weren't permitted inside without adult supervision, but the staff always made an exception for William, letting him slip in through the private employee door.

At its center, beneath the soft overhead lighting, a protective glass case housed the most prized volume in Shelley's collection—a chronicle of American exploration. The book rested atop a velvet-lined pedestal, its worn leather cover bearing only a modest inscription. But inside, on the title page, its full name stretched across the paper in elaborate, 19th-century lettering:

*History of the Expedition Under the Command of Captains Lewis & Clark to the Sources of the Missouri Thence Across the Rocky Mountains & Down the River Columbia to the Pacific Ocean. Performed During the Years 1804-5-6. By the Order of the Government of the United States. Prepared for the Press by Paul Allen, Esquire. Philadelphia: 1814.*

The book had been assembled by Nicholas Biddle, who had transformed the original journal entries of Lewis and Clark into a polished narrative. Few had ever been allowed to handle it. In Nightingale, it was the stuff of legend—rumors persisted that Presidents Thomas Jefferson and James Madison had once turned its pages.

Nestled in an alcove of the rare book room was William's favorite reading chair, where he could lose himself for hours. One afternoon, while exploring the dusty back shelves, he'd discovered a first-edition copy of *The Little Prince*. Inside was a delicate ink drawing and the author's looping signature. Like all the books in the room, it wasn't for sale—but Shelley's allowed trusted patrons to borrow them, as long as they were carefully returned.

On that same day, as William was leaving, he noticed a red-haired girl about his age sitting cross-legged on the floor near the architecture shelves. Her stack of books was nothing like his—thick volumes on bridges and buildings—yet she spoke with an easy confidence that drew him in.

One of the books she carried had the Prescott mansion on its cover, and she traced the lines of its towers with her finger as if committing them to memory. She told him she wasn't from Nightingale, but she knew about the mansion and loved its design.

Her gaze drifted to the book in his hands—*The Little Prince*.

"So," she said, raising one eyebrow, her emerald-green eyes bright with curiosity, "those are the kind of books you like, huh?"

William shrugged. "I guess so."

"What's your name?" she asked.

"Will, what's yours?"

"Ariya. But it's not spelled like the music."

"Oh," he said. "How do you spell it?"

Instead of answering, she reached into her backpack and pulled out a square of blue paper. "Don't look," she said with a grin, already folding. William turned away, unsure what she was up to.

When she told him he could turn back, she held out a small origami swan, its wings neatly creased, and placed it in his hand. In tiny print, she had written her name along one wing.

She slung her backpack over her shoulder. "Nice meeting you, Will. Enjoy *The Little Prince*."

It would be many years before he saw her again, but the memory of the girl—and the blue swan—stayed with him.

# Chapter Three

## *The Photograph*

Winwood's study could not have been more different. There were no fantasy books, no adventure stories—only rows of serious-looking volumes.

Then one spine labeled *Rodin* caught his eye.

Its cover bore a familiar image—*The Thinker*. The figure crouched in its eternal meditation. William's heart gave a small leap; he had seen the sculpture once in Paris, when his mother took him there for a family reunion.

He couldn't resist. He slipped the book from the shelf and opened it. Rodin's sculptures appeared one after another—bronzes, marbles, unfinished studies. He lingered over each, fascinated by the way the figures seemed to strain and twist, half-emerging from the stone. The book felt heavy, serious. Page after page paired Rodin's work with that of his many male students.

While Simon Penrose's piano lesson stretched on, faint scales and arpeggios drifting from the adjoining studio, William sank deeper into the book, letting the images pull him further into Rodin's world.

Then he stopped. A photograph of a young woman filled the page. It stood out—until now, every sculptor in the book had been a man. She stared directly into the camera, her hair slightly disheveled, loosely bound with a ribbon, as if she had been interrupted mid-task.

Her name was Camille Claudel, and she had been nineteen when the photo was taken, around the time she began working with the much older and more celebrated Auguste Rodin. Something about her expression held

William—a mix of confidence and melancholy. The book described her as a gifted artist, a budding genius well ahead of her time, whose brilliance unsettled many of her male contemporaries.

The book featured images of her sculptures—*Les Valseurs, Persée et la Gorgone, L'Âge mûr, L'Abandon,* and *La sirène ou La joueuse de flûte*—each one alive with movement and emotion. He lingered over them, surprised, feeling more drawn to her work than to Rodin's.

As William turned another page, he stopped cold. A black-and-white photograph filled the spread—a massive copper statue under construction. Workers swarmed the scaffolding, cranes towering above them as they pieced together the impressive fifty-five-foot figure.

He recognized it instantly.

The *Lady of Light.* The much-beloved sculpture that graced the heart of Nightingale, near the banks of the Makah River, admired by thousands each year. He had never seen it like this before—a giant in pieces, its copper panels being carefully fitted into place amid towering cranes and bustling workers in 1922.

Another photograph captured the statue fully assembled, towering over a gathered crowd at its 1923 dedication. In the foreground, R.C. Prescott stood beside his daughter, Eleanor.

Beneath the image, the caption read:
*The Lady of Light, Nightingale, USA.*
*Sculpted by Camille Claudel, 1923.*

William blinked, his pulse quickening. *Camille Claudel sculpted the Lady of Light?*

He had admired the statue his entire life, yet somehow never known the name of the sculptor. Perhaps that was why Claudel's portrait had seemed so familiar—maybe he'd seen her name before, tucked away in some forgotten memory. Or maybe it was something more.

The *Lady of Light* wasn't merely a monument but a presence—stepping forward, emerging into a world of darkness. Unlike the Statue of Liberty's neoclassical grandeur, with its rigid drapery and unyielding stance, the *Lady of Light* felt almost alive—unfinished. Her lamp cast just enough glow to bring her partially into existence. Her expression wasn't one of defiant strength but of compassion. She didn't raise a torch for all to see but illuminated the path ahead—offering light to those in need, and guiding them forward, back into the light.

To some, she was simply "the lady with the lamp," but her true name—the name given by her Claudel—was *La Dame de la Lumière*.

He turned one last page of the book and found a black-and-white photograph taken from the wings of a small concert hall. At a sleek grand piano sat a woman with a calm, focused expression, her hands poised gently on the keys. Leaning casually within the curve of the instrument was Camille Claudel, facing the camera with serene composure, her hands resting lightly on the piano's polished edge.

The caption read:
*Madeleine Monnier at her Érard concert grand, Salle Érard Concert Hall, Paris, 1904. Sculptor and close friend Camille Claudel pictured at right.*

William studied the photograph, drawn to the woman at the piano. Something in her presence—the elegant dress, the slope of her shoulders, her serene expression—held him. And then he noticed the instrument itself: her grand piano, gleaming in the stage light.

Here was where it began, part of a thread that would pull him back to Madeleine Monnier again and again.

# Chapter Four

## *Transitions*

From the outset, Winwood proved ill-suited to teaching a beginner like William. His method was pure mechanics—Herz finger independence drills, Hanon exercises for speed and precision, Czerny etudes for pattern recognition. There were no beautiful melodies to explore, no room for improvisation, no invitation to discover the joy of music.

It wasn't that William didn't try. He practiced at home, dutifully repeating the exercises. But his fingers stumbled over the keys, never quite landing where they were supposed to. Adding to the difficulty, William's lesson always followed that of Simon Penrose, Winwood's prized protégé. Simon was everything Winwood admired—technically precise, disciplined, methodical. William would listen from the waiting room as Simon's flawless scales floated through the door.

He tried to mask his struggles, not wanting to disappoint his mother or grandmother. But the signs were undeniable: the reluctant practice, the lifeless tinkering at the piano, the stomach pains on lesson days. His mother soon caught on, noticing he only seemed to play mechanical drills—never a song with any real expression. Though he tried to hide his unhappiness, she could sense the discouragement in his eyes. Yet she hesitated to interfere, trusting that this highly regarded instructor knew what he was doing. But with each passing week, it became harder for her to ignore. The piano, once magical to William, had become a series of lifeless drills—each repetition draining a little more of his enthusiasm.

Winwood, a man of exacting standards, had little patience for students who fell short, and after several months, it was clear to everyone that the arrangement wasn't working. At the final lesson, he didn't mince words: "I don't think playing the piano is your thing, son. You should find something else that suits you better."

His mother was appalled by Winwood's callous dismissal. His rigid methods had nearly extinguished her son's love for music, and in that moment, she regretted ever deferring to her mother's judgment. She muttered under her breath, "*À quoi je pensais? Comment pourrais-je être aussi stupide?*"

At the door, Winwood hesitated. His gaze moved from his mother's tightened grip on William's shoulder to the boy's downcast expression, tears slipping softly down his cheeks. Something in his manner shifted. "You know," he said at last, his tone warmer, more measured, "my studio is pretty intense. But if he truly loves the piano… maybe you should see if Rosa Carreño is still teaching. She used to run a Piano Zen studio up in Imperial Heights."

The suggestion caught his mother off guard. The words blurred past, but something in Winwood's voice made her pause. She turned, her tone clipped but deliberate. "Could you spell her last name? *S'il vous plaît?*"

He stuttered as he spelled out "Carreño." His mother jotted it down quickly, determined not to let the lead slip away, then tucked the note into her purse.

Outside the studio, a breeze caught William's hair, brushing his cheeks. For a moment, something unseen seemed to shift—gently but decisively—nudging him toward a different future.

# Chapter Five

## *The Ancient Mystic Order of Samaritans*

Cecil Winwood was startled by how easily, how unexpectedly, the words "Piano Zen" had slipped from his lips. Speaking them without a trace of sarcasm felt strange. Yet here he was, recommending Rosa Carreño as if she were a colleague… even an old friend.

In his younger years, he had delighted in mocking her eccentric teaching methods. Rumors swirled about her use of a Tibetan singing bowl and the so-called "Zen mumbo-jumbo" she spouted to students. With smug amusement, he had once dubbed her The Guru of Imperial Heights. For any serious piano teacher, recommending Carreño was practically an admission that the student was a lost cause—someone who lacked the discipline or promise to merit real instruction.

To Winwood, her unorthodox methods explained everything—why her students lacked rigor, why they failed to thrive. Unlike his own protégés, who sharpened their skills like weapons and fed off the ruthless energy of the contest stage, Carreño's students lived in a dream world of improvisation and self-expression. Winwood dismissed them outright. They simply couldn't cut the mustard, he would boast, waving off any suggestion that her approach had merit.

And yet, decades ago, he had secretly gone to hear Rosa Carreño play for the first time, unable to resist a strange curiosity about her—just as he was beginning to savor his first real taste of success.

At the time, he had just claimed a hard-won victory at a major international piano competition in New Jersey—a triumph that came only after years of bitter disappointment. Winwood had finally secured first prize, thanks largely to his dazzling performance of Ravel's *"Gaspard de la nuit,"* a three-movement suite notorious for its difficulty. His near-flawless rendering of *"Scarbo"*—the demonic final movement—left the judges in awe. Critics raved about his precision and technical command, though they had little to say about the rest of his program.

His triumph on the international stage had brought him a flood of acclaim, particularly in his hometown, where he was celebrated as the Golden Boy of Nightingale—the most successful student Leopold Steinberg had ever produced. Winwood returned to Nightingale at the end of his international concert tour, set to perform the Khachaturian Piano Concerto with the Nightingale Symphony. Posters, interviews, and advertisements announced his arrival, and he relished the city's admiration. The *Nightingale Observer* even ran a front-page feature on his illustrious career, hailing the dashing young virtuoso as a "technical terror" at the piano.

Yet despite the citywide buzz surrounding his upcoming performance, a small, almost inconsequential notice in the *Nightingale Observer* caught his eye: a piano recital scheduled for the evening before his own concert, taking place at the Samaritan Temple in the Old Town District of Nightingale.

The temple itself had always been an object of fascination—its massive Parthenon-inspired portico and luminous tower, crowned with a golden ziggurat pyramid, dominated the skyline like a watchful sentinel. Winwood, however, had never set foot inside. The Samaritans' secretive rituals and lofty spiritual talk struck him as little more than theater.

Winwood scoffed as he skimmed the notice in the paper, dismissing the concert as amateur at best—and yet something about it unsettled him. The Samaritans were an all-male society, notoriously exclusive. And yet Rosa Carreño—a woman—had been invited to perform in their Memorial Hall. A gesture not bestowed on him, despite his status as the city's most celebrated virtuoso.

Whether or not it was intentional, the slight hit its mark. Resentment and curiosity tangled inside him until one overpowered the other. He would hear her play.

At the time, Winwood knew of Rosa only through his mentor, Leopold Steinberg. He'd heard she was a gifted pupil of Eleanor Prescott and had spent much of her early childhood in an orphanage in La Dama De La Luz, the Nightingale district where many Mexican families lived. Steinberg had never regarded Eleanor as a serious piano instructor but respected her devotion to sharing music with orphaned children like Rosa.

On the night of the recital, Winwood arrived early and purchased his ticket in secret. He lingered near the entrance, waiting until most of the audience had filed in before slipping inside unnoticed. As the hall darkened and the murmurs of the crowd faded to silence, he found his seat near the back—hidden, but with an unobstructed view of the stage.

The auditorium was modestly appointed, its rows of crimson velvet seats stretching toward the shiny oak stage. But it was the piano that caught his eye—a Bösendorfer Imperial Grand, its burr walnut case lit warmly under the lights like dark honey. His eyebrows lifted almost imperceptibly. A rare choice. Most concert halls in the region favored Steinways for their brightness and projection, but the Bösendorfer had a different voice—darker, richer, capable of deeper resonances. Its extra bass keys—a curiosity even among professional pianists—hinted at indulgence, as if the instrument itself invited exploration beyond standard repertoire.

What on earth was it doing here? Winwood's jaw tightened. How had she secured a piano of that caliber? He scanned the room, almost expecting R.C. Prescott himself to be lurking in the shadows. The very idea that Rosa Carreño would have access to something so exquisite gnawed at him. It was an instrument for the finest stages in Europe—not for this hidden enclave, and certainly not for her.

A ripple of applause broke his train of thought as Rosa Carreño stepped onto the stage in an off-the-shoulder dress embroidered with intricate Mexican patterns, the vibrant flowers seeming to bloom under the lights. A simple pendant rested at her collarbone, though from Winwood's seat, its details were indistinct. Her long, dark hair was clipped back, cascading down her back like a loose ribbon.

The audience greeted her with warm, familiar applause. Winwood bristled. The bold embroidery, her easy poise—it all struck him as too casual, too familiar, for a concert stage. As Rosa acknowledged the crowd, her warmth seemed to draw the entire room closer, transforming the recital into something intimate, communal.

To him, it looked more like a salon gathering than a serious performance—a scene better suited to a cocktail lounge than a hall with a Bösendorfer Imperial Grand at its center.

As Rosa settled at the piano, her fingers poised over the keys, a hush fell over the room. With the first notes of Claude Debussy's *"Arabesque No. 1,"* she wove an intricate tapestry of sound, as rich and expressive as the embroidery on her dress. In the professional circles Winwood frequented, such a piece was dismissed as pedestrian—a work reserved for intermediate students rather than accomplished performers. To him, the *Arabesque* had no place on the grand concert stage, where brilliance was measured in velocity, precision, and complexity.

Yet, in Rosa's hands, the piece awakened—reborn with unexpected depth. Her execution was flawless, not only in technical precision but in the way she infused each note with musical nuance. The audience leaned in, visibly moved by the delicacy and musicality of her playing.

Winwood, meanwhile, clung to his skepticism. Despite the obvious connection Rosa forged with her listeners, he dismissed her repertoire as unambitious. But beneath his composed exterior, an unease stirred. Her ability to draw such raw emotion from so little unsettled him, shaking the very foundation of what he believed made a musician truly great.

Rosa followed with Chopin's *"Ballade in F minor, Op. 52"*—a tour de force that swept up the audience in a whirlwind of emotion. Like a magician, she conjured sounds from the Bösendorfer that ranged from the most delicate whispers to a resonant, earth-shaking force—an entire spectrum of musical color and expression brought to life by felt hammers striking tightly strung metal wires.

Winwood squirmed inwardly. The *Ballade* wasn't merely a technical feat, it was a deeply expressive work. Rosa played it with an unrestrained emotion, every phrase felt alive. He couldn't deny the mastery in her playing, though he resisted admitting it to himself.

For her final selection, she turned to Maurice Ravel's *"Miroirs: Noctuelles"* (Night Moths), *"Oiseaux tristes"* (Sad Birds), *"Une barque sur l'océan"* (A Boat on the Ocean), and *"La vallée des cloches"* (The Valley of Bells). Her touch in the Ravel was so exquisite, so delicate, it defied description.

Though Winwood fancied himself a Ravel specialist, he knew he could never replicate the depth of color she evoked. Her control, her pedaling, the resonance of the Bösendorfer—together, they wove pure magic.

The opening measures of *"Noctuelles"* were like fluttering wings in the dark—restless, elusive. Rosa's touch was gossamer yet taut, every note part of a dance between beauty and chaos. After the first few passages filled the air,

Winwood's eyes drifted shut. The world around him dissolved as the music drew him into a dreamlike state. It seemed to bypass his intellect entirely, sinking into some unguarded corner of his being.

At first—darkness. Then, in the distance, a pinprick of light. He hovered near it, drawn forward, a desire to see. But a wave of unease overtook him, and he fell back into the dark. The light vanished.

The moment dissolved into the delicate strains of *"Oiseaux tristes."* He found himself transported high into the treetops, where the sorrowful calls of birds echoed through a shadowy forest, their songs weaving through the dense canopy above and around his heart.

Then came *"Une barque sur l'océan."* Winwood's senses were swept onto the deck of a tiny boat, adrift on a vast, endless ocean. Here, he felt his existence diminish to a mere particle amidst the immense sea, a profound solitude enveloping him from unfathomable depths.

As *"La vallée des cloches"* began, his consciousness soared over a verdant valley, where a chorus of church bells floated across hills and meadows. The air was fragrant with apple blossoms, the valley below carpeted in a blanket of white petals.

In this final vision, Winwood felt himself dissolve—no longer a man but a spirit, drifting among the resonating bells.

When Rosa's final notes faded, the hall fell into an almost transcendental silence, as if the entire audience held its breath in reverence, unwilling to break the spell cast by the music.

Then—thunderous applause.

The sound jolted Winwood from his reverie. The abrupt return to reality left him disoriented, the details of his ethereal journey fading like mist as the audience rose in a standing ovation. The applause swelled, a passionate outpouring that filled the auditorium with vibrant energy.

Rosa's solemn poise melted into a radiant smile as she bowed, basking in the ovation. The raucous crowd and bright lights stood in stark contrast to the mystical world he had momentarily inhabited.

Though the visions had been vivid, only fragments lingered in his waking mind. Clinging to rationality, Winwood told himself he must have dozed off during an uninspiring performance.

To the rest of the audience, however, the evening had been nothing short of enchanting—like glimpsing the elusive Resplendent Quetzal, rare and unforgettable.

# Chapter Six

## *Beacon Rock*

Willliam winced as the iron door to Winwood's studio shut behind them with a deep, metallic thud. He walked ahead, his footsteps dragging, shoulders slumped beneath the weight of his backpack. Aimée followed in silence, her gaze fixed on his drooping posture. Outside, the wind stirred the branches of the elms that lined the street, scattering leaves across the pavement.

"Willy?" she called out, catching up to him as he reached the white Chevy Trailblazer. He paused, hand resting on the door handle but not opening it. His eyes were far away, lost in a scrambled maze of emotions.

She placed a gentle hand on his shoulder. "Why don't we get away for a few days? Just you and me. Tomorrow's Friday. I'll take the day off work. We'll go to the coast, to Beacon Rock. It's been too long."

He looked up, eyes more focused. "You want to go to the coast?"

She smiled, brushing a strand of hair out of his eyes. "*Oui, mon chéri.* Let's do it. I think we both need this right now."

William nodded, a hint of relief softening his expression, though not quite a smile.

"Bien," she said. "We'll leave first thing in the morning. Don't forget your headphones."

William opened the door and sank into the passenger seat, his body slumping against the worn upholstery. Aimée climbed in beside him. While

William stared out the passenger window, eyes distant and unfocused, she unfolded the piece of paper with the name "Rosa Carreño" scrawled in her own hurried handwriting. A flicker of hope sparked in her chest, though she knew better than to say it aloud—not yet. If this teacher proved another dead end, she wasn't sure William's dream of playing the piano would survive. She looked at the name again, turning it over in her mind. After they returned from their trip to the coast, she would call Shelley's Bookstore and ask for the sheet music department. Surely, if Rosa Carreño still taught anywhere in Nightingale, someone at Shelley's would know.

She started the engine and turned onto the main road, leaving the shadow of Winwood's studio behind.

The next day, they made their familiar drive to the coast, following the ritual they returned to time and time again when they needed to rest and restore. Beacon Rock was always their first stop. The massive basalt formation, shaped by prehistoric lava flows, jutted into the ocean, its rugged surface blanketed in grass, shrubs, and wind-battered trees. William loved to perch on its rocky ledges, watching waves crash below from every direction. From up high, he could gaze along the Pacific Northwest shoreline, where hundreds of cresting waves rolled in formation toward jagged cliffs. To him, it was the edge of the world—raw, untamed, and yet somehow connected to the vast, eternal presence of the ocean.

With his headphones on, he lost himself in his favorite symphonic music, "The Planets" by Gustav Holst. The awe-inspiring union of ocean and Holst's symphony stirred something deep within him. As the music swelled, nature transformed into a grand ballet—the waves crashed in sync with the cymbals, soaring strings lifted flocks of birds gliding across the sea, and seagulls darted overhead in time with the flutes and woodwinds. Every movement of the symphony felt like a journey to distant worlds—Mercury, Venus, Mars, Uranus—each one a glimpse into celestial mysteries, all the while he remained tethered to his rocky perch on Beacon Rock.

On one particular morning, William watched a pod of gray whales feeding in the deep cove beside Beacon Rock. As they surfaced, exhaling towering plumes of mist, the bold French horn sections from the *"Jupiter"* movement swelled in his ears, perfectly mirroring the whales' majestic movements.

Before returning to Nightingale, his mother indulged him with one last walk along the shoreline in search of the perfect thinking stone. It was his ritual on the last day—to find a basalt stone. Not too rough nor too smooth. There was an instinct to it—an unspoken knowing that guided his fingertips as he sifted through the scattered basalt stones on the beach, waiting for one to feel just right. The chosen stone would then travel with him—an anchor, a weight in his pocket to steady his mind and gather his wandering thoughts.

William once showed his friend, Professor Anthony Burns Montgomery, one of his basalt stones. The retired professor, endlessly curious, took it in his hands and traced its surface with his fingertips, slow and sensitive—like a man reading Braille. Fascinated, William watched the blind professor's fingers as they caressed the stone.

"Ah," Montgomery had said, his fingers mapping the stone's curves and ridges. "William, I can tell this basalt has been carefully chosen. But did you know that this little piece of the earth has been on a journey for millions of years? It was born in ancient lava flows—seventeen million years ago— erupting from volcanic vents at the Idaho-Oregon border. Back then, it was molten fire, carving new landscapes as it flowed. Over eons, it fractured, tumbling through time, and was finally claimed by the ocean. The sea's relentless rhythm polished it, shaping it into what you now hold. And after all that—seventeen million years later—it waited patiently for you to find it."

He paused, letting his fingers follow the stone's worn, smooth edges before handing it back. Then he added, "That ancient stone has traveled through time and space just to be with you. Take good care of it, William. It has chosen you as well."

William held the stone, rubbing its surface with his thumb, mirroring the professor's motion. Its weight in his hand felt different now—heavier, as though it carried the story of its long journey. He slipped it into his pocket, where it would remain as a quiet companion.

# Chapter Seven

## *Journey to the Gate Lodge*

That same stone rested in his pocket as the white Trailblazer climbed the twisting roads of Imperial Heights, carrying him toward Miss Rosa's studio for the first time. They wove through the district's tangled streets, doubling back more than once, and the journey quickly became more complicated than expected.

His mother checked the time, biting her lip. "*Mon Dieu…* Willy, we should have been there by now."

She had been so relieved when Rosa Carreño agreed to meet with William that she barely remembered scribbling down the directions. Now, as they wound through Imperial Heights, she cursed herself for leaving them on the kitchen counter in their rush to get out the door.

"*Bon sang!*" she muttered under her breath. "Why didn't I put them in my purse right away?"

Her fingers drummed the steering wheel, eyes flicking between the hedged streets and the dashboard clock. Imperial Heights had always been a labyrinth of winding lanes—and without directions, nearly impossible to find your way through. House addresses were often obscured by overgrown hedges or tucked behind hidden driveways. Strangely, there wasn't a single pedestrian in sight to ask for directions, and the thick morning fog hanging over the narrow, curving roads like a ghostly veil only made it harder.

The SUV lurched as his mother tried to downshift for yet another steep incline. The gears protested with a grinding noise, and the engine gave a low groan. Her knuckles whitened on the wheel as she wrestled the gearshift into place. "*Merde alors... cette fichue boîte de vitesses,*" she muttered, giving it a sharp tug. "Your father was the only one who could drive this thing."

Still fumbling with the manual transmission, she scanned the winding road ahead, looking for street signs, easing the Trailblazer to a crawl.

"I remember the street had a woman's name, and it's supposed to be near the Prescott Mansion," she continued, squinting through the dusty windshield. "The studio was called something with 'lodge' in it—just can't remember what exactly…"

William peered out the window, searching for any signs or landmarks that matched the few clues they had. The Prescott Mansion was no secret. Everyone in Nightingale knew of the iconic estate. Yet one could never see the whole thing—only fleeting glimpses through towering trees, its presence looming above the city. When the sun struck it just right, the red-tiled roof gleamed against the sky—a flash of color visible for miles.

Though his mother's frustration was growing, William's curiosity only deepened. He still wasn't sure he even wanted more piano lessons—not after Winwood—but something about Imperial Heights made him wonder what lay ahead. Maybe they'd catch sight of the Prescott Mansion.

A narrow road branched off from the one they were on. A towering Sitka spruce loomed beside the turn-off; its massive form shrouded in fog. Compared to the surrounding trees, it stood like a silent sentinel, marking the path.

She eased the car to a gentle stop and shivered, rubbing her arms. "*Peut-être que c'est la route...* Could this be it, Willy?"

"Huh... how do you know, Mom?"

"*Je ne suis pas sûre,*" she murmured.

William craned his neck, trying to read the street sign, but a thick branch obscured the lettering.

"*Mon chéri,* see if you can read it?"

William stepped out of the Trailblazer, its paint chipped and hood flecked with rust, still running strong—many years removed from his father's forestry days. The SUV had carried the family on countless camping and hiking adventures into the Fisher King National Forest.

His memories of those trips were faint, his father's presence a constant only in the earliest years of his childhood. Yet one image remained vivid: a photograph his mother had taken when he was barely three years old, perched in a toddler backpack on his dad's back. The Trailblazer was parked in the background, with gear strapped to the top rack. His father grinned at the camera, his smile broad and full of life, while little William sat high on his shoulders, head thrown back in laughter, tiny hands resting on his dad's head.

The snapshot, its edges frayed from years of handling, was one of William's most treasured possessions. On his tenth birthday, his mother had placed it into an ornate Art Nouveau frame, its edges gilded and etched with curling vines—a family heirloom from his great-grandmother's kitchen.

William stepped closer to the weathered street sign, its name half-veiled by dirt and overgrown branches. He squinted, trying to make out the name.

"It's hard to read, but I think it says 'Madeleine Way.'"

"*C'est ça*, Willy! That's the woman's name I had forgotten. It's spelled in *Français*, right?"

"Yes, looks like the French spelling... uh…" William's voice trailed off, his gaze resting on the sign. He then glanced at the road ahead. Something about the curve of it—the way it rose and disappeared into the trees felt... familiar.

He blinked, gave a small shake of his head, and turned back toward the Trailblazer, still lost in thought. His pace slowed, distracted—only adding to his mother's anxiousness about the time.

"Willy, come on… we're already quite late!"

He slid back into the passenger seat, eyes distant.

"What is it, *mon chéri*?"

"That name…" he said. "Madeleine." He paused. "I just saw a photograph with that name a few weeks ago... in Mr. Winwood's library. A woman at a piano. Her name was Madeleine—Madeleine Monnier I believe."

"*Oh oui*! Madeleine Monnier. Of course."

William turned to her. "Wait… that street sign is named after Monnier? The concert pianist?" The coincidence struck him as strange.

His mother wrestled the gearshift into place with a small grunt. "*Oui*, Willy, I do remember thinking there was something familiar about that street name in Miss Carreño's directions. I completely forgot. *Mais bien sûr*—Madeleine Monnier married R.C. Prescott."

Relieved to have finally found the right road, she released the clutch, and the Trailblazer lumbered forward. She hoped they could still make a good impression despite the delay.

As they rounded a bend, a utility truck and work crew suddenly came into view, blocking the way. A large ponderosa pine had fallen across the road, its branches sprawled over the pavement like a toppled giant. His mother let out a gasp, braking quickly. There was no way through.

As they slowed to a stop, a man wearing an orange hard hat approached, raising a hand. "I'm sorry, ma'am. This road's closed while we clear the tree."

His mother leaned out the window, explaining their predicament. The crewman listened, then nodded.

"Yeah, sounds like you're looking for the Gate Lodge," he said, gesturing toward the rise in the road. "It's only about half a mile up that way. If you're up for a short hike, you can park here and walk the rest of the way."

"*Bon sang*!" His mother sighed, tapping her fingers against the steering wheel as she weighed their options. "*Vous savez*, Willy, we've come this far, no sense turning back now, *oui*?"

William glanced at the blocked road, then back at his mother. The moment felt oddly significant, though he couldn't say why. "Yeah, Mom... let's do it."

Her expression tightened briefly before softening into a trace of amusement. She nodded. "*Mon Dieu*. This reminds me of those crazy adventures your dad used to take me on."

She parked the Trailblazer and stared out the windshield for a moment. "He never liked to plan things out, which always made me a little nervous. He loved being spontaneous, exploring new places in the wilderness. I usually had no idea where we were going, but the mystery of it all was fun."

She brushed back a strand of hair behind her ear. "It was good for me," she said, almost to herself. "I was always such a *casanière*... so many hours in the kitchen, conjuring up recipes..."

A moment of stillness settled in the Trailblazer. Then, with a shared nod, they stepped out of the car and began the uphill walk.

As they climbed the steep road, the sound of chainsaws and shouted instructions from the work crew gradually faded behind them. With each step, the noise of the world fell away, replaced by the muffled hush of the forest.

Rounding a bend, they paused, struck by the majesty surrounding them. Towering trees rose on either side, their trunks vanishing into a veil of fog that hung thick in the air above. Now and then, the mist thinned just enough for sunlight to break through, catching on the dew-laced pine needles and setting them aglow like tiny prisms.

Suddenly, they heard music drifting through the mist. At first, it was so faint they could barely tell if it was real. The notes floated on a gentle breeze, ethereal, distant. Then, clarity—piano music.

William stopped abruptly, listening more closely. His mother paused.

"What is it, Willy?"

"I think… I know that piece…" he said, brow furrowing as he squinted into the fog. The melody became clearer as they walked. William's ears sharpened, his expression open.

"I've heard it before, Mom. It's… French!"

"*Ah, intéressante,*" she said, resting a hand on his back to gently urge him forward.

But William hesitated, his steps slowing, his focus locked on the unseen source of the music. Recognition struck. "It's by Maurice Ravel, Mom. '*Une Barque sur l'Océan*!" he exclaimed.

His mother blinked. "What?"

"Yes! It mimics the waves, rolling up and down the keyboard. I could see this tiny boat, all alone on the open sea."

Aimée let out a soft laugh, shaking her head in admiration. "That's amazing, Willy. I'm always amazed by the things you know, but *s'il te plaît…* we must keep moving."

As William listened in rapt attention, Aimée found herself drifting somewhere else. She stared at the winding road ahead, but in her mind, she was alone on that boat—waves of chaos and fear crashing all around her. The sound stirred something deep within her, awakening memories she rarely allowed to surface.

Cooking had once been her refuge, a sanctuary from her personal struggles. In the kitchen, her mind grew still, aware. To her, food was stored sunlight, and each dish released that light into a world often shadowed by darkness.

Aimée's thoughts drifted back to the French town of Sarlat-la-Canéda, where she had spent her childhood under the care of her grandparents. The vine-draped lanes of Sarlat wove through her memory—the medieval town in the heart of the Dordogne, its cobblestone streets echoing with footsteps and laughter. It wasn't so different from the winding, misty paths of Imperial Heights.

Her heart thumped with familiar anticipation, mirroring the fluttering excitement she often felt as a child while weaving through the narrow cobblestone streets and secretive alleyways of Sarlat. Known for its Renaissance facades and Gothic archways, the town wasn't just a backdrop for her youthful adventures but a living museum. The tantalizing aromas of truffles and freshly baked cherry clafoutis floated from open windows and bustling market stalls, captivating her young senses.

Amid the vibrant market displays of cheeses, foie gras, and seasonal mushrooms, Aimée's passion for cooking first took root. Each dish, from the earthy richness of duck confit to the sweet simplicity of walnut cake, was a celebration of the region's culinary wealth and ignited her love affair with food.

Aimée's cooking style was different from her grandmother's—more akin to that of a jazz musician. To her, the recipe was like a lead sheet, a simple outline with which she could create her own culinary melodies. Sometimes the recipe felt like an unfinished poem, something that launched a journey of discovery.

It would begin with a trip to the market. Then, touching the ingredients with her fingers, smelling, and tasting, came wild abandon in the kitchen. It was as if she were giving new life to raw ingredients harvested from the earth, pollinated by wind, and nourished by rain and sun.

Through some culinary alchemy—blending spices and seasonings, marinating, then sautéing by heat of flame—she could bear witness to a new creation. Cooking, for her, was a connection to life itself. As a result, without fail, each person who tasted her cuisine invariably inquired about some mystery ingredient. There always seemed to be an item in every delectable dish that no one could quite identify; her own secret signature.

But that world—her kitchen—had gradually faded into the background, swallowed by personal struggles and the responsibilities of life. Now, Aimée's only therapy for her darker moods was simply to keep moving. She exhaled, pushing the memories aside—shrugging off the weight of her thoughts as she quickened her pace to the Gate Lodge.

The piano music grew clearer, weaving through the neighboring forest like something out of a dream. The tree branches swayed, as if carried by the rhythm of the music. As they approached a turn in the road, the Gate Lodge emerged from the mist.

Aimée caught her breath. "Willy, this must be Rosa Carreño's studio!"

The Gate Lodge stood before them, an Italianate-style craftsman home reminiscent of the old Emerald District of Nightingale. Vines curled hungrily up its walls, as if nature were reclaiming the structure, and a substantial wisteria climbed toward the second floor, its lavender blooms cascading over window boxes and mingling with lush petunias. Higher still, a balcony stretched from the third floor, its French doors ajar, letting the music spill into the morning air.

"It looks like a Monet painting, Willy. That wisteria... it's just like the one that climbed the walls of *Grandmère* and *Grandpère's* home back in Sarlat."

William and his mother pressed on, hurrying around to the front of the Gate Lodge. But as they rounded the corner, they stopped dead in their tracks.

The Prescott Mansion rose before them, its red-tiled roof glimmering in the sunlight. Its sheer grandeur felt almost unreal. At that exact moment, as if orchestrated by fate, the sound of Rosa's piano surged into a mighty crescendo, its notes swelling and cresting like waves, washing over the mansion in Ravel's *"Une Barque sur l'Océan."*

For a moment, neither of them spoke. William's chest tightened as he tried to take it all in. His mother's lips parted slightly, her expression suspended between awe and disbelief.

"Mom!" William finally managed, his voice a mix of wonder and shock. "The mansion… it's huge!"

Aimée pressed a hand to her chest. "Oh, *mon Dieu…* Miss Carreño said the Gate Lodge was near the mansion, but…" She swallowed hard. "I didn't think she meant this close!"

The heavy fog wove around the estate, softening its edges, veiling its true immensity. Only glimpses of its towering structure emerged through the mist—stonework, spires, shadowed archways—half-seen, half-hidden. A ray of sunlight pierced the cloud cover, catching the sheen of its red-tiled roof.

William wanted to stay and drink in the sight, but his mother's anxious glance at her watch pulled him back to reality. They were late. With one last look at the mansion rising through the mist, he quickened his pace and followed her toward the door of the Gate Lodge.

# Chapter Eight

## *Rosa Carreño*

Breathless, Aimée rang the doorbell. The music stopped mid-phrase. Moments later, Rosa Carreño appeared at the door.

She was an elegant, petite woman, seemingly in her mid-seventies. Her silver hair, streaked with a striking white flare, was brushed back from her face as if caught by the wind.

"Hello. My name is Rosa, and… ah…" She paused, scanning the area behind them. "Is everything okay? Where's your car?"

Aimée stepped forward, offering a polite but flustered smile. "Ah, oui, I'm so sorry we are late. We got lost in Imperial Heights. We found Madeleine Way, but just near the turn-off… a large tree had fallen across the road." She paused to catch her breath, brushing away a bit of perspiration from her forehead. "And we… we had to walk the rest of the way."

Miss Rosa's hands flew to her cheeks. "My word, what an ordeal! I'm so sorry you had to go through that."

Aimée managed a shaky laugh, then placed her hands gently on William's shoulders, guiding him forward a step. Her eyes softened as she looked from Rosa to her son. "Miss Carreño… this is William."

She bowed her head slightly. "Ah, a pleasure to meet you, William." With a small flick of her hand, she added, "And please, call me Rosa. Miss Carreño is much too formal. Please come in. I was getting a little worried," she said, ushering them inside. "I'm relieved you're both safe. The Prescott Mansion is undergoing renovations; it's usually quite loud by this time of day. The construction workers arriving this morning must have noticed the tree was down and called in a crew to clear it. No wonder it's been so quiet."

As Miss Rosa closed the front door, something soft brushed against William's leg. He looked down to see a fluffy cat rubbing up against him. When he bent to pet her, she immediately flopped onto the floor, exposing her furry belly.

"That's Misha," said Miss Rosa. "And it appears she's taken an immediate liking to you, William. Quite a compliment. She doesn't roll over like that for just anyone, let alone a stranger."

William rubbed Misha's tummy, scratching her neck and ears.

"She's beautiful," his mother remarked. "What kind of cat is she?"

"Misha is a Himalayan, a cross between a Siamese and a Persian."

Misha's long fur was a mix of creamy white and light brown, with darker shades on her face, paws, ears, and tail. But her most striking feature was her large, piercing blue eyes. As William stroked her, Misha let out an endearing sound—part purr and part meow.

As he stood, Misha's eyes flicked open, and in one swift motion, she flipped back onto her paws. She gazed up at him, meowing softly before rising onto her hind legs and reaching out, gently gripping his leg.

"She wants you to pick her up," Miss Rosa said with amusement.

William lifted Misha into his arms, and to his surprise, she wrapped her paws around his neck, hugging him like a baby. He stroked her back, charmed by her affectionate nature.

"My word, Misha!" Miss Rosa chuckled. "What has gotten into you?"

His mother leaned over his shoulder to get a closer look at Misha's dark face and vivid blue eyes. Scratching Misha's cheeks with both hands, she cooed softly, "*Quelle jolie petite chatte, oui, tu es vraiment magnifique.*"

"Himalayans are a fascinating breed," said Rosa. "It's hard to explain. There's something about their calm presence and observant nature. Eleanor Prescott adored them; always had one curled up beside her piano. So did her mother, Madeleine Monnier-Prescott. I loved seeing Eleanor's Himalayan during my piano lessons, and I suppose I've just continued the tradition."

Misha cooed, drawing William's attention. Their eyes met, and he found himself momentarily entranced by her electric-blue gaze.

Rosa gestured toward the studio. "Make yourselves at home. I should call my other students about the fallen tree."

Misha leapt from William's arms and sauntered over to a corner of the studio, curling up in a gray beanbag bed, large enough for two cats, yet clearly reserved for her alone.

Aimée took in her surroundings. The room carried a calm, understated beauty. Like the exterior, the home's interior was simple yet inviting. The refinished wood floors bore the marks of time; a blend of rich tones, worn patches, and scattered cracks that told their own story. Above, exposed oaken beams framed the ceiling, adding to the studio's charm.

At its center stood a Mason & Hamlin baby grand piano, its mahogany surface carrying a satin sheen, warm rather than showy. The instrument seemed to anchor the space, in harmony with the room's weathered elegance.

Above the fireplace, a striking slab of reclaimed redwood served as the mantel. The grain swirled in deep, warm hues. Its shape was subtly irregular, a little thicker at one end, a touch uneven along the edges.

To the left of the entrance, a wooden staircase led to the floors above and below. Miss Rosa's voice floated from the kitchen as she made calls to students.

Curious, William drifted to the French doors, left slightly ajar, and stepped onto the balcony to take in the view.

Aimée lingered by the fireplace, her attention caught by the mantel's natural uneven grain. She traced her fingers along its surface, following the gentle ridges and dips. A sunbeam poured through the window, igniting the wood's deep red and orange hues.

Near one end of the slab, a small, charred indentation caught her eye. Curious, she reached out and touched it, her fingertips grazing the blackened groove.

"*Wabi sabi.*"

Aimée flinched slightly. "Ah… pardon?"

"*Wabi sabi,*" Rosa repeated, nodding toward the mantel. "That piece of redwood."

Aimée hesitated. "Wabi… saah… I'm not sure. What does that mean?"

"The beauty of imperfection," Rosa explained. "It's a Japanese aesthetic."

Aimée studied the wood's weathered surface. "I've never heard that term before."

Rosa stepped closer. "You could sand this wood down, refinish it—make it perfect. Some might prefer that. But in doing so, you'd erase its history, its character. This piece of redwood, like people, is shaped by time and experience."

Aimée's fingers touched the charred mark on the slab.

"For me, that's the essence of *wabi sabi*," Rosa said. "This mantel piece came from a treehouse. There was a fire years ago. The treehouse was mostly destroyed…"

Aimée gasped and pulled her hand away.

"Oh, don't worry." Rosa said. "It was a long time ago. No one died. The treehouse was built for Eleanor Prescott, the Prescotts' only child. Fortunately, the estate had a modern plumbing system. Mr. Prescott and the groundskeeper managed to put out the fire before it spread. They saved the Gate Lodge and probably the mansion itself. Eleanor's thumb was injured, and that, too, is part of the mantel's *wabi sabi*. You see," Rosa said, "without that fire, I wouldn't be here today, teaching piano in the Gate Lodge."

The mention of the treehouse fire pulled Aimée elsewhere—to another fire, another place. She could still see the scorched remains of the Angel Crest Ridge fire near Lost Lake, where a once-vibrant forest had been reduced to a graveyard of blackened old growth pine trees.

But one image stood out among the devastation, preserved in her memory. A massive Sitka spruce stump, its hollowed-out core burned away, loomed like a gaping mouth. The fire had eaten through its center, leaving behind only a skeletal shell. Two deep notches marked where lumberjacks had once placed their springboard planks, standing on them nearly a century before to fell the giant tree. Now, those dark indentations looked like hollow, staring eyes, as if frozen in a primal scream.

That forest had been a place of adventure. When Aimée was younger, it had been Phillip who first drew her out into the wilderness, coaxing her from the familiar sanctuary of her kitchen to explore Angel Crest Ridge. Over time, it became something they shared. They would venture deep into the national forest, weaving through ancient trees until they reached Rogue River Falls, a secluded escape from the outside world.

Their courtship had been brief but intense, a fusion of passion and spontaneity that neither had questioned. Together, they'd leaned into life's unpredictability, never pausing to question where it might lead.

When William was a toddler, Phillip would carry him in a backpack on their hikes, the boy's laughter ringing through the trees. Phillip always called him *Sparky*, his voice playful and teasing. The two had been inseparable.

Aimée could still picture it—the way Phillip would twirl around, making William squeal with delight, his tiny hands tangled in his father's hair. She used to watch them from a few paces behind, smiling to herself, savoring the simple joy of the moment…

An uneasy stillness hung in the room. Aimée had gone silent, her eyes distant and unfocused, fingers lingering over the charred wood. Rosa had paused, studying Aimée's faraway look, before deciding to shift the conversation.

"Aimée, there's something else I'd like to show you. I think you might find it interesting." She motioned toward a nearby shelf. "This vase over there is a different kind of *wabi sabi*. It's an example of the art of *kintsugi*. Let me show you."

Still a bit dazed, Aimée followed Rosa across the room.

Rosa lifted a small vase from the shelf and tilted it slightly, letting the light catch the delicate gold seams running through its fractures. A single orchid, its petals a light shade of purple, rested inside.

Aimée leaned in, drawn to the gold cracks threading through the vase like veins of metal. "C'est beau," she said.

Rosa gave a small nod, encouraging her to hold it.

The glaze was cool beneath her touch, blue-gray with subtle variations in tone. Along each repaired fracture, the seams rose slightly, the lacquer forming a raised, irregular texture.

"It's real gold," Rosa said. "It may look fragile, but in spirit, the repair has made it stronger than before. The philosophy behind it is to honor what was broken, not hide it. Some would say it's even more beautiful this way." Rosa continued, "There's a wonderful story about that vase…" But before she could finish, William burst back from the balcony into the studio, breathless.

"Mom! The view from the balcony is incredible! You can see Mt. Drake,"

Rosa gestured toward the doors. "Go ahead, take a look, Aimée. This visit is mostly a meet-and-greet. Enjoy the view. I have one more phone call to make."

From the Gate Lodge balcony, the city of Nightingale stretched below, a patchwork of rooftops and winding streets. Beyond it stood Mt. Drake, its snow-capped peak rising through the distant mist, glistening in the sun.

"I've always wondered what it would be like up there," William said, leaning over the railing.

Aimée's eyes stayed on the peak. "Your father summited it several times before you were born."

William turned, astonished. "Dad climbed Mt. Drake?"

She nodded. "It's dangerous, Willy. A couple of his friends nearly died attempting it. I worried every time he went." Her voice grew softer. "He stopped after you were born…"

A breeze drifted across the balcony, carrying the crisp scent of pine. The city lay bathed in the midday light, rooftops gleaming beyond the winding roads.

William shifted his weight against the railing, eyes still on the mountain. "I wonder what it's like at the top? Maybe when I'm older I can climb it, like Dad?"

Aimée exhaled, brushing a strand of his hair off his face. "Maybe one day, but let's start with piano lessons first, mon petit." She squeezed his shoulder gently, guiding him back toward the studio.

Rosa stood at the piano, waiting. She beckoned William closer. "So, let's see. You are quite interested in the piano, yes?"

William hesitated, shuffling his feet. "Well, I love the piano… but I don't know if I'm cut out for it."

Rosa dismissed his doubt. "Pish posh. A student's harshest critic is usually the one in the mirror." Turning to Aimée, she said, "You mentioned that Cecil Winwood suggested you come study… with me?"

Aimée nodded. "He said you were a Piano Zen teacher, with a studio in Imperial Heights."

Rosa rested her chin in her hand. "Hmm… that's interesting." She gazed out the window for a long moment, her expression unreadable, then turned back to William, composed again.

"Here, William," she said, pointing to the piano bench. "Come, sit down."

As he stepped toward the piano, his eyes fell on the bench. It was unusual, unlike any he had ever seen. The four metal legs were etched in the shape of cranes, embossed in gold leaf. They stood back-to-back, their tail feathers intertwined in an intricate design.

"There's quite a history with that piano bench," Rosa said. "Eleanor Prescott passed it down to me. Before her, it belonged to her mother, Madeleine Monnier. For more than two centuries, it has been handed down from one Piano Zen teacher to the next."

William's brow furrowed. "Madeleine Monnier? She was also a Piano Zen teacher… like you?"

Rosa nodded. "Yes. She was both a concert pianist and a Piano Zen teacher. She performed all over the world."

William eased himself down onto the piano bench, afraid of damaging an antique.

"Don't worry," Rosa said. "It may be old, but it's surprisingly sturdy. It was specially crafted in France, based on Tibetan designs brought back from the East in the early eighteenth century."

She pointed toward the carvings beneath the cushion. "The birds you see here are demoiselle cranes, remarkable creatures. Delicate in appearance yet strong enough to migrate across the highest peaks of the Himalayas. Each of these birds represents one of the Four Elements."

William tilted his head. "The Four... Elements?"

"Oh, yes," Rosa said. "The Four Elements are essential to the Piano Zen Method: Earth, Air, Water, and Fire. They've been recognized since antiquity—the Greeks, Romans, Chinese, and Vedic traditions of India, each in their own way. Piano Zen simply weaves them into Western piano training."

She gave a small wave of her hand. "But let's not get too far ahead of ourselves. You'll learn all about it soon enough. Tell me, William, do you like books?"

"Yes, I *love* books," William said, glancing at his mother with a grin.

"Ah, wonderful. Because I have a very special one you might like to see. It's quite rare." Rosa crossed to a bookshelf and drew out a volume, cradling it with a sense of ceremony. The book looked ancient, its deep-red velvet cover bound with ornate brass bindings. She set it gently on the piano's music rack.

"This is a first edition, printed more than a hundred and fifty years ago. Only a handful of copies survive. I thought you'd enjoy seeing where it all began—the book that first gave the name Piano Zen to the world."

"Of course," Rosa said, "I don't teach directly from this one. The language, the notation, even the illustrations belong to another age. Over time, I've prepared new versions for my students, weaving in several of Madeleine Monnier's own compositions."

His hands hovered over the cover, hesitant to touch something so precious. Rosa gave him an encouraging nod. As he eased it open, a tingling rippled across his skin, the same sensation he'd felt in the Modern Prometheus rare book room.

With his mother peering over his shoulder, William turned the pages carefully, his fingers gliding over the thick, timeworn paper. Page after page revealed mesmerizing illustrations—figures of people and animals, a tranquil Japanese garden, a man in an aikido uniform. Between them, musical notation unfurled like flowing water, familiar pieces alive with intricate phrasing and expressive markings.

He drew in a quick breath. "Mom, look at this bird!" he said, turning the book so she could see more clearly. A brilliant creature with emerald-green feathers and a crimson breast filled the page. Its impossibly long tail curled like a ribbon in the wind, as though the illustration might drift beyond the paper's edge.

Aimée leaned in closer. "C'est magnifique. What kind of bird is that?"

From just behind them, Rosa replied, "It's the Resplendent Quetzal of Guatemala."

William and Aimée exchanged a soft, synchronized 'Ah.'

"William, why don't you take the Piano Zen book home and explore it at your own pace," Rosa said. She closed the volume and placed it in his hands. "I know you'll be careful. Just bring it back for your first lesson, and I'll give you your own book to keep—an updated edition with some of the same songs, plus new ones and plenty of illustrations. That's the one we'll use together."

William blinked. "Wait… my first Piano Zen lesson? Does that mean…?"

"Yes, William. It means I'd love to teach you the piano." She rested a hand on his shoulder. "Something tells me Piano Zen is meant to be shared with you."

William hesitated, nervous at the thought of taking home such a valuable book. But Miss Rosa brushed off his concerns.

"Now, to prepare this week," Rosa said, "begin noticing your breath. Most people breathe in a shallow way without realizing it. But deep breathing is essential in Piano Zen. It opens the mind, relaxes the body, and connects you to the music."

She then added, "And one more thing—if you don't already have one, start keeping a dream journal. Write down your experiences. One day, you might find it more useful than you realize."

At the door, Rosa's parting smile was reassuring. Still, William wondered what lay ahead on this strange new path.

# Chapter Nine

## *The Tibetan Bowl*

Being entrusted with the rare and mysterious Piano Zen book made William feel both honored and slightly anxious. In the days leading up to his first lesson with Rosa, he carefully studied its pages— puzzling over the evocative illustrations of temples, people, and animals engaged in curious activities.

When William arrived for his first piano lesson, Misha was there to greet him once again, her sweet disposition immediately putting him at ease. He handed the Piano Zen Book back to Miss Rosa and thanked her for letting him borrow it. She placed the rare edition back on the bookshelf and presented him with a newer lesson book with a light blue cover. It would be his to keep during his first year of piano lessons.

William ran his fingers over the glossy cover, then flipped through the pages, smiling at the whimsical sketches. They weren't as detailed as the ones in Rosa's rare book, but he recognized the characters instantly—a monkey sailing through the air, a bear with a drum, and a bright green bird with a long, flowing tail.

Inside, the first piece was titled *Music of the Smiling Pond*, marked as an improvisation.

She lit a sandalwood-scented candle, its fragrance unfurling slowly into the room. "Sandalwood," she said, "helps calm the mind and sharpen focus. Before we begin your first Piano Zen lesson, let me put some water on to boil for tea."

As she stepped out of the room, William settled in and took a deep breath, savoring the woodsy sweetness of the aroma. He set his backpack down near the Mason & Hamlin baby grand, noticing a built-in shelving unit. Resting on a cushion of deep purple velvet was a silver and gold object, about six inches long—something he hadn't seen the week before.

Curious, William leaned forward and picked it up. Its etched designs caught the light. Tiny gemstones sparkled along its surface, casting tiny prisms onto the wall. He turned it over in his hands, feeling its surprising weight.

He was so absorbed that he didn't hear Rosa return. "That is a dorje," she said. "A sacred object from Tibet."

William quickly returned it to its place on the shelf. "I'm... I'm so sorry. I just wanted to look at it more closely."

Rosa smiled. "There's nothing to be sorry about. I appreciate your curiosity."

"How do you pronounce it?" William asked.

"Dor-jay," Rosa said. "In Tibetan tradition, the dorje is more than a jeweled scepter. It's said to symbolize a bridge between the physical and the unseen—something that cuts through illusion and reveals truth."

"The tea will take a few minutes," Rosa added, stepping past him. "In the meantime, let's do a relaxation exercise to focus your thoughts." She moved to a nearby shelf and retrieved a dark, copper-colored bowl. "This," she said, cradling it in both hands, "is a Tibetan singing bowl. Its sound helps soften the mind and prepare you for your Piano Zen lesson. Sit about halfway on the piano bench, feet flat on the floor, and rest your palms facing upward on your legs. We are going to begin with the Earth Element. It's the easiest and quickest entry point to soften the mind."

William studied the bowl with fascination. He'd never seen anything like it, certainly not as part of a piano lesson.

Her voice carried a playful lilt as she said, "It's time to wake up the Tibetan singing bowl." Holding the bowl steady in one hand, she struck it twice with a simple wooden mallet wrapped in soft suede. The bowl gave a dull, metallic thud.

Rosa grinned. "Ah! That should wake it up."

She turned toward William who sat motionless, even more unsure of what to expect.

"The Earth Element is all about your contact points," she said. "Where your body makes contact with the world around you: your feet on the floor, your sit bones on the bench, even the backs of your hands resting on your legs."

Her words slowed to a calm cadence. "Close your eyes and focus your attention on those contact points. They'll help you become more aware of your body."

William had never thought much about his contact points before. He noticed the light pressure sensation in the soles of his feet against the floor, the solid weight of his sit bones on the bench, and the backs of his hands in his lap.

There was a long pause, then Rosa said, "Now, let's see what happens when the Tibetan bowl wakes you up." She struck the bowl again, this time circling the mallet around its rim. It resonated with a full, rich sound, deeper and more textured than he expected.

She let the vibrations hum through the room. William matched his breath to the steady tone, each exhale a little slower than the last. When Rosa spoke again, her words slipped easily into his awareness. "Notice the tingling sensation in your hands." He concentrated, and soon a faint current of energy spread through his palms.

"Imagine them growing heavier… and heavier. As they do, notice how the tingling sensation increases."

Her voice grew more faint. "I'm going to keep ringing the Tibetan bowl, and as I do, feel its vibrations inside your body."

She swirled the mallet around its rim, drawing out a deep, resonant tone. Sunlight streamed through the French doors, its warmth settling on William's face.

Then, the room began to undulate—walls stretching apart, the ceiling lifting. His eyes twitched uncontrollably as the air grew light with a mix of sandalwood and the scent of damp earth, reminiscent of a forest after rain.

Reality loosened its grip.

Time softened.

And then… he slipped into a world of dreams.

# Chapter Ten

## *The Whispering Woods of the Tall Pines*

When William's eyes fluttered open, he was no longer in Miss Rosa's studio. The shift was seamless; a new reality had quietly slipped into place. Unaware he'd entered a dream world, William accepted the scene before him as real, as though he had simply stepped through an unseen door.

He found himself on a rustic wooden bench before a pond that looked as if Monet had brushed it into being—soft edges, colors bleeding into one another, beautiful but lacking clarity.

As William adjusted to this blurred world, a small jolt of unease broke through. Something was off. The familiar weight of his father's Master Samaritan Ring no longer pressed against his chest. He instinctively reached for it, only to grasp at nothing. The ring was missing. His pulse quickened. He always wore his dad's ring. Had it fallen off somehow? He reached into his pocket for his basalt stone, but his pocket was empty. The stone was gone as well.

In a panic, he slipped off his backpack and rifled through the compartments, desperate to find the missing items. Instead, he found only one thing: his Piano Zen lesson book.

Dazed, he looked around, but the garden melted into blurred brushstrokes. Only the object beside him on the bench came into focus: a small, dark wooden box—worn with age, its edges smooth from time. William hesitated. Had someone left it?

Drawn by an inexplicable urge, he reached for the box and carefully lifted the lid. Inside lay a tightly rolled piece of parchment tied with a thin gold string. He unknotted it and smoothed the paper open.

*Place this Dream Dorje around your neck. It will help you navigate the dream world. In time, it will stir your memory—to remember.*

*Wu Wei – Master of the Fire Element.*

William stared at the strange note. *Who is Wu Wei? And what's a… Dream Dorje?* He peered back into the box and noticed a folded piece of deep purple velvet. Unwrapping it, he uncovered a small object that glowed silver and gold. Yet it wasn't reflecting the sunlight; it pulsed, as if alive. He recognized the shape. It resembled the dorje in Rosa's piano studio. But this one was smaller, affixed to a chain—a pendant meant to be worn.

William lifted it gently, watching as it cast tiny prisms of light across his skin. A faint harmonic chime seemed to resonate from within, so soft it was almost imperceptible.

With a sense of surrender, he placed it around his neck. As the dorje settled against his chest, a gentle surge of energy rippled through him. Suddenly, the world around him sharpened. Colors deepened. Sounds became more textured. The luminous garden around him felt impossibly clear, as though a hidden veil had been lifted.

To his left, a waterfall bubbled and rushed over jagged rocks into the pond, its sound blending with the lingering tone of the Tibetan bowl, the vibrations weaving through the very fabric of his consciousness, heightening his senses until every rustle of the leaves and every ripple on the water near him was sharp and alive, as though the world had shifted into a higher resolution. It was the most exquisite Japanese garden he had ever seen, more serene than any place he could remember. Flowering shrubs and trees grew in abundance, their colors rich and brilliant. Black rocks of varying sizes lay scattered on the ground, each one blanketed in thick, lush moss. Across the pond stood a massive weeping willow, its branches sweeping low and wide, far larger than any he could recall. Beyond it, rising in quiet majesty, towered an endless expanse of evergreen trees.

He didn't question how he had come to this dream world; it simply felt natural… as dreams often do.

As he gazed upon the water of the pond, a smile spread across his face. Every negative thought seemed to vanish. He tried to think of something bad but simply couldn't, and the futility of it made him laugh out loud. The vibrant sensations of the garden wrapped around him, sharpening his senses. His mind felt exceptionally clear—and there was a lightness in his step.

A light breeze picked up and caressed his face, carrying a sweet hint of citrus from the blooming magnolia tree nearby. The willow's branches swayed gently in its wake.

William rose from the bench and moved toward the pond. Several large stones lay at the edge, their surfaces blanketed in thick, green moss. The water itself was perfectly still, like a sheet of liquid silk, reflecting the landscape with mirror-like precision.

Drawn by an inner nudge, he reached out and touched the pond with his finger. To his amazement, the contact produced a beautiful tone, soft and clear, like the chime of a bell. Light sparkled where his finger met the surface, and tiny waves radiated outward in concentric circles. The ripples seemed to awaken the still water, breathing life into the serene pond.

William froze, eyes wide. *How is this possible?* He glanced around, half expecting someone to appear—someone who might explain it. But he was alone.

He touched the surface again, in a different place, and noticed the tone had changed. Kneeling, he experimented with each finger's contact on the surface. Every touch produced a unique sound, yet the tones blended in perfect harmony. Since no one was watching, William let himself go, tapping across the pond's surface and exploring this way of making music. As his fingers danced on the water, his thoughts and emotions seemed to flow out effortlessly.

As he improvised melodies, the water beneath his fingertips began to clear, revealing brightly colored koi fish—living jewels, gliding in rhythm to his music.

Nearby, a wooden post stood beside the pond with a small box attached to it. A sign on the front read "Please Feed the Koi." Intrigued, William approached and opened the box. Inside the lid was another smaller sign: "Fish Food," with an arrow pointing down. Peering inside, he found tiny objects in a rainbow of colors, each one shaped like a musical note.

Grinning with excitement, William grabbed a handful and hurried back to the water's edge. With a sweeping gesture, he scattered the colorful notes across the pond's surface. The moment they touched the water, a rich, cascading strum reverberated, like fingers running across the strings of a Japanese koto.

William tossed another handful. The sounds shifted subtly with each scattering, creating a symphony of delicate, melodic tones. The koi began to surface, drawn to the food. As they ate, their scales shimmered with bright, iridescent colors, illuminating the pond in a dazzling display of light and sound.

William stood transfixed, until a thought floated into his mind. Wasn't he supposed to be at his piano lesson with Miss Rosa? Before he could dwell on it, a resonant sound rolled through the air—the distant strike of a great gong, its voice deep and commanding, as if calling him forward.

William noticed a stream flowing away from the pond, winding in the direction of the sound. He decided to follow it.

The path soon sloped downward, curving as it hugged the stream. Farther on, a moss-covered stone lantern caught his attention. Its golden glow shone softly beneath a canopy of branches. William paused and leaned in to examine it, expecting to find a candle and flame inside. To his surprise, it was empty. The soft, ethereal light radiated from nothing at all. Shaking his head in disbelief, he continued on.

The narrow path soon merged into a broader one, sloping more steeply. Beside him, the little brook tumbled over a low rock wall and joined a wider stream, its waters weaving around moss-covered stones in a lively, gurgling song.

"Good morning to you, sir!" a tiny voice rang out. "Are you heading to Master Shinichi's home?"

William halted mid-step, startled, and spun around, but no one was in sight.

"I didn't mean to surprise you," the childlike voice continued. "You must be coming from the Smiling Pond. Did you enjoy it? I love spending time there. It's one of my favorite places."

William turned once more, scanning the trees, the path, the stream. The voice felt real, yet no one was there.

"Up here, in the tree!"

He looked up. An enormous apple tree towered over the path, its wide branches bursting with white blossoms. Its size was unlike any he'd ever seen. His eyes darted from branch to branch until he saw it: a small creature nestled among the blossoms. It looked like some kind of monkey.

"Hello!" the little animal exclaimed, hopping down to a lower branch. "My name is Densho—the White-Tufted Marmoset."

William swallowed hard, bewildered. "Uh... hello?"

The little monkey had striking white tufts of fur behind his ears. His black-and-brown head was streaked with gray, and a white patch adorned his forehead. His long, ringed tail twitched and curled as he spoke, adding to his animated demeanor.

The apple tree, overflowing with fragrant blossoms, swayed gently as Densho leapt from branch to branch. His movements were light and nimble, as though gravity had only a gentle claim on him.

The same soft breeze from the pond returned, stirring the branches. A cascade of apple blossoms drifted down like snowflakes, filling the air with sweet perfume.

"Ah..." Densho remarked, closing his eyes and flaring his tiny nostrils. "Nasim is having a bit of fun, I see—putting on quite a show for you, releasing all these petals for your enjoyment!" Densho's tail twitched as he raised his eyebrows. "Nasim must be quite taken with you, my friend."

William glanced around. "Naah… sim? Who?"

"It's pronounced *Nah-SEEM*," Densho corrected gently.

"Oh. So… Nasim isn't a person?" William asked.

"Correct. She's a Wind Spirit." His tail curled and uncurled quickly. "So, what's your name, young sir?"

"Ah, William... Em-em-merson."

"William Emerson, huh? That's a fine name. Do people call you *Will* sometimes?"

"Um, yeah… sure."

The gong rang out once more—deep and resonant, rolling through the trees like distant thunder. Densho closed his eyes and grew very still, swaying gently with the sound. When the tone finally faded, he opened his eyes.

"Gongs often announce special events. That's actually what brought me here." He leaned in. "I love gongs, by the way. Their sound helps quiet my thoughts. We marmosets are naturally anxious and excitable—our minds race so much, it's hard to relax and stay... ah... focused..." As he spoke, a bee buzzed near Densho's head, darting among the apple blossoms. Instantly, his attention shifted. His head jerked back and forth, tracking the bee's erratic movements as though hypnotized. William watched, bemused, as Densho seemed to forget their conversation entirely. After a moment, the bee flew off.

Densho blinked and gave a little shake, snapping back. "Sorry about that! Where was I…?" He angled his head to the side and tapped his little fingers together quickly while he gathered his thoughts. "Ah, yes! I need a lot of help to calm my mind, and gongs seem to do that. We call our big gong the Densho. When you strike it with a mallet, it rings for quite a while."

As if on cue, the gong rang again from deep in the forest. Densho closed his eyes once more, savoring the sound. His fingers stopped tapping, his tail stopped twitching. His entire expression shifted, still and at peace as he sat motionless on the apple branch. When the sound finally faded, Densho opened his eyes and continued as if he'd never paused. "...and that's why everyone in the Whispering Woods calls me Densho." He grinned proudly. "Because I like the big gong so much."

William glanced around. "You mentioned the Whispering Woods... is that where we are?"

"Oh, yes, I'm terribly sorry. I got so excited meeting you that I forgot to introduce you properly." He spread his little arms wide. "Welcome to the Whispering Woods of the Tall Pines!"

"Thank you. I've never seen anything like it."

William started to ask another question but paused, tilting his head, listening intently. *Is that music?* A faint thread of melody drifted through the air, so soft it seemed imagined. He almost dismissed it, but then it returned—a delicate, harmonious sound that seemed to rise and fall with the breeze, like the faint strains of a string orchestra. It didn't seem to come from any specific direction; instead, it felt as though it were everywhere at once.

Densho grinned, watching as William scanned the Tall Pines. "How do you like the music of the Whispering Woods?" he asked.

William straightened up. "So, you hear that music too?"

"Well, yes and no," Densho replied with a thoughtful twitch of his tail. "I hear it in the mornings when I wake up or at night as I'm falling asleep. But during the day, my mind gets busy, and I don't notice it."

Then, with a sudden shift in energy, Densho darted to another topic. "So, Will Emerson, you must be here to see Master Shinichi!"

"Master... Shinichi?" William repeated, the name stirring a faint recollection from earlier.

"Yes, yes!" Densho chattered, his tail twitching with excitement. "He's the Earth Element Master—very wise. He works in the gardens, trains in martial arts... and best of all, he teaches the piano!"

William's ears perked up. "Piano?" he murmured, then looked at Densho. "Yes, I think I'm here for a piano lesson."

"That's wonderful!" Densho said, leaping to another branch directly above him. "I'll take you to his home. It's just a short way down the Crooked Path of the Laughing Brook!"

# Chapter Eleven

## *The Wabi Sabi Teacups of Master Shinichi*

Before William could respond, Densho darted into the trees, flying from branch to branch like a nimble squirrel. William hurried after, struggling to keep pace along the Crooked Path.

Soon, they arrived at Master Shinichi's home, a traditional Japanese-style house, its dark gray tiled roof curving elegantly at the edges. Perched on a ridge above the Laughing Brook, it was surrounded by several smaller buildings nestled among neatly pruned shrubs and flowering trees. William paused to take in the sight, wondering about the man who lived within such beauty.

A neatly arranged path of rectangular stones led up to the entrance. To one side of the walkway stood a seven-tiered stone pagoda lantern, each level glowing in a different color. The base emitted a soft green light, followed by pink, orange, blue, purple, yellow, and finally white at the top. William leaned in to examine the lantern closely, intrigued by its mysterious illumination. As before, he found no light source within to explain the radiant colors.

Densho scurried ahead to the entrance, where a carved stone bench sat to one side. Hanging from the eaves was a set of bamboo windchimes, their hollow reeds bearing the gentle patina of age. Densho reached up with his tail, ready to give them a good shake, but before he could, a playful breeze stirred the air, striking the bamboo chimes into a spontaneous chorus of notes.

"Nasim!" Densho grumbled, squinting at the sky. "I was going to do that." The breeze rustled through the nearby trees in reply and then seemed to vanish.

Master Shinichi opened the door. A broad smile spread across his face, as though greeting an old friend he hadn't seen in years. He wore a gi and hakama—the traditional uniform for aikido practice. His long, dark hair was bound into a ponytail, and there was a quiet strength in his posture, a calm steadiness in his gaze that immediately put William at ease.

Before he could speak, Densho interjected with excitement, "This is my new friend, Will Emerson. I found him up near the Smiling Pond."

"Ah, greetings, Dream Traveler," Shinichi said. "I sensed our paths would cross today." He bowed deeply.

William gave an awkward bow in return. "Pleased to… ah… meet you, sir."

Master Shinichi gave a short bow toward Densho, who answered with a quick nod.

"Well, I think my work here is done," Densho said. He glanced skyward. "Nasim, can you give me a lift to Ning Jing's Treehouse? I promised Ukumari I'd help him pick mangos today, though I'll probably have to wake him from his nap first."

A gust of wind swirled around the little monkey, carrying with it a flurry of leaves and blossoms. With a delighted laugh, his tail curled as the breeze caught him, and he soared like a kite to the top of a towering pine tree. Moments later, he vanished out of sight.

William shook his head in disbelief. "Densho can… fly?"

Shinichi laughed. "Yes, I know—it's not every day you see a flying monkey. The truth is, Densho is skilled in both the Earth and Air Elements. He's learned to alter the vibration of his body, making himself lighter, a skill he picked up from Master Zaria Rumi at the Palace of Ubar."

Shinichi gently put his hand on William's shoulder. "Please, come inside."

William followed him through the entry, leaving his sneakers behind, and stepped into the washitsu—a large, open room with tatami flooring. Scrolls of Japanese calligraphy with bold, sweeping brushstrokes adorned the walls. On one side stood traditional Western chairs and a sofa, while the other held a short table surrounded by eight cushions.

An ancient painting hung on a far wall, its faded hues depicting a father and son in traditional robes standing at the edge of a misty canyon. Above them, a tree stretched its branches, heavy with indistinct fruit. Across the chasm, half-veiled in haze, a red temple with a golden roof emerged.

"The tree above the people in that painting is a persimmon," Shinichi said, his voice drawing William's focus. "Some believe it symbolizes transformation. Green fruit is acrid and bitter, representing inexperience.

As it ripens and turns orange, it becomes sweet, symbolizing wisdom gained through change."

William leaned closer, studying the image. Its faded hues made it difficult to tell whether the fruit was green or orange.

Shinichi moved to the *irori*, a sunken hearth used for cooking and heating. A kettle hung from a lever shaped like a metal bird. He turned back to William, extending a hand. "I was just about to enjoy some tea. Would you care to join me?"

William moved over and knelt on one of the mats. Shinichi lifted the kettle above the hearth and poured hot water into a teapot. A ribbon of steam curled and wound its way upward.

As they waited for the tea to be brewed, Shinichi spoke. "It might help you to know there are many dream worlds. Each mirroring the other. They borrow shapes, languages, and traditions—but never exactly. Like reflections in the rippling water of a pond, they resemble one another yet are not the same."

"There are... dream worlds?"

"Oh, yes. In this dream world, for instance, the people of the East often think in circles, while the people in the West prefer straight lines. These are only tendencies, not rules—but the contrast teaches us something about balance."

William noticed two teacups resting on the edge of the hearth. Their forms were irregular, as if handmade. There was something simple but beautiful about them.

"Have you ever heard of *wabi sabi*, William?"

"I think so... but I can't remember where."

"Well, these teacups you see here are an example of *wabi sabi*, and they may help explain what I mean." Shinichi lifted one and angled it toward the light. "If we look more closely, the glaze reveals a complexity of tones—the upper half brighter, the lower half steeped in shadow. From this contrast in the glaze, a deeper meaning begins to reveal itself."

He placed the teacup in William's hand. It was cool to the touch, its surface and rim uneven.

"*Wabi sabi* is an aesthetic that can be difficult to define—the beauty of things flawed, transient, unfinished. In this world, it stands in contrast to the Western notion of beauty, which favors the flawless and enduring. In the West, people strive for linear progress, a continuous search for light and clarity, always moving forward. This desire is reflected in the brighter tones of the glaze. In Eastern thought, the path is often more circular—returning, revisiting, finding meaning in cycles and subtle variations. That sensibility lives in the darker parts of the teacup, in its shadows and subtleties.

"Light and darkness—East and West—they may seem opposed in this world, yet they must coexist, as they do in every world a traveler may pass through."

Shinichi poured tea into William's cup and then his own. William lifted the cup with both hands, imitating Shinichi's careful gesture. The first sip was sharp, almost bitter, but as the warmth spread through him, a mild sweetness followed. The contrast lingered on his tongue.

For a while, they drank in silence. William studied the teacup as if its glaze might yield an answer. He traced the uneven rim with his thumb, searching for meaning in the play of light and shadow across its surface.

Shinichi watched him quietly. "I can tell you are struggling. These teacups have puzzled many before you. Would you like some help from Nasim?"

"Nasim…?"

"She can offer you some insights, a shift in awareness we call the *Winds of Change*."

William lowered his eyes to the cup in his hands. He felt as if he stood at some kind of threshold—like the boy in the painting on the cliff. One path was safe, familiar. The other leapt into mystery, toward the hidden temple with the gold roof across the canyon. Once he chose, there might be no turning back.

He looked up, meeting Master Shinichi's gaze, and gave a small nod. "Yes. I would like her help."

All at once, a breeze drifted through the open window and brushed against his face. In that instant, a sudden illumination rose within him. A sharp focus took hold of his mind, and he found himself thinking and feeling with unusual speed and clarity. He looked again at the wabi sabi teacup. For a fleeting moment, he understood the balance between the opposite forces of Eastern and Western aesthetics—philosophical insights of this dream world beyond the reach of an eleven-year-old boy.

His eyes widened. "I understand," he whispered. "It's so obvious." But as quickly as the breeze entered, it slipped away, out another open window, and the clarity vanished with it.

William shook his head. "That was… strange. I understood for a moment, but now it's… gone."

"Ah, gone for now, William—but not forgotten. When the time is right, you will remember."

# Chapter Twelve

## *Stepping Stones*

After they finished their tea, Shinichi slid open a shoji door at the back of the living room, revealing a pathway that led to several traditional Japanese looking buildings nestled behind his home. Near the doorway, a small, wooden platform—the genkan—held neatly arranged pairs of outdoor slippers.

Shinichi motioned toward them. "You can put on a pair to walk outside."

But just as he was about to slip on his own, he paused and raised a hand. "On second thought… let's skip the slippers. Let's take off our socks and go barefoot. It's the best way to truly feel the Earth beneath you."

"Sure!" William said without hesitation. Going barefoot was something he always did at the ocean near Beacon Rock. He loved the cool press of wet sand between his toes.

As they stepped out of Shinichi's home, William noticed a large, white stone block just outside the door. It served as the first step down to the ground.

"This marks the beginning of the path," Shinichi said. "The steppingstones ahead are called *tobi-ishi*. Each one is raised slightly above the ground, surrounded by moss, which represents flowing water," Shinichi continued. "When you walk across, it's as if you're crossing a stream—without getting your feet wet. But you must tread carefully. Each stone has its own shape and feel. Just like every step we take in life."

Shinichi moved ahead with deliberate grace, stepping slowly and fluidly from stone to stone. His movements were unhurried but precise—so light he seemed to glide, like a martial artist in slow motion.

William had to tread carefully. Some stones tilted at odd angles, others bore ridges that made footing uncertain. It was easy to lose balance, and keeping Shinichi's steady pace proved difficult. At one point, he wobbled and planted a foot firmly on the soft moss.

Shinichi glanced back with a chuckle. "Ah… I see you got your foot wet. Lower your center of gravity by sinking down just a bit. That will help you maintain your balance as you move slowly. Focus on each stone as you step. Take your time and enjoy the shape beneath your foot. This is how your Earth Element training begins."

William watched Shinichi's flowing movements with renewed attention. They reminded him of Densho leaping effortlessly through the apple tree, and he imagined himself moving just as lightly. To his surprise, as he envisioned it, he began landing more softly on each stone, as if thought and motion were beginning to merge.

"Walking barefoot over uneven surfaces like this," Shinichi said, "draws your attention to your feet and strengthens your connection to the Earth. The raised stones slow your pace, and as your movements slow, so does your mind. This path, these tobi-ishi, invite mindfulness—an awareness of something we often take for granted… walking."

He watched William's careful steps. "But you don't need a special path to practice this. Anytime you walk, simply slow down. Focus on each step. Feel the weight of your body shift from one foot to the other. This awareness of your contact points is fundamental to the Earth Element."

Shinichi's tone softened. "As you walk in a mindful way, you may begin to notice other qualities—lightness, expansion, even serenity. These belong to the Air Element. You'll learn more when you meet Zaria Rumi. She is a true master of Air—and a remarkable piano teacher as well. For now, simply feel the ground beneath your feet."

Shinichi led William across a grassy lawn, where a group of students were practicing a martial art, their white uniforms bright against the mossy green. William studied the students. Their slow movements seemed almost meditative, each shift intentional and connected.

He noticed other people milling about who weren't part of the class—dressed more casually, standing at the edges or wandering among the buildings. They looked different somehow, expressionless, easy to spot.

Then, at the edge of the lawn, a reclining figure materialized into view, and William watched as the person, clearly asleep, began to stir and slowly sat up, blinking as though trying to remember. Then they rose to their feet and started walking, eyes unfocused.

William raised his hand as they passed him and said, "Hi." The person looked at him and gave a faint nod, eyes still distant, before moving along. Shinichi gently moved William aside as another figure nearly walked into him from behind.

"Who are those people?"

"Dream Walkers," Shinichi said. "They drift through our world, observing but barely aware."

"Oh. But where do they… come from?"

"Many places, really. They are like tourists in this dream world, mostly moving through it as if sleepwalking."

Shinichi then directed William's attention toward the students practicing martial arts. "That is nekkara, a discipline I developed to help students connect with the Earth Element. It begins with a grounded stance and awareness of the breath. When students sink down into their nekkara stance," Shinichi explained, "their breathing naturally deepens. The two are interconnected: The stance roots the feet to the Earth, while steady breathing expands the mind. Together, they create a harmony often lost in the more goal-oriented culture of the West."

William tilted his head. "What do you mean, *the West?*"

"The western part of the continent of Ulandia—that is the main landmass of this world. The Whispering Woods, where we are now, lies in a remote region that borders the great division of East and West."

When one student wobbled in their stance, Shinichi paused. "Excuse me, William," he said, stepping away to assist. William watched as he moved among the students, adjusting their posture with a light touch or a quiet word.

A moment later, Shinichi motioned for William to join the class.

"I see my lower body as the roots of a willow tree," he said, "and my upper body as its flexible branches. This is the second stage of nekkara: rootedness with fluidity."

Sinking into his stance, Shinichi stood like a tree, immovable. One student stepped forward, pushing against his upper body. Shinichi swayed effortlessly, redirecting the force so the student tumbled to the side. More students tried, only to find themselves off balance as Shinichi's movements rippled like water.

"Your turn, William," Shinichi said, motioning him forward with an encouraging smile.

William hesitated, unsure. "I'm not really good at sports or martial arts..."

Shinichi rested a hand on his shoulder. "Skill is not the doorway, William... it is your imagination. Let it guide you. You might be surprised."

He knelt beside him, gently adjusting William's stance. "Widen your feet... good. Now sink your weight." He tapped the tops of William's feet. "Feel your connection to the earth." Then he stood again and added, "Imagine roots growing from the soles of your feet, deep into the Earth. You are a willow—flexible above, unshakable below."

William drew a breath and closed his eyes. Unsure how to begin, he clung to Master Shinichi's words. In his mind's eye, he pictured roots spreading downward from his feet, anchoring him. Slowly, he allowed himself to become the trunk of the willow, centered and still.

When he opened his eyes, he found himself surrounded by several students pushing against him—but he didn't move. No matter how hard they strained, his stance held firm.

Shinichi's eyes widened. "Exactly, William—you did it!"

Startled by the praise, William lost focus. The image of the tree dissolved, and he stumbled, sending himself and the students tumbling to the ground.

Shinichi helped him up, laughing. "Rarely have I seen someone use their imagination so naturally. Hmm... can you try that again?"

William nodded, still nervous but steadier. He closed his eyes and returned to the image of the willow tree, its roots anchoring him deep into the Earth.

This time, Shinichi stepped forward, placing his hands gently on William's shoulders. He began to push. Nothing happened. Shinichi deepened his stance and pressed harder. A subtle sound of disbelief escaped with his breath as William remained immovable. Around them, William could hear the students beginning to stir, their whispers rising in low, uncertain tones.

Finally, Shinichi stepped back, shaking his head in wonder. "Amazing. I haven't seen this level of natural ability since..." He paused, catching himself, then finished softly, "...well, in a very long time."

But the murmurs grew louder, carrying a single name—*Florestan.*

William opened his eyes and glanced around, catching fragments of their voices. *Who's Florestan?* he wondered.

"William," Shinichi said, his tone firm but calm, cutting through the rising whispers. "Let's take it a step further. Imagine your upper body as the flexible branches of the willow, while your lower body remains rooted."

William nodded and closed his eyes again. This time, when a student pushed against his shoulder, his upper body swayed like branches in the wind, redirecting the force. The student lost balance and toppled over. More students joined in, but one by one, they fell as William's body bent and flowed effortlessly, while his feet stayed firmly planted.

Shinichi watched with growing amazement. "William, you're combining rootedness and fluidity is as if you've been practicing for years."

One student leaned toward another and whispered, "Could he also be aware of the Fifth Element?"

The other shook their head. "Impossible. Only the Masters know about it. How could he?"

Shinichi stepped closer, a flicker of hesitation crossing his face. "Let's try once more—this time, with greater force. Let's see how deep your roots truly go."

Sinking into his stance, Shinichi began softly but soon pushed harder—then more aggressively. William imagined the pressure as a powerful wind and allowed his body to sway and bend with it. Gasps spread through the students as they watched his body undulate, leaning nearly horizontal while Shinichi moved quickly above him, searching for resistance.

When Shinichi finally stopped and stepped back, his expression was a mixture of awe and disbelief. "William... your imagination is powerful—and yet, so intuitive."

The whispers of *Florestan* and the *Fifth Element* grew louder.

Shinichi raised an open palm, and the students fell instantly silent. After a pause, his voice softened. "The kind of imaginative power you're tapping into lives in everyone. But after childhood, most forget. Elements training is not about gaining abilities, really—it is about remembering what was always there."

He turned to the others. "Please, continue with your nekkara practice." Then, gesturing toward a pavilion in the distance, he said, "William, let us move to the piano dojo. I think you are ready to carry the Earth Element to the keys."

William slapped a hand to his forehead, "Oh—that's right. I'm here to take a piano lesson with you, aren't I?"

Shinichi smiled. "Indeed. Come."

# Chapter Thirteen

## *Cristofori's Dream*

As they walked along the moss-covered stone path toward the piano dojo, a high, flute-like melody drifted through the trees—delicate and spiraling beneath the forest canopy.

William paused. "What is that music?"

Shinichi glanced up toward the treetops. "Ah… yes, that is Quetzal. She's one of the most beautiful birds in the Whispering Woods and a good friend of Densho's. Her songs drift through the forest like a wandering piccolo."

As the final note from the Quetzal faded into the trees, they reached the pavilion. Shinichi motioned toward the entrance.

Inside the dojo stood a grand piano, its ebony surface gleaming in the light. The intricately carved bench beside it, with delicate inlaid details, lent the instrument an aura of something ancient yet untouched by time.

The room was filled with soft, natural light. A window opened onto the Laughing Brook, its gentle murmurs blending with the faint scent of incense and fresh blossoms. A few simple artworks adorned the walls, enhancing the stillness of the space.

Shinichi beckoned William to take a seat at the piano. William lifted the keyboard lid, revealing a span of luminescent keys that reminded him of the Smiling Pond.

He settled onto the bench, which seemed to send a gentle charge of energy through his body, softening the edges of his thoughts.

"To begin, place your attention on your contact points," Shinichi said, "where your body meets the world—your sit bones on the bench, your feet on the floor, your hands in your lap."

William focused on those points of contact. The simple act of noticing them quieted his thoughts and slowed his breathing.

"Now," Shinichi continued, "imagine both of your arms growing light, as if filled with helium. Let them float up and allow your fingers rest gently on the black keys."

William raised his hands slowly, the movement unhurried.

"Your fingertips," Shinichi said, "are sacred contact points in Piano Zen. To begin understanding this, you must heighten their sensitivity." He gestured. "Caress the black keys lightly. Tiny circles. Imagine the surface of each key as water."

William touched the keys delicately. His fingers traced slow spirals across the ebony surface, barely grazing them.

"With just a bit more weight," Shinichi continued, "the hammers will strike. In Piano Zen, this sensitivity is called *Touching the Pond*. It teaches the fingertips to hover at that edge—supple, aware, responsive. Touching the Pond keeps both mind and body soft as you play."

He stepped back, watching William for a moment. "You see, Piano Zen uses the Four Elements to deepen our awareness when playing the instrument. Most students chase speed and precision through endless repetition. That builds technical skill, yes—but often at the cost of a true connection with the piano. When you slow your movement, your breath, even your thoughts, you create space for harmony to emerge between mind and body. That's when the real magic of the Elements begins to unfold."

Shinichi gave William a moment, then said, "Let us move to an improvisation piece called *Music of the Smiling Pond*. Do you have your Piano Zen lesson book with you?"

William blinked. "Oh… yes, just a second." He opened his backpack and found the lesson book. When he flipped it open, it landed on the very page. At first, the illustration seemed ordinary, but then it stirred to life. Brightly lit koi began gliding through clear water, white apple blossoms drifted across the surface, and tiny points of light sparkled in the ripples.

Off to one side sat the wooden bench by the pond.

"For this improvisation," Shinichi said, "press and hold down the sustain pedal. Stay on the black keys and use the same light touch you have been practicing."

As William's fingers moved, he experienced an echo of that moment in the Whispering Woods when he first touched the surface of the Smiling Pond. The luminescent keys of Master Shinichi's piano seemed to mirror that memory—tranquil, alive, ever-shifting. Now, each note shimmered like ripples across the water.

Shinichi watched for a moment, then added, "Do not think too much about what to play. Let your heart guide you."

The improvisation felt freeing. The more he released control, the more expressive his playing became. The sensation of floating, of discovering music by touch, shifted something inside him.

After some time, Shinichi raised his hand. "Excellent, William. Do you see how heightened sensitivity in your fingertips transforms your playing?"

William nodded. He held the sustain pedal until the final improvised notes dissolved into silence.

"Rest for a moment," Shinichi said, moving to an open window. For a while, he stood in silence—the gurgling of the Laughing Brook the only sound in the room.

"You know, there is more to the piano than meets the eye," he said at last, turning back toward William. "It holds a secret—one that most students find impossible to believe. But I think, to assist you on your journey with Piano Zen, it's time you heard the truth. The piano is more than just an instrument—it is a gateway."

William looked at him. "A gateway?"

"Yes. And to understand that, we must return to the very beginning—to Bartolomeo Cristofori's original dream of the piano. In that vision, he crafted his masterpiece, but he went much further."

Shinichi rested both hands on the piano's shiny, ebony surface. "He embedded within it a mathematical code—a matrix weaving all the Elements into a single, harmonious expression, allowing the player to reach something deeper... something timeless."

Shinichi's hand glided across the curve of the piano. "To truly understand this instrument, you must realize that Cristofori was not merely an inventor—he was a mystic."

A crease formed between William's eyebrows. "A *mystic*... Cristofori?"

"Yes," Shinichi said softly. "Cristofori believed, as Pythagoras once taught, that numbers form the bridge between the visible and the invisible. He built his piano to mirror that hidden order. To Cristofori, music was the language of all the dream worlds, and he wove that belief—the harmony of numbers drawn from Pythagorean geometry—into the piano's mechanical design, a hidden code that still lives inside every instrument."

William scratched his head. "That sounds like the piano has some kind of… magic in it."

Shinichi nodded. "Yes, it does."

While William was still pondering Shinichi's words, the master retrieved a Tibetan bowl from a nearby shelf. The sight of it stirred a faint memory. Without a word, Shinichi began to circle a wooden mallet along its rim, releasing a low, resonant tone. He started to speak, but William couldn't hear the words. The sound of the bowl deepened as the edges of the room began to blur—until everything dissolved into silence.

In the darkness, disoriented, he caught a familiar scent—the warm aroma of sandalwood from Miss Rosa's candle. A soft breeze brushed past, carrying the fragrance of flowers and pine needles. These comforting sensations drew him steadily back toward consciousness.

"Okay, William," Miss Rosa's voice called gently. "You can open your eyes now. William? Oh… William?"

He blinked several times, as though rousing himself from a deep sleep.

"Ah, there you are!" Rosa said. "You looked so relaxed, I thought you might have nodded off. Ready to dive into your first Piano Zen lesson?"

He responded, his voice groggy. "Um… yes, definitely."

"Wonderful. Have you had a chance to look through your Piano Zen lesson book yet? Was there anything that caught your eye?"

He mopped his face with his hands, still in a haze. "Yes, I—I think so." He took a deep breath. There was something on the tip of his tongue. Then his eyes lit up. "Could we start with *Music of the Smiling Pond*?"

Rosa brightened. "Why, of course. Beginning with an improvisational piece would be perfect."

As she spoke, a flicker of panic crossed his mind. His hand flew to his chest—his father's Master Samaritan ring. For a heartbeat, he thought it was gone. Then his fingers found the familiar shape, cool against his skin. He exhaled, relieved.

That's when it struck him—he must have drifted off during the ringing of the Tibetan bowl.

"Miss Rosa," he said, "could I have just a moment? I need to write something down."

"Of course," she said, setting the bowl aside. "Take your time. I'll gather a few materials for our lesson."

William took out his dream journal from his backpack and began to scribble notes, desperate not to lose the fragments and fleeting impressions already fading—Japanese gardens and buildings, a talking monkey, a shiny black piano, teacups. Disconnected as they were, he captured as much as he could before the images slipped away.

When he looked up again, Rosa was waiting patiently. She simply smiled. "Well," she said, "let's see where this Piano Zen journey takes us, shall we?"

# *Air*

# Chapter Fourteen

## *Valley of the Bells*

William realized he'd been walking with Rosa in silence for some time, lost in memories of the past year. As they continued their hike along the Wildwood Trail, it climbed to an elevated ridge. From this height, the view stretched for miles. The most stunning sight was Mt. Drake, towering larger than ever, its snowy peak glistening under the sun. The distant peaks of the Fisher King Range—usually hidden behind the city's rolling hills—rose into view, their jagged beauty cutting into the sky.

Rosa slowed her pace as they reached the ridge, pressing a hand to her side. She took a deep breath, letting the crisp air fill her lungs, and studied the sprawling view. The wind tugged at her hair, and she held it back with one hand, her other resting on her hiking stick—its shape twisted and knotted. William stood beside her, both of them taking in the panorama in silence.

After a while, Rosa's eyes drifted downward to a deep ravine, its floor hidden beneath a dense canopy of trees. A smaller path branched off from the Wildwood Trail, marked by a weathered wooden sign: *La Vallée des Cloches*.

William stared at the trail sign, the name triggering a memory. "Isn't '*La Vallée des Cloches*' from Ravel's '*Miroirs*?' It's a piano suite that means Valley of the Bells, right?"

Rosa gave him a curious look. "Yes, it is. How do you know that piece?"

"I… I'm not sure," William admitted, his voice trailing off.

"R.C. Prescott named this path Valley of the Bells many decades ago," Rosa said. "It leads down into the ravine." She hesitated, peering into the depths below. "I had planned to show you something down there. It's quite magical, really. But as much as I would like to take you there, I'm afraid I don't have the energy for it today. The hike down and back is steep, and, well… I'm not as young as I used to be." She offered a faint smile. "We'll save that mystery for another day, when I'm feeling up to it." Gesturing ahead, she promised, "I still have a few surprises I can share with you today. Let's follow the trail a little farther."

"Sure," William said.

As they moved on, he cast one last glance toward the deep ravine. Whatever was down there would remain a mystery—for now.

He followed Rosa as the trail curved gently downward, leaving the ridge and its hidden ravine behind. Their footsteps softened as the trail led them into a grove of birch trees. Sunlight filtered through the leafy branches overhead, creating shifting patterns of light and shadow on the forest floor.

A clear, mournful music drifted through the air, and Miss Rosa raised her hand, tilting her head toward the sound. "William, listen…"

They both stood still as a symphony of birdsong filled the air.

"Those are nightingales," she whispered. "They're native to this region. It's the only place in America where they're found. That's how the city got its name."

"I didn't know that," he said. He closed his eyes, listening as the notes drifted through the branches, blending with the rustle of leaves.

"It's magical, isn't it?" Rosa said. "I love this spot. I could stay here for hours, I imagine."

"Me too." Listening to the birds, he murmured to himself. "*Cela ressemble à des oiseaux tristes.*"

"Pardon?" Rosa asked.

"Oh... I was just saying it sounds like the birds are sad."

"Ah." Rosa smiled. "'*Oiseaux tristes*,' another Ravel piece from '*Miroirs.*' I suppose you grew up with French music at home?"

"When I was little, there was always music playing—my mom singing in the kitchen, my dad with his old records."

"What kind of music?" Rosa asked.

"All kinds, I think. But there was this one old record my dad used to play for me. And I remember asking him to play it over and over again."

"A record? Do you mean an LP?" she asked. "I didn't know kids your age still listened to those things."

"Yes... he had an old portable record player from when he was a kid. It had its own speaker. You could put it on the floor and sit and listen."

"Well, now I'm intrigued. What was the name of this record you listened to over and over?"

"It was called Sparky's Magic Piano."

"That was the title? Oh, I see… it was a story album. I recall they made those in the 1950s. Kind of like the old radio shows back in the day—sound effects, character voices, music."

William nodded. "It was about a boy named Sparky. He's pretty young. I'm not sure. Maybe six or seven years old? He falls asleep and has this dream where his piano comes alive and talks to him."

"I love it." Rosa laughed. "Tell me more. What happens with this talking piano?"

"Well, it had this strange voice. Its words came through as musical notes. I remember the sound of it was kind of creepy. Anyway, the piano said it would play any piece of music Sparky wanted. All he had to do was request a song, then run his fingers over the keys, and the piano would play all the notes for him."

"Oh, I see. What kind of music did he make the piano play?"

"It was all classical music: Beethoven, Chopin, Ravel…"

"Hmm… interesting," Rosa said. "I wonder if that's where you first heard Ravel's music, his 'Miroirs' suite, perhaps? Anyway, what happens next?"

"Sparky starts touring around the world with his magic piano and becomes very famous. He finally makes it to Carnegie Hall. But then it got a little… scary."

"How so?"

"He's about to play a Beethoven sonata, and his magic piano refuses. Like as if the time was up for any more magic. He pleads with the piano on stage and hits the keys, but the piano won't play for him, and it makes the audience uncomfortable."

"Oh, my. Losing the magic on stage at Carnegie Hall… that sounds like it turned into a nightmare."

"Yeah," William chuckled. "I never liked that part of the story. But when he wakes up, Sparky decides to learn to play the piano for real."

Rosa's expression softened. "How old were you when you listened to that?"

"I guess about three years old. I remember that's where my dad got his nickname for me."

"What nickname?"

"Sparky. My mom said he always called me that."

"That's so sweet, William. Maybe that is where your love for the piano was born—with 'Sparky's Magic Piano'."

"Maybe."

"We should pick up our pace," Rosa said. "I noticed some clouds on the horizon earlier. If it turns into a storm, we may have to cut our hike short."

# Chapter Fifteen

## *Walden Lake*

As the two of them continued their walk along the trail, the birch forest thinned, giving way to rolling green hills. Wildflowers dotted the slopes, swaying in the breeze, as the trail curved toward the western edge of Imperial Heights.

Before long, they reached the base of a grassy embankment, where the trail climbed steeply in a zig-zag pattern. Rosa paused at the base, planting her stick for balance, gauging the climb before starting up. The ascent was slow and steady, William keeping close behind.

When they reached the top, the view dazzled him. Below lay a vast body of water—so clear and blue it seemed almost unreal. Its surface was smooth as silk, a perfect mirror reflecting the snowcapped peak of Mt. Drake looming on the horizon. The water's image was so sharp, it was hard to tell where the mountain ended and its twin began.

Rosa motioned below. "That's Walden Lake. And we're in luck. I thought it would be windier today."

"I've never seen a lake look so… blue," William said.

"It's a mix of rainwater and snowmelt from Mt. Drake. The basin used to be an old limestone quarry."

William stood still, as if he had stepped into a dream—afraid to speak and break the spell cast by the mountain's image upon the surface. What had once been an environmental scar at the turn of the century—a quarry that left a gaping wound in the heart of Imperial Heights—had become something beautiful, almost surreal: a pure, clean source of water for the people of Nightingale.

Rosa signaled for William to follow her down a winding path to the shoreline.

"I've never heard of Walden Lake before."

"That's because the city officially calls it the Prescott Reservoir. Walden Lake was Eleanor's name for it."

"Oh. Yeah, I've heard about this reservoir—I just never knew where it was."

As they neared the lake, they passed by the weathered remains of a small cabin. The porch sagged to one side, part of the roof missing. Moss lined the eaves, and the whole structure looked as though it had been abandoned for years.

William studied the cabin. "Who lived there?"

"Prescott. Built it himself. Eleanor told me he used to come here to think. Often stayed there for days."

Puzzled, William reached into his pocket, fidgeting with the basalt stone as he peered through a broken window. A chill ran down his spine. For a moment, it felt as if the ghost of Prescott still lingered there.

"Rumor has it," Rosa said, "that once the mansion opens to the public, the McFarland Sisters Restoration Company plans to return the cabin to its original state. I think it's a wonderful project—especially after seeing it in ruins for so many years." She paused, leaning on her walking stick. "Eleanor once considered restoring it herself, but she was always busy with her philanthropic work. Still, she found time to place a bench down by the water in honor of her father— crafted from Imperial Heights limestone, the very stone once quarried here."

Rosa gestured toward the bench by the lakeshore. "Come, William. Let's rest a while."

As they sat together quietly, a cool breeze drifted over the rim of the old quarry, carrying the scent of pine and blooming wildflowers. Ripples spread across the surface, catching the sunlight like scattered jewels.

Rosa's thoughts drifted—back to the orphanage, to a time when she was painfully shy and kept mostly to herself. She had rarely played with the other children. Words had been hard in those days, especially in a language not her own.

Eleanor Prescott had often found her sitting alone in the garden courtyard. She would speak to her in Spanish—gently, patiently—but Rosa rarely replied, sometimes even running away.

Over time, Rosa's English had improved. And, like William, she grew to cherish books, tucking herself into corners, lost inside their worlds.

One day, a book appeared on her bed: *Little Women.* She knew who had left it—the woman with the missing thumb.

Reading it, she imagined herself among the March sisters—a family that chose virtue over wealth, tenderness over ambition. She admired Jo's fire, but it was Beth's quiet love of music that stayed with her. Beth was the reason she began piano lessons with Eleanor.

Moved by the memory, she reached for the locket on her necklace—a small, bronze oval etched with thorny vines and a golden phoenix. Inside was a photograph of her mother, a link to the family she barely remembered.

As the Great Depression deepened in the 1930s, a wave of repatriation swept across the country. Fueled by President Hoover's rhetoric and headlines in *The Saturday Evening Post*, families of Mexican descent—citizens and non-citizens alike—were rounded up and sent back to Mexico.

Rosa's parents had been among them. Though they were U.S. citizens, they were taken in the sweep, while Rosa, who had been visiting relatives, was left behind.

Someone had placed the locket around her neck that first night in the orphanage. She'd worn it every day since. Her fingers lingered there now as she sat on the limestone bench. Then, gently, she released the memory once more, as she always did, at the edge of crystal-blue water.

Beside her, William sat quietly, eyes closed, the light breeze brushing across his face. "William," Rosa said softly, "the pilgrimage to Walden Lake is a tradition for all my students after a year of Piano Zen study. But there's something else I like to share. Many years ago, Eleanor Prescott selected a book for me, one I didn't realize I needed until I began to read it. I've continued the tradition with my own students ever since. As the year unfolds, I listen and wait until the right book reveals itself. And then I present it here, at the lakeshore."

The wind stirred across the lake as Rosa set down her backpack and withdrew a small wooden box. She opened it carefully in her lap, revealing an object wrapped in red velvet. Without a word, she handed it to William, nodding for him to take it.

He loosened the string and unfolded the cloth to reveal an old, worn edition of *Walden* by Henry David Thoreau.

"I know how much you love the rare book room at Shelley's," Rosa said with a faint smile. "R.C. Prescott had an extraordinary library of his own. This one was given to me by Eleanor when I was about your age."

He opened the cover and stopped short. The inscription inside was personal, addressed to R.C. Prescott himself:

*To my young friend, R.C. Prescott: Socrates once said that "an unexamined life is not worth living." May you endeavor to find Walden as Henry once did. Remember, all unrest is but the struggle of the Soul to reassure herself of her inborn immortality. — Amos Bronson Alcott, Concord, Massachusetts, 1885.*

"It was a gift," Rosa said, "from Amos Bronson Alcott to R.C. Prescott. The same Alcott who helped guide Thoreau and the other transcendentalists. They believed there was something sacred in nature, in silence—and about the journey within."

Rosa's hand drifted to her locket, caressing its contours as she watched William turn the pages, his fingers tracing R.C.'s margin notes in quiet wonder.

"Thoreau's *Walden* isn't a book you rush through—it's one you return to. The truths in it unfold slowly, like the seasons he wrote about."

William stopped at a passage that had been underlined, his fingers resting on Thoreau's words.

*"I learned this, at least, by my experiment: That if one advances confidently in the direction of his dreams, and endeavors to live the life which he has imagined, he will meet with a success unexpected in common hours."*

Rosa noticed the passage, then placed a hand gently on his back. "Making your dreams come to life doesn't happen without effort, William. But I can think of no worthier challenge."

William looked up at her, his eyes bright with excitement. "Thank you, Miss Rosa. I don't know what to say."

"You're so very welcome, William." She stood slowly, steadying herself with her hiking stick. "Thoreau believed that truth lives in stillness—and that each of us has to find it for ourselves."

As Rosa turned toward the water, William gently flipped to the back of the book. On the final page, written in delicate, looping script, were the words: *Dearest Rosa, never doubt that your life holds meaning, and that by living kindly, your light may help to mend this world. Yet fear is ever the shadow that lingers behind us—fear of failure, of abandonment, of losing what we love. At times, it presses upon the heart as if to still its beat. But in the dark night of the Soul, even the humblest act of mercy, the faintest breath of human kindness, can awaken us once more to the light.*

Below the inscription, there was a faint signature: *Eleanor Monnier-Prescott.*

# Chapter Sixteen

## *Strong Winds*

Just then, the wind kicked up, stirring the lake into waves as the sun slipped behind rolling clouds.

"It's time to go, William. Looks like a storm is brewing."

William carefully placed the *Walden* book back in the wooden box and secured it in his backpack, before the two of them began a quick retreat up the slope of the old quarry.

The wind pressed against his face, tossing his hair, stirring a memory— a windy afternoon, many months earlier, when a sudden rush of air burst through Miss Rosa's studio, interrupting one of his Piano Zen lessons.

It had been the day he first began learning the piece "Across the Dunes of the Rub' al Khali"—a piece Rosa said required lightness of mind and body. He'd only been studying with her for a few months. He remembered his mother staying in the studio for that lesson, which wasn't unusual for her, as she often sat nearby with a book in hand, completely absorbed.

On that windy afternoon, a sudden gust had swept through Rosa's studio, flinging open the balcony doors with a crash. The banging sound startled Misha, the cat. Panicked, she tried to scurry out of the studio, her claws slipping on the polished wood floor. After much frantic spinning and a blur of her brown paws, Misha finally scrambled up the stairs and vanished into Miss Rosa's room.

The wind outside grew stronger. Branches swayed and thudded against the balcony rail, yet Rosa only seemed invigorated by the storm. Standing by the window, she quipped, "This looks like a good day to talk about the Air Element."

She lit her sandalwood candle. Its sweet, woodsy fragrance filled the room. William took a seat on the engraved demoiselle crane piano bench as Miss Rosa reached for her Tibetan bowl. Holding it gently, she began, "The Air Element is about expanding the mind. When I ring the bowl, close your eyes and imagine your thoughts becoming as light as the air around your head. Let them dissolve and ride upon the sound waves."

William shut his eyes, amusement flickering across his face. His schoolmates often teased him for his tendency to drift off into daydreams, earning him the nickname *airhead.* Yet perhaps that same trait would serve him well as he tried to grasp the Air Element.

The Tibetan bowl released a deep, vibrating tone that pulsed through the room. The sound enveloped him, easing his breath into a steady rhythm. He imagined his mind becoming as light as air—thoughts evaporating into the bowl's resonance, carried away on the invisible currents of the Air Element.

As the tone lingered, William felt a familiar breeze brush his cheek. It was cool, scented, soothing. For a moment, he wondered if a window had been left open in Rosa's studio. He tried to steady his focus, letting his thoughts dissolve once more into the air. Then everything shifted when a familiar voice called out to him.

"There you are, Will. I told Nasim we'd find you here at the Smiling Pond."

He opened his eyes and found himself on a wooden bench, with Densho perched on a branch of a willow tree nearby.

"Densho! It's great to see you again. How are you?"

"I'm doing quite well… quite well, indeed. But you, Mr. Will, are about to be late for your piano lesson with Master Zaria Rumi."

William blinked hard. "Wait—a piano lesson? Oh, I-I must have forgotten that was happening."

"Oh, yes and when you didn't appear on the palace bench in Ubar, Master Zaria sent Nasim and me to find you. I had a hunch you'd be here at the Smiling Pond."

"We should get going, then," William said.

"That's not going to be so easy," Densho said, nervously tapping his fingers. "You see, her piano studio is really… really far from here."

The little monkey paced back and forth on a branch, tail flicking. "Even if we left now, you wouldn't reach Ubar for days—on foot, anyway."

William scanned his memory but couldn't recall scheduling a lesson with Master Zaria Rumi. Embarrassed, he also realized he couldn't even remember who she was. Reaching into his pocket for his basalt stone to collect his thoughts, he found it empty.

Just then, Nasim's breeze swept through the willow branches, rustling their long tendrils. A swirl of air tousled Densho's fur, and the little marmoset paused, glancing upward, listening. "That's bold, Nasim, but Will's never even had a flight lesson," he said, stroking his chin like a tiny professor while muttering to the wind.

"Hmm... you really think so? Well, yes, I suppose that could work, though it's a bit dangerous for Will."

Nasim whooshed around William, and it made something inside him feel suddenly confident and light. His hand found the Dream Dorje against his chest, and he clutched it. The word *airhead* drifted into his mind, and he felt a nudge to focus on it. As he did, his body grew strangely weightless, as if gravity had loosened its grip on his bones. His thoughts, too, began to drift, unspooling like thread in the wind.

"Whoa," he murmured. "Wha-what's happening?"

"Ah... very good, Will," Densho said, flashing a grin. "Nasim is helping you lighten your thoughts. She's stirring the Air Element in you—like helium for the mind."

"But I feel weird," William murmured. "Like I'm... expanding?"

"Perfect," Densho said. "You're still new to the Air Element, but that might work to your advantage. Overthinking can weigh you down."

Densho gestured toward William's backpack. "Nasim asked if you brought your Piano Zen lesson book. It can help you harness the Air Element. She says your book holds magic in it—just enough to help you fly."

"Fly? What do you mean... fly?" William said, slipping off his backpack and pulling out the book.

"Good, you've got it," said Densho, clapping his tiny hands. "Now hold it out, arms relaxed—like you're about to read it."

William's expression froze as his heart began to pound.

"It's all right, Will. Nasim won't let anything happen to you."

A breeze began to gather, fluttering the pages.

"The book's magic is meant to help you when you're practicing the piano," Densho continued, "but we can use it for flying, too. Just keep a light grip and focus on the sensation in your fingertips."

William looked at him, bewildered. He felt as if he were standing on the edge of a high platform, moments before a bungee jump.

"Just trust me and be ready to let go," said Densho. "Again, it's better if you don't think too much."

The little monkey hopped onto William's shoulder. "Nasim says to use your imagination. Picture yourself as a kite on a windy day and let the book do the rest. Densho chuckled. "Just close your eyes, Will. You'll see."

For a moment, he hesitated, uncertain he could manage it. Still, he closed his eyes, focusing on the tingling sensation in his fingertips. The word *airhead* floated through his mind again. He followed the thought, imagining himself as a bright kite with a long tail.

Instantly, a sensation of lightness filled him—not just in his body but in his mind. A gust of wind surged around him, catching the open music book like a ship's sail. He felt the lift of the air beneath him, and something inside him surrendered.

The ground seemed to release its hold, and before he could even comprehend what was happening, he was rising—soaring into the sky. The lift carried him high above the Whispering Woods of the Tall Pines.

When he finally opened his eyes, he drew in a startled breath. The view below was dizzying. But any sense of fear gave way to wonder. For a moment, he imagined he had no body at all—weightless, no longer a boy, just a ghost adrift in the dream world.

As they soared higher, the massive pines of the Whispering Woods shrank below them, and the Smiling Pond became no more than a shimmering puddle. He glanced into the distance and gasped. Towering, snowcapped peaks glistened on the horizon.

"Densho! Those mountains. They're enormous!"

"Yes, those are the Pahadas, Will. You'd never spot them from the Whispering Woods—too many tall trees down there."

The wind picked up, swirling around them with sudden force. William tensed, his grip tightening on the lesson book. "Densho, what's going on? This feels different."

"High winds around the peaks of the Pahadas," Densho shouted over the growing roar. "The air currents up here are intense, but don't worry. Nasim will guide us through the Kali Gandaki Gorge. It's a narrow pass that cuts through the mountains and shelters us from the worst of it."

The high, snow-capped peaks of the Pahadas rose before him—majestic yet forbidding. Nothing could possibly survive up there, he thought. Then, in the distance, he noticed a strange formation: tiny black dots moving across the sky. Squinting, he realized they were birds, flying toward the highest peaks at an altitude that seemed impossible.

He shouted over the rushing wind, "Densho, look over there—birds."

"Yes, I see them. Demoiselle cranes. They migrate over the peaks of the Pahadas to reach their nesting grounds far to the east."

Densho pointed toward the highest, snow-laced peak. "See that mountain up there? That's Mount Parthena. It's where Parthenopolis is located."

"Parthenopolis?" William squinted at the towering cliffs, straining to make out anything unusual. "I've heard about that place from Master Shinichi."

"Yes! An ancient spiritual city," Densho called back, his voice nearly lost in the wind currents. "But you can't see it with regular eyes."

William scanned the rugged slopes, looking for any sign of the hidden city. For a moment, he thought he saw a faint outline of a great wall etched against the cliffside, but when he blinked, it was gone.

Densho nudged him. "Look over there, Will—the Kali Gandaki Gorge. That's our way through."

Nasim guided them lower, away from the turbulent winds, until they were gliding within the quieter depths of the gorge. Terraced rice fields and small villages appeared along the riverbanks, tucked like postcards into the valley floor.

The Kali Gandaki Gorge stretched before them—a deep chasm carved through the heart of the Pahada Mountain Range. Towering walls of jagged, moss-covered rock flanked both sides, their faces streaked with iron and clay hues. Far below, the river wound through the valley like a serpent.

William kept his grip light on the music lesson book, focusing on staying balanced. Glancing back, he caught sight of Mt. Parthena's snow-capped peak, its upper crest wrapped in a delicate band of white clouds.

The ride smoothed out as the trio glided just above the winding Kali Gandaki River. Mist from towering waterfalls filled the canyon, their cascading waters plunging into the gorge below. William felt the cool droplets on his face as they sailed past.

As they whisked along the bottom, he noticed a reddish, golden glow ahead, cutting through the gray, overcast light. The foliage along the riverbanks began to thin, and the jagged cliffs flanking the river softened into rounded slopes. Patches of wildflowers, vivid against the rocky terrain, gave way to stretches of barren ground as the basin of the gorge widened.

The cool, misty air they had traveled through was now shifting—warmer, drier, and tinged with a faint scent of earth and sand. The gorge was transforming, leading them into an entirely different world.

# Chapter Seventeen

## *Over the Sands of the Rub' al Khali*

The transformation of the landscape into a desert was startling. The glow he'd glimpsed earlier came from a vast expanse of golden-tangerine sand stretching endlessly into the eastern horizon. The dunes below rolled like frozen waves on a sunlit sea.

Behind them, the Kali Gandaki Gorge lay shrouded in mist. High above, Mt. Parthena stood sentinel—guardian of the gorge, its snow-capped peak clutching the clouds and marking the boundary of the world they'd left behind.

As they sailed across the dunes, William noticed something unusual. It wasn't just the visual beauty that struck him—it was the sound. Ringing chimes. Faint and ethereal, rising from the sand. The wind sweeping across the dunes seemed to shape the celestial music, as if the desert were an instrument played by invisible hands.

William closed his eyes, letting the unearthly sound wash over him, its rhythm lulling him toward sleep.

"Hey, Will," Densho said, tugging on his ear. "Don't fall asleep on us, buddy."

William's eyes snapped open. "Oh—yeah. Sorry."

"Careful," Densho said. "There are layers within the dream worlds. You can get lost in them if you drift too deep. Nasim says it's like a maze that can lead you into dark corners."

"Sure, I'll try to stay focused on flying," William said. He glanced out over the rolling dunes. "Um… I forgot to ask. Where are we?"

"This is the Rub' al Khali desert. Some call it the Empty Quarter because they think nothing is out here, just endless sand. But Nasim's taking us to a place hidden from sight—the Ubar Palace. It's where Master Zaria Rumi lives."

William was quiet for a while as they sailed high above the dunes. Then, out of the blue, he asked, "Densho, who's Florestan?"

Densho's eyes widened and his tail went rigid as Nasim's breeze faltered, their flight momentarily unsteady.

"Will, where did you hear that name?"

"Shinichi's nekkara students. They were whispering it—also something about a Fifth Element. That's all I caught."

"That's not a name you want to invoke lightly," Densho said. "Speaking it can draw his attention, and pull you toward the darker layers of the dream worlds."

*Darker layers?* William's thoughts raced, unsure whether to laugh or believe him. But something in Densho's tone—its sudden gravity—made his stomach tighten. Fear surged through him. His buoyancy faltered, and the wind beneath them collapsed. Densho clung to the collar of William's gray hoodie as they plunged in an uncontrolled descent, tumbling down the side of a crescent-shaped dune until they hit the base in a flurry of sand.

William staggered to his feet, groggy, shaking grit from his hair. "W-What happened?"

"You got spooked up there and lost control of the Air Element," Densho said. "Your mind has to stay light and open for this flying thing…"

Suddenly, Densho's voice trailed off, and without warning, everything shifted. The sky dimmed, and the celestial chimes and gentle breeze vanished, leaving behind an eerie void.

He found himself standing at the foot of a mountain, disoriented— forgetting the desert, forgetting all about Densho and Nasim entirely. He wandered a few paces across the mossy ground, unsure where he was or how he'd come to be there. A strange emptiness filled his chest, a sense of having misplaced something precious, though he couldn't recall what.

A sudden cry tore through the silence.

High above, a demoiselle crane was locked in a desperate struggle with an eagle. The crane tried to climb for altitude, its wings beating furiously, but the eagle was faster—striking, slashing, driving it down. Then another eagle dove from above, talons extended, and raked its wing. The crane spiraled toward the ground, twisting helplessly until it struck the earth.

William ran forward, heart pounding. The crane was still alive, one wing bent at an unnatural angle, trembling on the mossy forest floor. The eagles landed beside the helpless bird, edging closer to its crumbled body.

From a grove of tall trees near the mountain's base, a figure emerged from the darkness. Cloaked in a heavy robe of deep red, its hood shadowed their face, concealing their features. They moved with unsettling speed, a long staff in hand, its tip crowned by a jagged black stone, a faint ember seeming to smolder deep within.

"Begone," the figure commanded, raising the staff. A flash of red light burst from its tip, searing the air.

Blinded by the glare, the eagles shrieked and took flight, retreating into the forest.

The cloaked stranger knelt beside the fallen crane. From within his thick robe, he withdrew a jeweled, white glove and slipped it onto his left hand. William froze, watching as the figure passed the glowing hand slowly over the crane's body. A pale light rippled through the bird's feathers, and the twisted wing began to straighten.

"Is the bird going to be okay?" William asked.

The figure didn't answer. He held the bird's wing gently, and before William's eyes, it mended itself—whole again. The crane stood and fluttered, testing its wing several times. Soon, it lifted back into the air, climbing higher and higher until it vanished against the horizon.

The red-cloaked figure watched the crane disappear, unmoving. Then, turning toward William, he lifted his gloved hand and beckoned—inviting him to follow into the forest. "Come. You're not safe here," the figure said, his voice a low, rasping baritone.

Before William could take a step closer, a violent wind swept over the wet, mossy ground, carrying with it a rush of sand that seemed to rise out of nowhere into a swirling veil. The figure lowered his hand, and in the next instant, they were gone, swallowed by the storm.

The wind expanded, surrounding William, an he threw up an arm to shield his eyes. When at last the gale subsided, he lowered his hand. The sky had turned powder-blue again, the sun warm on his face. Nasim's gentle breeze returned, and the distant chimes floated through the air once more.

"Will! Will... are you okay?" Densho's voice broke through the haze of his thoughts. William blinked, disoriented. Densho tugged on his collar with his tiny paws. "You scared us! You just froze up—stiff as a board! What happened? Where did you go?"

William shook his head, his voice unsteady. "I must've been dreaming. It's all a bit hazy. I was alone." He paused, looked down at the ground, trying to collect the fragments of the experience. "There was an injured crane—maybe one of the demoiselle cranes. Then an eagle, two I think. And someone else... a figure in a red cloak. I couldn't see their face, but I think they healed the bird. It's all a... blur."

Densho glanced up toward the air above them, where Nasim hovered silently. "What kind of eagles were they?" he asked.

"I'm not sure. They moved fast and... I think they injured the crane."

"Oh, dear. That sounds like Deimos and Phobos," Densho said. "They're golden eagles, Will. And the figure in the cloak... that was Florestan. Speaking his name must've drawn you into one of the darker layers of the dream world. Nasim managed to bring you back, but you gave us quite a scare."

William's hands tightened around his Piano Zen book as a shiver passed through him. "What does he want with me?"

Densho wrapped his arms around William's neck in a reassuring hug. "Don't worry about that now, Will. We're taking you to the Palace of Ubar. It's safe there."

William nodded faintly, still shaken, and Nasim's breeze stirred gently, coaxing them forward. He took a deep breath and softened his mind once more. As he opened the Piano Zen book, the wind lifted them back into the air.

They glided eastward, the stark beauty and silent danger of the Rub' al Khali lingered in William's mind—until his thoughts turned to the mysterious Palace of Ubar, where Master Zaria Rumi awaited.

# Chapter Eighteen

## *The Palace of Ubar*

"Nasim says we're just about there," Densho said. "She wants to know if it's okay to activate your Dream Dorje."

"The dorje? Oh, um… what will that do?"

"It'll help tune you to Ubar's frequency so you can see the palace."

"Ah, sure," William said. "Go ahead, Nasim."

He felt a gentle warmth at his chest and looked down. The dorje beneath his shirt had begun to glow.

As they drew closer, the heavy thoughts that had weighed him down earlier seemed to dissolve into the air. His mind felt lighter, freer, expanding outward into the endless sky.

The travelers glided up over a final dune. As they crested the ridge, violet and pink lights bloomed across the horizon. The Palace of Ubar emerged like a mirage made real—its towers and domes shimmering in a cascade of rose, amethyst, and gold.

At first glance, the architecture of the Ubar Palace blended Middle Eastern elegance with Western grandeur, forming a harmonious and otherworldly aesthetic. Two circular towers rose at either end, their cone-shaped roofs extending outward like burnished vermilion umbrellas. Long corridors connected them, their arches adorned with Moorish curves and symmetrical patterns. At the center rose a vast dome, reminiscent of a Renaissance cathedral, painted in rosy hues and crowned with a golden cupola that caught the last light of the sun.

The palace grounds spread out lush and vibrant—gardens blooming, palms swaying, a bubbling spring feeding a tranquil pond. Jasmine and wisteria perfumed the air, their blossoms cascading over pergolas that lined the walkways.

Nasim set the travelers down gently on a manicured slope.

As William and Densho began walking toward the palace, Densho gestured toward a marble bench near the edge of the pond. "That's the bench where dream travelers like you usually arrive when they visit Ubar," he said.

William furrowed his brow. "Then why didn't I show up there? How did I end up at the bench at the Smiling Pond instead?"

Densho scratched the back of his head. "Yeah, you're right. That was… unexpected. You should ask Master Zaria Rumi."

As they passed beneath archways of flowering vines, William spotted a group of demoiselle cranes roaming the gardens, their elegant black and white feathers stunning.

"Densho, are those the same birds we saw flying over the Pahadas?"

"Yes, they often stop in Ubar to rest before continuing their migration east."

William exhaled. The sight of so many brought a quiet kind of relief. Deep down, he felt certain it was the same kind of bird he'd seen in his dream—the one the red-cloaked figure had healed and set free.

As they climbed the grassy slope toward the palace veranda, a young woman appeared beneath one of the ornate horseshoe arches and descended the stone steps to meet them on the lawn. She wore a turquoise-blue silk sari adorned with gold Khari palm leaves, draped gracefully over a brown choli blouse. Her dark brown hair was tied back in a neat ponytail, revealing delicate gold earrings shaped like lotus blossoms that glinted in the fading sunlight. A small, red bindi marked her forehead—subtle yet striking. Her presence radiated calm and vitality in equal measure.

"Greetings, William, and welcome to the Palace of Ubar! We've been expecting you. I'm Amara, a student of the Air Element and apprentice to Master Zaria Rumi. I can only imagine the challenge of flying all the way from the Smiling Pond. I'm grateful Nasim brought you safely to Ubar."

Amara turned to Densho. "Hello, my sweet Densho!" She cupped his furry cheeks in both hands. "I've missed you. It's been far too long."

Densho went unusually quiet, avoiding her gaze as his cheeks puffed out slightly in embarrassment.

"Maybe I should visit you and Ukumari in the Whispering Woods. How is that old bear these days?"

Densho's eyes lit up. "Ukumari would love that! You know him—still the same. Playing his djembe drum, eating mangos, sleeping all day."

Amara pressed a hand to her mouth, then burst into laughter. "That old bear, my word!"

She turned back to William. "I know you've had quite a journey. Please come inside the palace and rest. Master Zaria is just finishing a class on the Air Element in the rotunda. It should be wrapping up soon."

She led Densho and William through the veranda into the grand rotunda. The sheer scale of the space took William's breath away. High overhead, a majestic dome arched above them, casting intricate patterns of light and shadow across the polished marble floor.

Dozens of guests were seated below, listening intently to Master Zaria Rumi as she stood in the center of the rotunda. Amara gestured toward a staircase winding along the right side of the rotunda.

"Let's sit up on the balcony level," she whispered, leading them upward.

As they climbed, William ran his hand along the smooth marble rail. Beneath it, delicate carvings of vines and leaves coiled in elegant patterns. Densho perched on his shoulder, his tufted tail swishing.

From above, William got a clearer view of Master Zaria. She carried herself with effortless grace, her brick-red gown brushing the floor and a loose-woven brown hijab draped across one shoulder, cascading past her waist.

The acoustics were extraordinary; even from the balcony, her voice reached him as if she were standing only a few feet away.

"I could simply tell you that the secret of life is a never-ending expansion of consciousness," Master Zaria said. "But every young student needs a place to begin—a first step toward awakening to this reality."

She paused, her gaze sweeping over the crowd before it settled briefly on William. A small, knowing smile played on her lips, and he shifted uneasily in his seat.

"The Air Element you seek to master already resides within you. Like angels in slumber, you only need to wake up to realize you can fly and be free."

Her expression softened. "My task is not to give you power but to help you remember the boundless abilities you already possess."

She stepped into one of the aisles between the students. "Let's close with a brief contemplation to stretch our imagination. Everyone, close your eyes."

There was a soft rustle as students adjusted in their seats. William glanced around. Amara and Densho had their eyes closed, their expressions serene. After a moment's hesitation, he exhaled, shrugged, and closed his eyes too.

"Now, breathe gently for a few moments," Zaria's voice continued, soothing and steady. "We are going on a little journey. Let your imagination guide you. Don't overthink. First, soften your mind and relax your body. Feel yourself becoming light—lighter still—until gravity no longer holds you. You are as free as a gentle breeze, the edges of your body dissolving into the space around you. Now imagine yourself lifting... floating above the palace dome... drifting higher and higher..."

Her voice grew melodic. "The palace glows beneath you, shrinking into the distance as you take flight. You glide past a flock of demoiselle cranes, their wings cutting gracefully through the air. Ahead, the Pahada Mountains appear—majestic and vast. You soar above Mt. Parthena and descend into one of the gardens of Parthenopolis, fragrant with jasmine. You walk among towering temples—grander than the rotunda here at Ubar. You feel small beside them yet perfectly at peace. The people of Parthenopolis bow slowly, greeting you with warmth. You notice other dream travelers on the grounds. Let your imagination stay in that place...."

Her words lingered, and for a long moment, the room remained completely still.

She stepped back to the front of the room, her tone playful now. "It's time to come back. Slowly return. When you're ready, open your eyes."

One by one, the students opened their eyes, their expressions quiet and introspective, as if they were waking from a deep, inner journey.

"Your imagination is far more creative and limitless than your conscious mind," she said. "When you imagine something vividly, your subconscious cannot tell the difference—it begins to make that vision real."

"It is time to conclude our class," Zaria said. "Thank you for coming, and, as always, *doret begardam!*" She turned to leave, but Amara's voice rang out from the balcony, sharp with alarm.

"Master Zaria!"

Zaria stopped mid-step, her gaze snapping upward. A hush fell over the rotunda as every head turned, then a wave of gasps swept through the crowd.

William was no longer in his seat.

His body floated high above the floor—arms extended, eyes closed, serene and unaware that he was suspended in midair.

From the balcony, Densho and Amara clung to the edges of their seats, motionless, their eyes wide with disbelief and panic.

# Chapter Nineteen

## *A Dream Within a Dream*

As William hovered, unaware, the fabric of the dream world began to shift. The palace faded from his senses—the veil of that dream world lifted, revealing a deeper layer beneath. A surge of light flooded his senses, piercing through his closed eyelids—brighter than the sunlit shores of Beacon Rock. A cascade of tinkling bells filled his ears, not loud but all-encompassing, as if the sound resonated through his very being.

William opened his eyes. The light was blinding. Shielding his face, he stumbled toward a colossal temple looming nearby. From what he could make out, the structure resembled the Roman Pantheon, only far larger, monumental, as if built by giants. Its heavy metal doors, etched with intricate designs, rose several stories high. They looked impossible to open.

Feeling his way along the smooth stone wall, he found a smaller, less imposing side door. Relieved, he slipped inside, escaping the glare and the sound outside. The air within was cooler, still. William paused, breath ragged, as his eyes adjusted to the muted light.

It looked like a waiting room—bare stone walls, a long bench running along one side.

Then, without warning, a young girl appeared on the bench. One blink, and she was simply there.

The name Ariya surfaced in his mind before he could place it. A girl from a bookstore, somewhere.

Her red hair was tousled, as if she had just woken from sleep. Her eyes slowly moved around the room before fixing on him. "Where am I?" she asked, her voice hoarse with confusion. "Do I know you?"

"Ariya," he said, half-relieved, half-bewildered. "I'm glad you're here. I just arrived too. But I don't really know where *here* is."

She stood unsteadily, scanning the stone walls. "I need to go home," she murmured, mostly to herself. "My parents will be worried."

"Well, don't go that way," he said, gesturing toward the door he had entered. "It leads outside, but the light is really—"

Before he could finish, she reached for the handle and pulled the door open.

"Ariya—don't."

A white blaze flooded the room. In an instant, she vanished, gone as suddenly as she'd appeared.

William struggled forward, shielding his eyes as he pushed the door shut. For a moment, he just stood there, heart pounding, staring at the empty bench where she had been.

He paced back and forth, uncertain what to do next. Then he noticed another doorway on the far side of the room. With nowhere else to go, he crossed to it and eased it open.

Beyond the door was a classroom. Rows of transparent pianos rested on clear stands, making them seem to hover above the floor, their black and white keys suspended inside. There were no strings, no wires within the instruments.

Students sat before the instruments, each wearing a small, crystal earpiece, eyes closed, hands moving in slow motion across the keys. The room felt like an ashram for piano instruction.

Candles ringed the walls, their flames swaying in the gentle current of air. The faint scent of bergamot drifted through the space. At the front of the chamber stood a man in a white robe threaded with intricate gold patterns. A long, dark ponytail trailed down his back, his bald head catching the candlelight.

"Oh… sorry," William whispered, easing the door shut, not wanting to interrupt the class.

He returned to pacing the vestibule, trying to steady his thoughts, wondering where he was and what had happened to Ariya.

The same door opened again, and the teacher stepped through, closing it softly. He approached with a calm smile. "Greetings, dream traveler. You must be William Longfellow Emerson."

"I'm sorry I interrupted your class," William said.

"Quite all right," the man replied. "I am Wu Wei, the abbot here at Parthenopolis. Welcome. Let me guess—Master Zaria Rumi had you doing an imagination exercise, and you ended up here."

William hesitated. "That sounds familiar. I just remember closing my eyes, and when I opened them, I was here. Wait, did you say Parthenopolis? I've heard of this place."

"Yes. You stumbled into the Praetorium Temple—a place for musical training. It is also the location of Cristofori's Dream Piano." Wu Wei stroked his chin thoughtfully. "Your senses are not yet accustomed to the higher vibrations of Parthenopolis. It takes time."

"I saw my friend, Ariya," William said. "Then she opened the door and the light—it swallowed her. She just disappeared."

"She is safe, I assure you," Wu Wei said. "She is a dream walker and has simply returned to her own world. She sensed your presence, though, and was drawn to you here."

William exhaled, relieved, but something tugged at the edges of memory. He vaguely recalled a card with a cryptic note at the Smiling Pond:

*Place this dorje around your neck. It will help you navigate the dream worlds.*

Dorje… right. Now he remembered. As the memory settled, he felt a subtle energy pulsing near his chest. He noticed the dorje glowing underneath his shirt.

"You are in a dream within a dream," Wu Wei said. "A place where dream-walkers and dream-travelers sometimes meet, though few recall it when they return. Parthenopolis is one of the deeper layers among many in the dream worlds." Wu Wei's patient gaze rested on him. "In the dream worlds, the ordinary rules of time and space do not apply. You will understand soon enough, the further you go on your adventures here."

William tried to respond, but no words came.

He placed a hand on William's shoulder. "It is time to return to Ubar, dream traveler. Do not be alarmed when you wake. You are safe. Master Zaria is watching over you. Until we meet again…"

The room around him began to dissolve, fading into light, and the last thing he saw was Wu Wei's serene smile.

Then everything went dark.

# Chapter Twenty

## *Origins*

The next thing William heard was chairs screeching against the marble floor as students scrambled in alarm below. The commotion startled William. He opened his eyes, confused, and realized he was floating high above the floor of the rotunda, near the ceiling of the great dome. His heart raced as the reality of his predicament set in.

Before he could gather his thoughts, panic overtook him and he began to fall, plummeting like a stone. The air rushed past his ears as he raced toward the marble floor at terrifying speed. In that moment, time stretched—his mind flooded with images even as the cold certainty of his imminent death gripped him.

Master Zaria reacted swiftly. With a commanding gesture, she summoned a powerful current of air. A whirlwind roared through the rotunda, sending loose papers spiraling upward. The students gasped as the wind caught William, wrapping around him like an invisible net. He drifted downward and landed softly on the floor, light as an apple blossom.

For a moment, the rotunda held its breath.

Master Zaria approached William and knelt beside him, placing a steady hand on his shoulder. "Are you alright?"

William couldn't lift his gaze from the marble floor. He gave a faint nod. "I... I think so."

Amara and Densho rushed down the stairs, then leapt onto William's shoulder, his paw resting on the back of his head. Amara wrapped an arm around his shoulders.

Zaria stepped back, observing William. "Master Shinichi was right about you. It has been a long time since we have seen a dream traveler adapt so quickly to the Elements."

The students began to file out of the rotunda. A few paused to pat William on the back or offer a word before moving on. In the murmur of voices, someone whispered in passing, "They say Florestan is looking for him."

As the rotunda emptied, only William, Densho, and Amara remained. At Zaria's suggestion, they made their way down the main corridor.

The hallway was tall and narrow, lined with Corinthian columns and Moorish horseshoe arches. Above and below the arches were intricate geometric patterns, and the walls were adorned with biomorphic carvings of leaves, vines, and blossoms. The palette of rich blues, pinks, and golds seemed to glow, though William couldn't figure out where the light was coming from. It reminded him of the lanterns in the Whispering Woods that seemed to glow with their own mysterious energy.

"Many people call this a palace," Zaria said as they walked, "but it's more of an oasis—a retreat for musicians. Here, travelers from many realms gather to listen, learn, and share."

From the adjacent practice rooms, music spilled into the hall. The sound was a rich, dissonant harmony of overlapping textures. William recognized the familiar timbre of Western orchestral instruments—violins, trumpets, flutes—but woven among them were exotic melodies played on unfamiliar instruments, some with a distinctly Middle Eastern character.

As they passed each window, William and Densho glanced inside, glimpsing the source of the layered sound. In one room, a musician played the cello; in another, someone practiced the trumpet. But in several others, musicians played strange instruments he didn't recognize.

William tapped Amara on the shoulder. "What's this one called?"

Amara looked inside. "Ah, yes, that's the Arab rebab," she explained. "It's the ancestor of the cello." She gestured to another room. "And over there is the al-zurna. It evolved into what is known in the West as the trumpet."

They continued down the hallway, stopping outside another room, where a musician was practicing on a stringed instrument William had never seen before. Its intricate, rhythmic sound caught his attention—bright, bell-like, and oddly familiar.

He leaned closer, eyes widening. The musician sat on a low stool, striking strings stretched across a trapezoidal wooden frame with felt hammers. The motion was mesmerizing—fluid, precise, and the music stirred something in him.

"That's the Persian santur," Amara said, noticing his fascination. "It's an ancient instrument, like the European dulcimer but much older."

William studied the rows of tuning pins and the metal strings spanning the santur's soundboard.

Suddenly, it clicked. "It's like… a piano!"

Amara laughed softly. "Yes, exactly. The santur, a treasured instrument from the Muslim world, planted the seeds for the invention of the piano."

Master Zaria, walking just behind them, drifted into the conversation. "Long before he built his first piano, Bartolomeo Cristofori journeyed through the dream realms, studying the *musica universalis*—the teachings of Pythagoras."

"Does that have something to do with a special code he put inside the piano? Master Shinichi mentioned it."

"Indeed, it does." Zaria nodded.

# Chapter Twenty-One

## *Evolutions*

William lingered at the practice window, captivated by the musician playing the santur. The piece was complex—fast, precise, hypnotic. The hammers struck so quickly, they blurred, lulling him into a trance. For a while, he stood there, untethered from the passage of time.

When the piece ended, the musician glanced up and smiled, then winked. The spell broke.

But Densho was no longer on his shoulder, and Amara was gone. A jolt of panic gripped him. He turned sharply, relieved to find Master Zaria Rumi still there, standing behind him.

"I'm sorry," he said. "I guess I got a little… lost."

"Oh, for quite some time, actually," she said with a faint smile. "But you are fine, William. I asked Amara and Densho to go on ahead. They are waiting for us."

She gestured down the corridor. "Shall we join them?"

As they walked down the long hallway, the clamor of the practice rooms faded behind them. "You may have noticed," Zaria said, "thoughts are lighter here. In Ubar, the mind is free to wander, to drift beyond logic. That's when intuitive awareness deepens and creative discoveries quietly arise."

For a time, they walked on in silence—then, faintly, the sound of piano music drifted through the air. The corridor ended at a pair of double doors.

Zaria gently opened them to reveal a spacious chamber with Moorish arches and inlaid patterns, bathed in the warm light of the setting sun. At its center stood an ornately carved white piano, its lacquered surface catching the amber tones of dusk.

Amara was already seated on the bench, her fingers dancing across the keys in a fluid, improvised melody, while Densho swayed atop the piano, tail twitching in rhythm.

William paused at the threshold, captivated. Amara's playing flowed with emotion and a sense of mystery.

"She's playing 'Across the Dunes of the Rub' al Khali'," Zaria whispered. "Many who study piano here learn that piece."

Amara's expression was serene, her eyes half-closed as she played. The music conjured vivid images in William's mind: shifting sands, moonlit dunes, and the soft violet glow of a desert sunset.

"Amara likes to get creative and improvise around the melody," Zaria explained. "Every time she plays the song, it is slightly different."

Amara's fingers slowed as she reached the final notes, letting the sound hang delicately in the air before fading into silence. She turned and smiled, surprised to see William and Zaria standing in the doorway.

"I didn't know we had an audience," she said, eyes bright. "I hope you enjoyed it."

"Very much. It was beautiful," William said. "It reminded me of my journey with Densho and Nasim, flying across the desert."

Amara glanced toward Densho. "I think Master Zaria is ready to give William a Piano Zen lesson. Want to keep me company while I tend to a few things around the palace?"

"Sure," Densho said, jumping up on Amara's shoulder. He turned back to William. "I've been telling my friends in the Whispering Woods about you, Will. They're all excited to meet you. Maybe next time?"

"Sure, Densho. I'd love to meet your friends."

After Amara and Densho departed, a soft hush settled over the room. Zaria invited William to sit at the piano.

He sat down, intrigued by the intricate gold designs on the fallboard and traced them with his fingers.

"I hear you did well with Master Shinichi and your Earth Element training."

William nodded. "He taught me to place my awareness on my contact points. He said to play very slowly, so I could stay aware of my breath and my body."

"Yes, very good. Air and Earth are opposites—mind and body. But they balance each other. Imagine flying a kite," Zaria said, gesturing lightly. "The wind lifts it, but only because someone on the ground holds the string." She smiled. "Many study the Air Element for years and never find its freedom— not from lack of effort but because they try too hard. What they need is a child's imagination, a sense of wonder."

After a pause, Master Zaria tapped her lips thoughtfully. "Let me show you something." She motioned toward William's hand. "Make a fist. Hold it tight."

William clenched his right hand into a fist.

"Tighter," she said.

His knuckles whitened as the tension built.

"Focus on the sensation," Zaria said. "Notice how your fist affects the rest of your body—your shoulders, your breath. Everything contracts because of that one point of tension."

William nodded but stiffly—his neck had locked up and a small twitch formed beneath his left eye.

"Your fist is like the mind in a state of contraction," Zaria said. "This is what happens to it when we try too hard at the piano."

She placed her hand on William's shoulder. "Now hold your fist just as tightly, but relax everything else: your arms, shoulders, your breathing. Let go of tension everywhere else but the hand."

William exhaled and allowed his body to soften, all except his clenched fist, which remained tight as a stone.

"Good," Zaria said. "Keep breathing deeply. Observe the fist from a detached point of view while the rest of your body completely relaxes. This is how the mind looks in contraction—a knot of anxiety, anger, fear."

She paused, letting the thought settle. "Now, slowly begin to soften your fist. Imagine your fingers unfolding like the petals of a lotus blossom. Let your fist become an open palm. This is the image of the mind letting go, releasing its grip, surrendering the need to control. It represents expanded awareness. Your thoughts are light, spacious, and free. That is the Air Element principle."

As William slowly opened his fist, a translucent lotus took shape above his palm—its petals faintly aglow, made of light itself. He stared in wonder, mesmerized by its delicate radiance.

Master Zaria noticed. "What are you feeling?"

"My palm is tingling, like there's some kind of energy inside," William said.

Zaria's eyes softened. "Very perceptive, William. You are feeling the current of the Fire Element—the life energy that flows through all things."

William closed his eyes, focusing on the prickly sensation in his palm. When he opened them again, the lotus blossom had vanished.

Master Zaria leaned against the piano. "In Piano Zen, the mind should be like your open palm—soft, receptive, creative. When we let go of tension and control, music flows through us effortlessly."

William looked down at his open palm. "Airhead!" he suddenly blurted out.

Zaria blinked. "I beg your pardon?"

"Oh! I just remembered something. Airhead. It reminds me to keep my mind light, like the Air Element."

Zaria threw her head back, laughing. "If that image works for you, then use it!" A trace of amusement lingered in her expression as she turned to a nearby shelf and retrieved a Tibetan bowl, cradling it in her hands.

The sight of the bowl sent a ripple through his mind. As he focused on it, the room began to spin. Instinctively, his fingers closed around the Dream Dorje as Zaria struck the bowl, releasing a deep, resonant tone that expanded outward in waves—dissolving the dream world around him.

He shut his eyes, and colors flickered in his mind, swirling, shifting, merging with the bowl's vibration. Then a gust of wind swept through.

"Nasim?" he called out.


A faint trace of sandalwood curled through the air—warm, earthy, familiar. William's eyes snapped open. It was Miss Rosa's studio, but his mind hovered above, caught between the two worlds, unsure which one was real.

Across the room, Rosa hurried toward the French doors, pulling them shut against the sudden rush of wind. "I must not have latched the door properly," she said. "The wind's really picking up out there! You have to be careful—weak branches tend to fall when it blows like this through Imperial Heights."

William blinked, his surroundings gradually coming into focus. Yet the echo of the dream world lingered in his mind.

As Rosa secured the doors, he grabbed his journal from his backpack and scribbled down what fragments he could remember: flying over a desert, a talking monkey, a palace with a white piano, a bald man with a long ponytail.

His eyes landed on his mother, still sitting by the table with the kintsugi flower vase, her book open in her lap. A wave of relief swept through him, though he wasn't sure why.

Aimée set her book down and began to rise, intending to help with the balcony doors, but Miss Rosa was already waving her off. As she settled back into her chair, her eyes met William's. For the briefest moment, she caught a fleeting expression on his face—a distant, bewildered look that stirred a memory she hadn't revisited in years.

He had been just three years old, and they were visiting the Marrakech West Bazaar in the Old Town District of Nightingale. While Aimée was buying him a glass of fresh lemonade from a street vendor, William had wandered off, disappearing into a sea of people, drawn by the sound of Middle Eastern music from nearby street performers.

The moment she realized he was missing, a bolt of panic ripped through her. The rush of adrenaline had been immediate, fierce—an ancient, primal force that eclipsed all reason. For those few agonizing minutes, time behaved strangely: racing forward and standing terrifyingly still all at once. Her entire world narrowed to a single, searing imperative—find William.

Thankfully, the ordeal had been brief. Above the bustling crowd, William's cry rang out, sharp and clear. She followed the sound, pushing past bodies, the crowd parting as she closed in on him.

A young woman crouched beside William, gently reassuring him between his sobs while keeping an eye on the stroller where her own toddler sat. When the mothers' eyes met, no words were needed.

Aimée scooped William into her arms, holding him close, wiping away both of their tears. For a long moment, the world beyond their embrace ceased to exist.


After Rosa latched and secured the doors, she turned to William with a curious look. "You said something just as the bowl stopped ringing, but I didn't catch it."

Still a bit dazed, William drew in a slow breath. "Yes, you're right. There was a name on the tip of my tongue, but I can't quite… remember."

Rosa tilted her head thoughtfully, then smiled. "Well, today we'll explore the Air Element. Let's start with a piece from your lesson book—'Across the Dunes of the Rub' al Khali'."

William opened the book. The illustration showed a mystical palace rising from the sands, its domes and towers bathed in the rose-tinged light of sunset.

Outside, the wind gave a final push against the windowpanes, and then fell still.

# Water

# Chapter Twenty-Two

## *The Journal*

The wind picked up, stirring Walden Lake into restless waves as the scent of rain thickened in the air. A sharp, cold gust cut through William, pulling him back into the present—out of his memory of the Air Element.

Rosa quickened her pace up the slope of the quarry. "We should hurry if we hope to reach the Gate Lodge before the storm hits."

At the rim, William paused for one last look, drawn once more to the lake's beauty, even though in a previous life it had been a scarred, limestone quarry. He turned and hurried after Miss Rosa, already descending the far side in haste along the Wildwood Trail.

Few words were exchanged on the return trip. Rosa, focused and quiet, moved at a measured pace through the thickening mist, her steps careful but steady. Before long, they reached the vista overlooking the ravine. He was still curious to know what might be down there, underneath the thick canopy of branches, but the wind picked up, carrying a light dusting of rain. They both pressed onward, toward the safety of the Gate Lodge.

As they hurried along in silence, William's thoughts drifted back to where it all began—to the moment Rosa accepted him into her studio and placed the rare Piano Zen book in his hands. That quiet act of trust had opened something in him, a door to wonder.

He had pored over the book for hours that week, searching for any clue to this mysterious discipline. The pages offered musical passages framed by exquisite illustrations, yet few answers. Unsatisfied, he had set off for the Modern Prometheus rare book room at Shelley's, determined to uncover more.

At first, William found nothing. He visited Shelley's several times that week, combing the rare book room on his own, scanning shelves and index records for any mention of Piano Zen. Eventually, he asked the staff for help, but they came up empty too.

A few days later, an unexpected phone message arrived from Shelley's. One of their part-time staff members had come across something she believed might be exactly what he was looking for. That same evening, near closing time, his mother agreed to drop him off. He made his way up to the rare book room, ushered in through the employee entrance and introduced to Lina Bauch, a soft-spoken Austrian woman with silver-streaked hair and a gentle, steady gaze.

Her voice carried a faint Austrian lilt, and now and then she'd slip in a soft *ach so* or *bitte schön*. Lina was gentle, unhurried, and curious. As she led him toward a weathered mahogany table near the hearth, she offered a few glimpses into her past: her early childhood in Herzogenburg, Austria; her family's flight to America just before the outbreak of the Second World War.

William recognized her from his recent visits to Shelley's. Though they'd never spoken, she was often nearby, reshelving books, mending bindings, or quietly organizing the index card drawers in the rare book room. Most of the store had long since been computerized, but the rare book wing still relied on the older system—index cards typed decades ago, still quietly doing their job. Tactile, dependable, and free of screens.

Flames from the fireplace cast flickering hues across the carved woodwork, bathing the room in an amber glow. The air smelled of aged paper and leather bindings. On the table, a single volume waited. William's pulse quickened as he stepped closer, his fingers working the surface of the basalt stone in his pocket.

"I overheard the staff talking about you," Lina said, watching him closely. "You've been asking about Piano Zen?"

William nodded. "Yes. I wanted to understand what it is and where it comes from."

Lina tilted her head. "Those words—Piano Zen. *Ach so.* They triggered something in me... a memory from childhood. *Ja,* my Oma and Opa used to tell stories, strange ones. There was talk of a mysterious piano school in Vienna, very old, from the early-1700s. Run entirely by women. They were keyboardists, enthusiasts, proponents of Cristofori's piano invention, but they practiced something more..."

She hesitated. "*Was sagst du?*" Lina searched for the word. "*Entschuldigung... ja. Überirdisch.*"

William frowned. "*Über...* what?"

She smiled faintly. "Otherworldly."

William straightened. "So, Piano Zen... it's really old. Some sort of secret society? I've read about these things."

"That, I don't know," she said. "But my grandparents said the traditional Viennese schools dismissed them as charlatans, and the religious authorities were even harsher, calling them spiritually dangerous. Eventually, the group disappeared. Some said they disbanded, others claimed Piano Zen went... underground."

"Underground?" William squinted into the fire. "I wonder if Rosa Carreño, my new teacher, is somehow connected to them."

"Rosa Carreño?" Lina echoed. "Hmm... I'm afraid I don't know her. I'm still new to Nightingale. So, you study piano with her?"

"Well, not yet. We just met last weekend. She let me take home a rare Piano Zen book. It was unlike anything I'd ever seen, even different from the rare books here."

William glanced down at the floor. "I just hope piano lessons go better this time."

"*Oh je...* what do you mean by that?"

"Well, my last teacher was Cecil Winwood. Things didn't go so well. He had to drop me from his studio."

Lina raised her eyebrows. "Winwood? Now that is a name I know." She stroked her chin. "Yes... I believe I saw him perform once in the Mozart-Saal at the Wiener Konzerthaus—a concert hall in Vienna. It was years ago. Brilliant technique, as I recall, but his playing struck me as rather... cold."

She trailed off for a moment, her gaze drifting toward the hearth, then folded her arms, as if collecting her thoughts. By now, the store had quieted. Only a few staff members moved about, preparing to close.

Lina glanced briefly over her shoulder and then lowered her voice. "When the staff mentioned your questions about Piano Zen, something stirred in me. I started searching everywhere: the rare book room, the catalog, even our old ledgers. But I found nothing. It felt like I was chasing shadows of the stories my grandparents used to tell. But, *ach so,* I couldn't let it go."

She placed a hand gently atop the book on the table. Its brown leather had weathered to a deep umber. Etched faintly on the cover was the outline of a small bird, and beneath it, the words *Die Nachtigall.*

"What does that say?" William asked.

"*The Nightingale,*" Lina replied. "It's a bird well known throughout Europe. The clasp once held a working lock. I imagine whatever key it required has long since been claimed by time."

The firelight danced across her face, softening her features. "I don't usually speak this way," she said in a hush. "I was trained to find books through records and references—not feelings. But something about this was different. I had a strong sense there was a book about Piano Zen here, somewhere in the building."

She looked at William, as though weighing whether to speak the next part aloud. "At first, I thought it was just wishful thinking. But then I had a vivid dream that was strangely… specific."

She lightly tapped the book with her finger. "I saw this very book—the nightingale etched on its cover, the broken lock—tucked in a dark corner of the attic. No one ever goes up there. And yet, in my dream, it was there, in a wooden crate, buried beneath a heap of damaged books no one ever thought to explore."

She hesitated, then added, "The McFarlands are known for scouring Europe in search of rare books to bring back. Maybe the title on the cover caught their attention. It could easily have been acquired decades ago."

She lifted the book and held it out to him. "When I woke, I went straight over to Shelley's. Access to the attic isn't easy, it requires a special key. But I found a manager who knew where to get one and went to the exact spot I'd seen in my dream. And there it was, just as I'd pictured it. *Ach und lieber…* I still can't quite believe it."

A young staff member passed nearby, reshelving a book. Lina fell silent, watching them go. Only when they were out of earshot did she continue, more softly now. "It's never happened to me before, William. And I don't know what it means. But it felt…" She set the worn book gently back on the table, her fingers lingering on the cover. "It felt like this book wanted to be found."

A tingling sensation spread across William's skin, his thoughts spinning. He leaned closer, studying the brown, leather-bound volume. "So… what kind of book is it?"

"That's the strange part," Lina said. "It's not a published work. It's a personal journal—handwritten, bound in soft calfskin. Very old. The text itself is in an older form of *Deutsch—bitte*, I mean German—and written in a flowing, ornate hand. Beautiful, gothic Kurrent script, but not easy to read or decipher. Fortunately, I speak several languages and read in a few more, which helps, because the author drifts between tongues: German, Italian, some Greek, a little French—though my French is not so good. Between the water damage and the elaborate script, reading this journal has been a challenge. But also a fascinating glimpse into the mind of its author."

She rested her hand on the cover again. "Here's the mystery, William: I don't know how it ended up at Shelley's. It belongs in an archive or a museum. Or..." she paused, her voice lowering, "...perhaps it was meant to be found. By you."

"By me?" William's brow furrowed. "I don't understand. Why would you say that?"

She drew a breath. "Carl Jung called it *Synchronizität*—when something meaningful happens that logic can't explain."

"Synchron... what?"

"*Ja*. Synchronicity. Two meaningful events that are causally connected but feel deeply connected nonetheless."

She opened the journal and withdrew a slip of paper tucked inside. "I looked this up before you came and made a note for myself. This is interesting. Jung once wrote: *'The meeting of two personalities is like the contact of two chemical substances: if there is any reaction, both are transformed.'*"

Her gaze lifted to his. "It doesn't always have to be a person. Sometimes it's a book—appearing at just the right moment, and everything shifts."

"So... do you know whose journal it is?"

Lina carefully opened the front cover, revealing the delicate inside page. "*Ja*. Her name is written here—Katarina von Paradis. I'm almost certain this is her personal journal."

She turned to one of several bookmarked pages. William recognized the souvenir bookmarks Lina used. They were only found in the Modern Prometheus book room: thick, sepia-toned stock embossed with an old engraving—a torch resting inside an open book, its stem wrapped in a climbing rose.

William rubbed his neck. "Katarina von Paradis. That name sounds familiar."

"I thought the same thing," Lina said. "I looked into it. You're probably thinking of Maria Theresia von Paradis—the blind pianist and Salieri's protégée, who moved in Mozart's circle. But Katarina, judging by internal dates in the journal, was active around 1705—roughly a generation earlier. They could well have been relatives. From what I can tell, Katarina was a highly regarded performer on both the harpsichord and the organ."

William leaned back, eyes narrowing in thought. "You know... this is kind of a strange coincidence."

"What, William?"

"Well, Miss Carreño. She told me to start keeping a dream journal, something like Katarina's."

"*Ach so.* That is interesting." A flicker of concern crossed her face. "Unfortunately, Katarina's journal is badly damaged—water, age, neglect. Pages are stuck together. Ink badly faded. And her handwriting..." She gave a soft laugh. "So beautiful... just not easy to read."

She turned another delicate page, pausing at one of the sepia-toned bookmarks. "I garnered all that information about her from the early entries, written when she first began the journal. But the later entries?" She gave a faint nod. "That's where things become more intriguing."

William shifted in his chair as his heart began to race. Lina removed another bookmark, carefully turning past the fragile pages. "I think she began writing around age ten or eleven—probably about your age, William. Most of the early entries are too damaged to read, but I was able to glean that around the same time she started journaling, she also began organ and harpsichord lessons in Vienna with Johann Baptist Peyer."

She paused on one of her bookmarks and pointed to a faded entry. "Here, she is five years later—dated 12. März 1725. Katarina writes: '*Heute war mein sechzehnter Geburtstag*'." Lina translated. "Today was my sixteenth birthday."

She squinted at the next passage. I can't make out some of the details, but later she continues: '*Herr Cristofori ist endlich angekommen. Er bringt das neue Instrument, das er das Gravicembalo col piano e forte nennt...*' She's saying *Herr* Cristofori has finally arrived. He brought the new instrument he calls the *gravicembalo col piano e forte*."

William scratched his head. "What is a *gravicembalo... ah... col piano e forte?*"

"*Ach so*, that was something I came across in my research," Lina said. "It was Cristofori's original name—*harpsichord with soft and loud*. An instrument that could finally express dynamics through touch, something the harpsichord and organ could never do. In her entry, she uses the name Cristofori gave it. But over time, historically, it became known by a much simpler name. The piano."

"I get the sense," Lina continued, "that she was a prodigy—already well known in Vienna and Europe. Respected enough that Cristofori took notice all the way from Florence. I think he may have been a bit desperate, too. Katarina writes: '*Cristofori hat Schwierigkeiten, die italienischen Höfe der Medici-Familie von seiner Erfindung zu überzeugen. Sogar Händel und Bach bevorzugen das Cembalo*.'"

Lina gave a small nod. "*Ja,* this is revealing. She says Cristofori is having trouble convincing the Medici family in the courts of Florence to take his invention seriously. Even Handel and Bach prefer the harpsichord."

She turned another page, scanning the faded ink. "I can't make out all the details, but from March 13$^{th}$ to 20$^{th}$, she seems quite taken with Cristofori's piano—writing about her practice sessions nearly every day."

Lina flipped to the next bookmarked page, her eyes widening. "Now, in this entry... she switches to Italian. It says: '*25 marzo 1725: Quando tocco i tasti... è come se qualcosa dentro di me si risvegliasse. Vedo luci e colori*.'"

She looked up at William. "She's saying, 'When I touch the keys, it's as if something inside me awakens. I see lights and colors.'"

She continued flipping through a few more bookmarked entries. "It's 22, April 1725. Here, she writes about performing at a private performance in Vienna. It doesn't say which hall, just 'for members of the House of Habsburg.' She mentions Prince Eugene of Savoy and Emperor Karl VI himself. Cristofori was there too, she writes—watching, evaluating the audience's reactions."

Lina gave him an excited look. "Here, now, this is where things get fascinating." She carefully turned to another bookmarked page. "Dated 3. *Juni* 1726. More than a year later. Katarina writes about having dinner with Cristofori after another concert."

She squinted at the faded ink. "*'Er sprach mit solcher Leidenschaft... sagte, dass die Welt seine Erfindung noch nicht versteht*.'" She glanced at William. "That means: 'He spoke with such passion... said the world does not yet understand his invention'."

She traced her finger along the vellum paper. "Ah, here. A line in Italian. '*Mi ha detto delle teorie di Pitagora... della Musica Universalis.*' 'He told me about Pythagoras' theories—Musica Universalis'." Lina looked up, curious. "Pythagoras was an ancient Greek mystic and mathematician. What would he have to do with Cristofori's invention, I wonder?"

She tilted the book toward the firelight. "Then she writes something in Greek, though the script is faint. Only part of it is legible: '*mēkos, harmonía, psychē*—length, harmony, soul."

William leaned in. "What do you make of all this?"

"I think she was beginning to sense something… *wundersam. eh…was sagt man auf Englisch*… something *magical* about the piano. But I don't think she fully understood it yet."

She turned another page. "Another year has passed. 13. Mai 1727. Katarina mentions traveling often to Florence—sometimes alone. She describes Cristofori's studio above a violin maker's shop. She writes that she spent hours there—playing, listening, dreaming." Lina read an entry, then translated aloud: "'*Quando suono… il mondo si ferma. C'è qualcosa che brilla nei tasti, come se ogni nota avesse un riflesso segreto*'. 'When I play… the world stops. There's something that shines in the keys, as if each note carries a secret reflection'."

Lina paused for a moment. "It's so strange. It's as if the piano is casting some kind of spell on her."

"I kind of know how she feels," William said. "I've felt that way about the piano my whole life. What happened next?"

She opened to another marked page, blotched and wrinkled.

"5, August 1728. This part's nearly unreadable… but she writes of preparing for a concert tour. There's mention of Constantinople, China, a stop in Tibet." She paused, adjusting to the light. "And ending her journey in Kyoto, Japan."

"So… Katarina took the Cristofori piano all the way to… Japan?" William asked.

Lina nodded. "It appears so. He arranged the shipment himself. She says Cristofori told her: '*A Kyoto troverai ciò che non si può insegnare*.'"

William looked up. "What does that mean?"

"'In Kyoto, you will find what cannot be taught'."

Lina and William exchanged a look, their eyebrows raised but words failing them.

"I also found this," Lina said, gently removing something tucked inside the journal. She drew out a faded envelope laced with intricate designs, then carefully unfolded a fragile piece of parchment from within. "I'm surprised this letter survived inside the journal all these years. The string binding must have held it in place. It's written to Katarina from a metalwork artisan in

France, I believe. My French is a bit rusty. I haven't yet asked anyone on staff to translate it."

"Oh, that's okay," William said. "I can read French. Can I see it?"

"Well, it's not just the French," Lina said, squinting at the page. "It's the way she writes, the Kurrent calligraphy is hard to—"

"No, actually, I've got this. I can read it," William interrupted, already leaning in. "It's okay."

"Wunderbar," Lina said, gently handing it over. "I'm curious. It seems to be some kind of order for a piece of furniture."

William carefully held the letter and began to read.

"*Paris, le 4 novembre 1732*

"*Chère Katarina,*

"*Le banc est en cours de fabrication. Je me souviens encore des longues soirées passées avec Bartolomeo à discuter des proportions secrètes, lorsque je l'ai aidé à construire son pianoforte.*

"*J'ai suivi de près vos dessins tibétains et j'ai commencé à forger les pieds du banc selon votre motif des grues demoiselles. Le métal que j'utilise provient des anciennes mines d'Alsace—réputées pour leur résonance.*

"*La spirale dorée est en place. Le métal répond bien.*

"*Il sera prêt dans quinze jours. — Étienne Moreau.*"

"It says, 'Paris, November 4, 1732. Dear Katarina, The bench is underway. I still remember the long evenings spent with Bartolomeo, discussing secret proportions and the power of sound when I helped him build his piano.

"'I have followed your Tibetan drawings closely and have begun forging the legs of the bench in your demoiselle crane design. The metal I'm using comes from the old Alsatian mines—renowned for their resonance.

"'The golden spiral is in place. The metal responds well.

"'It will be ready in fifteen days. — Étienne Moreau'."

William placed the letter back in the envelope and sat back in his chair.

"Why would she keep such a strange letter about a bench in her journal?" Lina asked.

"It's not just any bench," William said. "It's a piano bench. And I know this sounds crazy, but I think Miss Carreño has that very same bench in her studio."

Lina blinked. "Your teacher has Katarina's piano bench? *Gott im Himmel.*" She let out a shaky laugh. "William, honestly, at this point, I could believe anything."

They both fell silent, staring down at the journal.

After a pause, William said quietly, "So… what happened when she came back from the East?"

Lina turned another page. "Yes, there are a few more entries that I can still read. Katarina seems changed, very different, after her return to Vienna."

She paused to review the Italian.

"*'4 settembre 1732*

"*'Oggi ho saputo che Cristofori è morto mentre ero via. Il mio cuore è spezzato.*

"*'Avevo così tanto da dirgli—così tante domande, così tante scoperte da condividere, nate dalle visioni che ho avuto in Tibet e dall'addestramento ricevuto a Kyoto.*

"*'Non ho ancora tutte le risposte, ma qualcosa si è aperto dentro di me. Una chiave invisibile. Il Metodo Zen del Pianoforte. Il Quinto Elemento.*

"*'Lui avrebbe capito.'*"

She nodded gently. "*Ach so*," she murmured, as if acknowledging the weight of the words.

"It reads, 'September 4, 1732. Today, I learned that Cristofori died while I was away. My heart is broken. I had so much to tell him—so many questions, so many discoveries to share from visions I had in Tibet and the training I received in Kyoto.

"'I don't yet have all the answers, but something has opened within me. An invisible key. The Zen Method of the Piano. The Fifth Element.

"'He would have understood'."

Lina closed the journal and rested her hands on top of it. "That's as far as I could go with what was preserved. There were more entries, but they're too damaged to read."

William was only half listening. He felt dazed, as if he'd just woken from a dream. "Rosa Carreño only mentioned Four Elements," he murmured. "Not five."

Around them, the staff were dimming the lights in the rare book room. It was past closing time. He thanked Lina, gave her a quick hug, and made his way downstairs, where his mother sat waiting in a chair, reading.

In just a few days, he realized he would take his first true step into the mystery of Piano Zen—not as a curious observer but as a student.

The staff unlocked the front doors, and he and his mother stepped out into the night.

The crisp air of Nightingale had turned to rain.

# Chapter Twenty-Three

## *Marrakech West*

A hard rain had persisted for days after his meeting with Lina, but as the weekend approached, it softened to a light drizzle, typical for that time of year in the Pacific Northwest. That meant Marrakech West would be open again, and with it, the sound of live music filling the air.

Located in Old Town Nightingale, the bazaar was a vibrant, noisy, labyrinthine marketplace. The scent of roasted almonds always hit William first. Then came the swirl of cardamom, orange blossom, and slow-burning incense.

Each weekend it reassembled itself like a living mosaic—rugs from Uzbekistan, lanterns from Marrakesh, flutes from Iran, saris from Jaipur. Vendors sold embroidered caftans, polished brassware, leatherwork, jewelry, spices, and carved wood accessories. You could buy fig pastries from an old Turkish man, then turn the corner and catch a Senegalese band covering Bob Marley. Food carts lined the walkways, filling the air with the scent of sweet pastries, roasted nuts, and meats sizzling with saffron, sumac, and cumin.

Street musicians played traditional instruments—an oud here, a ney flute there. Somewhere, shimmering notes rose from the hammers of a Persian santur, dancing above the steady pulse of an Egyptian hand drum.

This was Marrakech West. If Shelley's was William's sanctuary, this was his escape.

One thing became clear about Piano Zen: he'd wandered into something much deeper than he realized. If anyone had answers, it was the Professor, and William knew exactly where to find him—performing on the main stage.

The grand entrance was an elegant archway of white stone inlaid with sparkling green tiles, known as the Gateway of the Moors. Beyond it, a series of horseshoe-shaped arches fanned out, supported by columns that looked ancient. Originally constructed for the *Spirit of Lewis and Clark Exposition* in 1912, the Gateway was the only surviving structure from the event.

Built from R.C. Prescott's Imperial Heights Limestone, it had once welcomed visitors to the grand exposition. Over time, the site had evolved into what was now the bazaar—a bustling marketplace inspired by the legendary Moroccan trade city.

Though rooted in Moroccan design, over the decades, Marrakech West had absorbed influences from across North Africa, the Middle East, and beyond—a tapestry of languages, colors, and traditions all its own.

William had loved Marrakech West for as long as he could remember. Even as a young boy, he'd been drawn to its winding alleys and shadowed corners, the way each visit felt like discovering a secret. But no part of the bazaar fascinated him more than Professor Anthony Burns Montgomery.

Though he'd earned a Ph.D. in Education, everyone simply called him "Professor." The name fit: his encyclopedic memory, his knack for weaving history and music into every conversation. Now well past retirement, he was a legend at Marrakech West, his presence as integral to the bazaar as the Gateway itself.

A musician, historian, and storyteller, he could often be found on the main stage near the Gateway of the Moors, singing in a voice that reminded some of Ray Charles—soulful, rough-edged, and unmistakably his own—as his fingers danced across the strings of a well-worn guitar or hammered out bluesy rhythms on a baby grand piano.

Between sets, he held court with visitors and locals alike, discussing history, politics, and philosophy—many drawn by tales of his photographic memory. He'd been profiled in the *Nightingale Observer*, and television crews occasionally filmed segments on the city's beloved "Professor." Tourist brochures ranked Marrakech West among the "Top 10 Things to Do in Nightingale," always including a blurb about Montgomery.

Though nearly blind, he could still make out shifting shadows—just enough to sense movement around him. He was always impeccably dressed: pastel button-downs under tailored blazers, a black trilby fedora with a grosgrain ribbon and bright side feather, and most famously, his retro gold-rimmed sunglasses.

William had been captivated by Professor Montgomery for as long as he could remember. As a child, he had watched him perform with fascination—but always from the safety of the crowd. His mother often encouraged him to go and say hello, but William never could.

A few summers ago, summoning his courage, William had stepped up to the Professor's merchandise tent and bought a CD. A staff member handed it to him while Montgomery stood nearby, deep in conversation. He was close enough to approach—close enough to speak to. But William couldn't do it. He was just too shy, too in awe.

For the first time in his life, though, William mustered the courage. He was going to talk to the Professor.

# Chapter Twenty-Four

## *The Professor*

As William arrived that afternoon, a soft mist had settled over Marrakech West, cloaking the bustling bazaar in a dreamy, silvery veil—like an impressionistic painting coming to life.

He was in luck. Professor Montgomery was just beginning his final song of the day. William darted through the Gateway of the Moors and climbed onto a cement block for a better view.

"Good afternoon, friends. Just a reminder, all proceeds from my performances, t-shirts, and CD sales go to The Saint Teresa Orphanage over in Nightingale's La Dama De La Luz District. I truly appreciate your support and kindness—your generosity makes a real difference in their lives."

Montgomery launched into his closing number, "Above the Fray." One of his originals, it carried a folk-gospel feel, rich with soul. His voice, weathered by time, had a warmth and authenticity that made people hang on every lyric.

Strumming a steady rhythm on his guitar, he leaned into the harmonica strapped around his neck, drawing out a flourish of bluesy notes before he began to sing:

*No one knows the wisdom*
*That's packaged in our shoes*
*Walking streets indifferent*
*And singing the drifter's blues*

*Here's a note now sing it*
*Let it carry you along*
*Some roads twist and some roads break*
*But the journey pulls you on*

*Along the way*
*Above the fray*
*Hope you make it*
*Make it someday*

The crowd swayed with the rhythm, some clapped in time, others sang along. A few called out in encouragement as Montgomery's fingers danced over the guitar strings, his foot tapping out a hard beat on the stage.

*My mind is set on history*
*Got to find my place*
*Got to get beyond it all and*
*Free of this rat race*

*There's gold left in them memories*
*You're sure to hear someday*
*But the sun shines now upon your face*
*Please stay for one more day*

With a flourish on the harmonica, he then lifted his voice, drawing in the crowd's energy. Some raised their hands, caught in the song's growing intensity flowing into another chorus.

*Along the way*
*Above the fray*
*Hope we make it*
*Make it someday*

Montgomery closed his eyes as his strumming gained force, his voice lifting across the marketplace like an old hymn sung at a tent revival.

*There's a land that's overflowing*
*God give it back to me*

*Rainbows, ribbons, and violins*
*Lord, play your symphony*

*At times I'm sad and lonely*
*At times I think of you*
*Go ahead, don't believe me—your heart can't deceive me*
*You're the only love I knew, that was true*


The music seemed to weave itself into the misty air, settling over the bazaar. With one final flourish, he unleashed the last refrain, repeating and improvising until the final chord faded into the hum of the bazaar.

*Along the way*
*Above the fray*
*Hope we make it*
*Make it someday*


The crowd erupted in cheers, applause rippling through the plaza. Montgomery grinned and offered a slight bow in acknowledgment. While the crowd gradually dispersed, he shook hands and exchanged a few words with tourists and longtime friends before finally beginning to pack up his gear.

William watched the Professor closely, turning his basalt stone nervously between his fingers as he waited for the last of the lingering fans to move on. He took a deep breath, his heart pounding.

Finally, he stepped forward. Circling behind the stage, he approached the Professor with quiet resolve. His voice wavered slightly, a whisper barely rising above the hum of the bazaar.

"Ah… Professor Montgomery?"

The Professor turned at the sound of William's voice, tilting his head slightly. His gold-rimmed sunglasses were speckled with mist. A slow grin spread across his face.

"Well now… hello, Mr. Emerson! What a pleasant surprise. Did you enjoy the show?"

William froze and felt his stomach drop. He hadn't introduced himself—had never even spoken to Montgomery before. So how did the Professor know his… name?

William swallowed, trying to steady his voice. "Uh… ah, yes. I-I always enjoy your music, sir."

Montgomery chuckled. "Oh, please… don't call me 'sir.' That's way too formal."

As Montgomery packed up his harmonica and guitar, William struggled to make sense of how this blind musician—someone he'd admired from afar for years—could possibly know who he was.

Montgomery worked in silence for a moment, fastening latches with the ease of muscle memory. Then, without looking up, he spoke again—his tone friendly. "I can tell you've got some things on your mind, Will. How about I treat you to some of the finest *m'hanncha* you'll ever taste outside of Morocco? There's a place called Sweet Muejanat."

William just stood there, blinking through the mist. The whole moment felt slightly unreal. Still, he managed a nod. "um… ah, sure."

Montgomery grinned. "Oh, and they also serve the freshest, sweetest pomegranate juice you've ever tasted. It's called Pomegranate Bliss." He leaned in slightly, as if sharing a secret. "There's a hidden ingredient." He paused. "*Ma zhar.* That's orange blossom water." He gave a light shrug. "Eh… not much of a secret if you're from Morocco, though."

He turned to William. "If you'll give me a hand, I've got a storage unit over yonder where we can stash my gear before grabbing a bite."

As they talked, a young woman in a colorful headscarf approached from the merchandise tent. "We did well today, Professor! We sold out of your newest CD. I'll need to order more—and more merch—hopefully in time for next weekend's show."

"Thank you, Layla," said Montgomery. "Couldn't do this without you."

Layla smiled and hurried back to the tent, where CDs, shirts, and posters bearing Montgomery's image were still neatly stacked. William glanced at the display—it was the same spot he'd stood years ago, trying to summon the courage to speak to the Professor, but slipping away with only a CD instead.

Montgomery hoisted his guitar and harmonica cases with practiced ease, while William fell in step beside him, carrying a weathered microphone case. They wove through the thinning crowd toward a nearby storage locker tucked behind the stage tents.

Once there, William helped stow the last few items while Montgomery fastened the padlock.

"Thank you kindly, Will," he said, turning with a warm smile. With a wry tilt of his head, Montgomery added, "Pray to God, yes… but tie up your camel."

He snapped the lock shut with a firm click. Then, unfolding his long white cane—red at the tip—he gestured for William to follow.

Together, they set off into the winding, bustling alleys of Marrakech West.

# Chapter Twenty-Five

## *Sweet Muejanat*

"Where we're going is a little hidden," Montgomery said, navigating confidently through the crowd despite his limited sight. "It's in the more traditional Moroccan section, off the beaten path." William followed close behind, weaving between vendors and passersby, doing his best to keep up.

"Marrakech West..." Montgomery said, slowing a little as they passed a cluster of musicians playing oud and flute, "It's a symphony of voices—half a dozen languages swirling in the air. Music everywhere, colliding and drifting. Charles Ives would have a field day."

William glanced over. "Who's Charles Ives?"

Montgomery's face lit up. "Ah! One of the great American originals. A composer who believed that life was too rich, too layered, to be captured in a single melody. He'd write pieces where two or three different tunes played at once—marching bands clashing with hymns, folk songs brushing up against dissonance. He wanted you to hear the chaos and beauty of the world as it really is. Messy. Overlapping. Alive."

He paused for a moment, letting the air around them speak for itself: the bustle of voices, the drumbeats from the square, the scent of cumin and cardamom on the breeze.

"That's why I love this place," Montgomery said. "It's like living inside an Ives symphony. Every voice has a place. Every sound has a story."

"I've never thought about it that way before," William said. "But maybe that's why I love it too?"

"Well, that's certainly obvious to me, Will. You come to Marrakech West all the time. I remember two summers ago, you bought my *Heartland Café* CD..." Montgomery paused. "Didn't say a word though, just slipped away."

William's step faltered. *Wait... how could he possibly know all that?* Thrown off by the remark, he caught his foot on a loose brick in the walkway and tripped.

Montgomery's gold-rimmed sunglasses caught a glint of light as he smiled. "Careful, Will, eyes on the road."

They reached an intersection where the bazaar's main walkways converged. Montgomery paused, angling his head as if listening to the flow of people, then tapped his cane forward. "This way."

William stayed close as greetings echoed from stalls and alleyways, "Hello, Professor!" "*Salām 'alaykum*, Montgomery!" And from the old-timers, with affection, "Anthony!"

Just ahead, a distinguished-looking older man in a tailored blazer stood outside an office pavilion, speaking with a few well-dressed men clustered in a semicircle. When he caught sight of Montgomery, his face lit up. Raising a hand in greeting, he called, "Monty! What time should we plan on dinner?"

Montgomery smiled, instantly recognizing the voice. "How's six-thirty sound? I need to stop by the farmers market. We're short on a few things."

As they passed, he leaned toward William. "That's Winston McFarland. He's the only one who calls me 'Monty.'" A chuckle escaped him, as if at some unspoken inside joke.

"Winston's family has been in Nightingale a long time, even before old Prescott. His nieces run the McFarland Sisters Restoration Company. They buy up old buildings and bring them back to life—beautiful work. Winston, though, he's the numbers guy, always has been. He keeps the books balanced, manages the investments, handles the logistics. His sisters and nieces are the ones who run the construction side of things." Montgomery chuckled. "We split the chores at home too. He balances the check book, and I keep track of the appointments."

William glanced over. "You said 'old Prescott'? Do you mean R.C. Prescott? The guy who built the mansion on Imperial Heights?"

"The very same," Montgomery said with a grin. "And the McFarland Sisters Restoration Company? They've been restoring half the buildings he left behind."

He gestured ahead and veered them toward a narrow corridor lined with mosaic tile. The hum of the main plaza faded behind them, replaced by the softer rhythms of neighborhood life. Here, the walkways narrowed and the crowd thinned. Clotheslines hung between balconies above, fluttering like flags in the breeze. A boy darted past with a tray of mint tea, while orders called out from a kitchen hidden behind a carved wooden door.

The scent of saffron, charcoal, and fresh bread mingled in the air. Musicians still played, but now it was a seated oud player in a shaded alcove, improvising with two older men on hand drums. A woman stitched leather sandals at her stall, while an elderly man dozed behind a stack of handwoven baskets.

Montgomery moved easily through it all, tapping his cane lightly with each step, as though the alleyways themselves whispered directions.

He tilted his head back, nostrils flaring slightly as he inhaled. "We're close now, Will. I can follow my nose from here."

Guided by the scent of warm pastry and honey, they wound their way toward Sweet Muejanat, a small, hand-painted cart adorned with turquoise and cobalt arabesques, its awning stitched in faded saffron and crimson stripes. Brass lanterns dangled from the corners, and the air was rich with the scent of rosewater and toasted almonds. The display case overflowed with fruit juices and Moroccan pastries: *ghoriba, maamoul, baklava, m'hanncha*.

Montgomery grinned. "*Wa-alaykum assalaam*, Hadiya!"

"*Kaifa al-hal?*" she asked.

"*Alhamdulillah*," he replied, then gestured toward William. "Hadiya, I'd like you to meet my friend, Will."

William gave a small nod. "Hello."

"Nice to meet you, Will." She studied him for a moment. "You look familiar. Do you come to the bazaar often?"

"Oh, yeah. I've been coming here since I can remember. I love Marrakech West."

"Me too. I like to hang around after work, grab food with friends, and catch the bands playing on the main stage."

After a bit of small talk, Montgomery placed their order. "Hadiya, we'll have two lemon-almond *m'hannchas* and two Pomegranate Bliss drinks, please."

"Coming right up, Professor!" She quickly got to work.

As she prepared their food, Montgomery turned to William. "This pastry is filled with a lemon-flavored almond paste. After baking, they dip it in honey and coat it with powdered sugar and pistachios. Absolutely divine."

Moments later, Hadiya handed them their order, setting the pastries on small paper plates with practiced ease.

Montgomery nodded. "*Shukran!*"

"*La shukran ala wajib,*" Hadiya replied with a smile.

William smiled back, not quite sure what she'd said, and added, "Thank you very much!"

"Oh, you're welcome, William. Enjoy! Come back and visit again."

With their food in hand, they set off, Montgomery leading them through narrow back alleys and down a flight of stairs.

William glanced back. "I thought I knew the bazaar pretty well, but I've never been in that area before. I didn't even know Sweet Muejanat existed."

Montgomery leaned back a little and chuckled. "Well, you'll find I'm full of surprises, Will."

William looked over, curious, but Montgomery had already turned his attention back to the path ahead, his cane tapping with renewed purpose. Soon, they emerged from a tunnel near the banks of the Makah River, close to the towering fifty-five-foot statue, the Lady of Light.

# Chapter Twenty-Six

## *Sky-Blue*

The iconic statue, cast in copper, had taken on a rich, dark, almost mahogany-like color, depicting a beautiful woman emerging from an uneven wall of copper. The *Lady of Light* gazed downward toward the docks of the Makah River. Only half of her figure was visible, sculpted to appear as though she were emerging from shadow. She drew a shawl close around her neck and held a lamp in her left hand that burned with a real flame—by decree of the sculptor, the flame of her lamp had to remain eternally lit.

"See any free tables by the river, Will?" Montgomery asked.

William didn't respond. He had stopped in his tracks, fixated on the statue. He had always known about her, everyone in Nightingale did. She was an icon. But something about her now felt different.

Montgomery noticed the hesitation. "Will… what's up?"

"I was just standing here, admiring the *Lady of Light.*"

"Ah yes. *La Dame de la Lumière.* I remember this statue well. I used to come down here all the time when I was young, years before my accident. She's lovely, isn't she?"

"Yeah, I love this statue."

William then scanned the riverside. "There's a couple just getting up from a bench."

"Well then, lead on, my friend. Lead on."

They weaved through the thinning crowd, making their way to a quiet bench tucked beneath the statue's shadow. The sun had finally broken through the clouds, casting light across the waters of the Makah River. Ripples glinted like scattered coins.

For a while, they sat in silence beneath the statue's watchful gaze. William let the almond-and-honey sweetness of the *m'hanncha* linger on his tongue, occasionally sipping his Pomegranate Bliss while the soft murmur of the river mingled with the distant hum of the bazaar.

The silence wasn't uncomfortable, exactly, but it felt suspended—as if both of them were waiting for something, for one of them to speak first, for the right words to arrive.

Montgomery sat quietly, gently breaking apart the flaky pastry with his fingers. After a moment, he cleared his throat. "You know, we were talking about R.C. Prescott earlier—did you know he commissioned the *Lady of Light* statue as a memorial to his late wife? I've always found something quietly moving about her presence here, as if she's only half in this world and half somewhere beyond it." He paused, then added, "Bit of personal trivia for you—my grandfather led the team that helped reassemble the statue on this very spot back in 1922."

William looked up, surprised. "Wait, really? That's kind of crazy. I just saw an old picture of that in a book at Mr. Winwood's piano studio. The scaffolding, the crates..."

Montgomery smiled faintly. "So, you're studying with Cecil Winwood? I actually know him quite well, he's Winston's cousin."

"Oh, I was. At least for a little while. He... well, he had to let me go. I wasn't making much progress."

"I wouldn't take that to heart, Will. Like I said, I know Cecil well, maybe too well. I hope that didn't put you off completely. Are you still studying?"

"I am—well, not yet. I'm starting with someone new next week. That's actually what I wanted to talk to you about."

Montgomery tilted his head. "Who's the teacher?"

"Her name is Rosa Carreño," William said. 'She teaches in the Gate Lodge up in Imperial Heights. She uses something called the Piano Zen Method."

Montgomery's lips curled into a knowing grin. "Ah yes, I know Rosa. A bit of a recluse but deeply devoted to her students." He leaned back slightly. "She didn't perform often, but when she did, it was unforgettable. The kind of playing that affects you deeply, touches something inside." He paused, his voice softening. "I know this because I heard her in concert once. Years ago. It has stayed with me ever since.

"But Piano Zen…" He shook his head. "That's something else entirely. I can't tell you much about it. Like Rosa, it's quiet, mysterious—a blending of Eastern mysticism and Western music instruction. But if Rosa has accepted you, Will, you're indeed fortunate. She doesn't choose lightly."

William's eyes lit up. "I just met her last week for the first time. She let me take home this old Piano Zen book. It's over a hundred and fifty years old, filled with these beautiful drawings—I'm supposed to bring it back for my first lesson."

Montgomery nodded. "Ah. I know the book. I'm surprised she let you take it home." He stroked his chin. "Hmm… interesting. Well, if you've been spending time with that book, I can understand why you're so curious."

For a while, they sat quietly beneath the towering statue, the rustle of wind blowing over the surface of the Makkah River, mingling with the distant call of reed flute from somewhere deeper in the bazaar. William nibbled on his last bit of pastry and then finished his drink, but his thoughts had drifted elsewhere.

"Professor Montgomery, I'm really confused about something. Can I ask you a question?"

"Of course."

"After your show, when I walked up to you, how did you know it was… me? I never said my name."

Montgomery paused, rapping a slow, steady rhythm against the side of his cup, as if weighing the moment. His voice softened, turning more personal. "Will, I'm a member of the Ancient Mystical Order of Samaritans." He held up his Master Samaritan ring on his right hand. "I first saw you at a family gathering at the Samaritan Temple. All the local lodges were there. You were just a baby, maybe a few months old. Your parents brought you."

William's brow furrowed. "You knew my… dad?" He reached beneath his shirt and pulled out his father's Master Samaritan ring.

"Not well. Phillip belonged to a different lodge, but I did meet him and your mother."

William raised his eyebrows, the information settling in, but something still didn't add up. "So that's how you recognized me now? I still… I still don't understand."

Montgomery tapped his cane lightly against the ground. "Well, that's complicated, Will." He turned slightly, facing the river. The sun had pierced the misty cloud cover from earlier, brightening the copper tones of the statue. William studied Montgomery's face, searching for a reaction behind the round, gold-rimmed sunglasses, but they revealed nothing. The lenses caught a gleam of water light and held it there, opaque and unreadable.

"The truth is…" Montgomery said at last, "my sight isn't completely gone. I can see shapes and outlines in my left eye. But over the years, something else developed."

"Like what?"

Montgomery didn't answer right away. He kept his face turned toward the water. "Will, when I lost my sight after an accident in a chemical engineering lab, something else woke up in me…" He fell quiet again.

William waited, the soft rustle of the river filling the silence as a nearby rowboat creaked against its mooring.

"When I hear music, I see dancing colors in my left eye. Over time, I realized that I could see the vibrations of people as well. Every person has a unique aura, a frequency—like a personalized musical tone—alive with color."

William blinked. "You can see people's auras?"

Montgomery let out a quiet, almost embarrassed chuckle, as if surprised by his own words. "Yes, and yours, Will, is the most piercing sky-blue light I've ever seen. That's how I've always recognized you. Even in a crowd."

William stared at him, unsure how to respond.

"I saw your mother holding you at the temple," Montgomery continued. "That's when I saw your baby-blue light for the first time. I couldn't look away. I had to come closer. That's when I learned your name. Your mom let me hold you for quite a while. You were glowing in my arms, like a ball of pure blue light."

Professor Montgomery tilted his head upward, as if scanning the sky. "I saw that beautiful aura around you, but I kept it to myself. Over the years, I've come to see that losing my sight was a strange kind of gift. It allowed me to discover truths and insights about this world—things that had once been hidden from me."

A sudden burst of Middle Eastern music broke through the ambient sounds of the bazaar. Montgomery shrugged. "I hate to cut this short, Will, but I've got to get going. Come find me again sometime. There's more I'd love to share."

William had more questions, but the Professor was right, it was getting late, and it was time to meet up with his mother. He thanked Montgomery for the *m'hanncha* and pomegranate drink, shook his hand, and set off toward the street where she would be waiting.

As he passed the *Lady of Light* statue, the sun emerged in full. Her eternal flame flickered softly against the backdrop of Imperial Heights. Something made William slow his steps. He had walked by this statue countless times before, but today, his gaze drifted toward the base.

An inscription. A poem engraved into a metal plaque for its 1923 dedication. He had never read it before, but for some reason, it caught his attention and held him there.

**The Lady of Light**
*May the light of my lamp*
*Serve as beacon and testament,*
*To the broken soulful wayfarers,*
*Wandering neath shelter of starry heavens,*
*In exodus from the dark places of tyranny and oppression.*

*Rest here, oh ye kindred spirits.*
*Find safe harbor, respite from stormy seas.*
*We open our arms and yield the truth*
*That all must tread harrowing trails*
*Amongst lofty mountain passes,*
*Aspiring to reach exalted dwellings*
*Where charity, love, and wisdom abide.*

Lower on the pedestal, his eyes rested on the sculptor's name, Camille Claudel.

Tearing himself away, William hurried on through the Gateway of the Moors toward the street beyond.

# Chapter Twenty-Seven

## *Memories in the Mist*

The storm was closing in fast as William and Rosa made their way back toward the Gate Lodge. The first drops of rain cooled his skin, more spattering against the leaves along the trail. A sudden drop in temperature sent a chill sweeping through the forest. He glanced up at the thickening clouds, their heavy gray swirls rolling in over the hills, blotting out the last hints of blue sky. A gust of wind whistled through the trees, bending the tops of the tall pines.

The drizzle turned into a light but steady rain. William yanked his hood up, tugging it low over his forehead.

Beside him, Rosa slipped off her backpack and pulled out a folded shawl, draping it around her shoulders. "I should have checked the forecast," she said, half to herself.

A deep rumble of thunder rolled in the distance, echoing off the valley walls before being swallowed by the hush of the forest. Fat droplets began sliding down branches, landing with wet plunks into the undergrowth.

Rosa slowed her pace slightly, careful on the slick stones, her shawl darkening as it absorbed the rain. The trail ahead blurred into softened greens and muted browns, as if a painter had brushed the scene with a hazy glaze. Moisture slicked the leaves, and droplets clung to fern fronds like tiny beads of glass. The air smelled sharp and clean, like pine needles and fresh earth.

Despite the thunder and rain, William felt an odd calmness. It had been almost a year since he came across Katarina von Paradis's personal journal in the rare book room. Back then, he'd imagined it might unravel all the secrets of Piano Zen. Though it revealed fragments of its history and even hinted at the elusive Fifth Element, many questions still lingered.

One time, he asked her directly about the Fifth Element. She looked amused. "Best to walk before you run, William. Master the Four Elements first. Then we'll see. Some secrets reveal themselves only when you're ready to see and hear them."

At first, her evasive answers frustrated him—but now, he understood. The wisdom of Piano Zen didn't come all at once. It arrived through doing. Through noticing.

"Looks like we'll just beat the worst of it," Rosa remarked, quickening her pace. "If I'd been better prepared, I would have packed our raincoats."

William didn't mind the rain. In Nightingale, it often came as a soft, misty veil—more atmosphere than weather. But something about the weight of these droplets tugged at another memory, carrying him back to a rainy afternoon months earlier, when Miss Rosa had first introduced the Water Element. That day, just before their lesson, she had taken him for a walk across the Prescott Mansion grounds, even as a light drizzle fell.

The estate had been buzzing with construction—scaffolding, tarps, the clatter of tools. "The McFarland Sisters Restoration Company has taken over and plans to turn the mansion into a museum," Rosa had said, dodging a wheelbarrow as they passed.

They made their way toward a newly restored waterfall that spilled into a koi pond. She waved at some of the workers, who seemed to recognize her. Raindrops pattered against the pond's surface, sending ripples outward in delicate, overlapping circles.

"This waterfall was part of the original design by Lewis Hayden Montgomery, Anthony's grandfather," Rosa said, gesturing toward the rock cliff at the back of the property. "It's built right into the natural landscape. See that small Chinese pavilion?" She pointed toward the structure nestled beside the falls. "It conceals a pump system that filters and recycles the water. R.C. Prescott and Madeleine Monnier saw something similar during her piano tour in Beijing, and he had it recreated here.

"The Water Element is essential to understanding the higher principles of Piano Zen," she said. "It teaches you to touch the pond—your fingers landing on the piano keys like raindrops on water—and to feel the flow, the way music moves from note to note without resistance, like a current carrying you forward.

"To appreciate the Water Element," she continued, "you must first understand Earth and Air, or simply think of them as body and mind. When both are in balance, you begin to sense the subtle nature of *The Flow*."

Miss Rosa then traced an infinity loop in the air, mirroring the continuous cycle of water—from the waterfall to the pond, through the pumphouse, and back again.

Suddenly, the drizzle turned into a heavy downpour, sending them hurrying back toward the Gate Lodge. Rosa laughed, throwing up her hands. "Well, it appears the Water Element has spoken."

Once inside the piano studio, they shook off the rain. Rosa slipped off her jacket and disappeared into the next room. William was tugging off his wet shoes when she called from the kitchen.

"William, come in here for a moment."

It caught him off guard. In all his months of lessons, he'd never stepped into Rosa's kitchen before.

She stood by the stove, setting a tea kettle over the flame. "You know what? I'm in the mood for hot chocolate today. How about you? Would you like some before we start your lesson?"

William nodded. "Ah… sure."

The informality of the moment made him feel at ease. He had always associated Miss Rosa with tea—jasmine, oolong, chamomile—but somehow, the idea of her indulging in hot cocoa was unexpected.

The kitchen was small and tidy, with a wooden table tucked against the wall near a window. As William looked around, something on a nearby shelf caught his eye—a framed photo of two Himalayan cats, curled up together on the familiar gray bean bag bed from the studio.

He stepped closer. One of them was clearly Misha, but the other had a darker coat, deep chocolate brown on her face, paws, ears, and tail. She looked wilder somehow, more exotic.

"I recognize Misha, but who's the other cat?" William asked.

Rosa glanced at the photo and gave a wistful smile. "Oh, that's Sasha. Misha's sister. They were from the same litter."

William nodded slowly. "Oh." He hesitated, unsure whether to ask what had happened.

Sensing the silence, Rosa offered gently, "Sasha was a wonderful cat. She and Misha were inseparable. They would curl up together in the cat bed or take turns sneaking up on each other like little hunters. They even played fetch."

"Fetch?" William echoed.

Rosa chuckled. "Yes! If I crumpled up a piece of paper, one of them would dash after it and bring it right back to me. They even competed to see who got there first." She shook her head, sighing at the memory. "It was something to see—two cats playing fetch like that."

Rosa stepped over to the shelf, picked up the picture, and studied it for a moment. "Misha has always been content living in the Gate Lodge, never interested in exploring outside. But Sasha… she had a bit of wanderlust in her." A faint smile flickered across her face before fading.

"Every chance she got, she'd dart out the door. At first, she never went far. I'd always find her nearby, chewing on grass. She was easy to retrieve. But each time she escaped, she ventured a little farther, and each time, she was harder to catch.

"One evening, my last student of the night closed the front door but didn't latch it properly. Sasha had learned how to work at the door with her claws—if she kept at it long enough, she could pry it open. I was exhausted after a long day of teaching and dozed off on the couch. When I woke up hours later, the door was open.

"Misha was standing on the stoop, just staring out into the Prescott woods. But Sasha was gone. I grabbed a flashlight and searched the woods, calling her name. The next day, I put up posters around the neighborhood, but there were no leads."

Rosa shook her head and let out a quiet sigh. "That was a couple of years ago. She never came back."

The hot water came to a boil, and Rosa poured it over the cocoa powder in two cups. As the rich aroma filled the small kitchen, Misha sauntered in and leapt onto William's lap. She let out a soft meow, placing her paws on his shoulders, rubbing her face against his chin. William scratched behind her ears and was rewarded with deep, vibrating purrs.

As they sipped their cocoa, Misha shifted contentedly in William's lap. He found himself maneuvering his cup around her tail, which kept swishing up into his face. Between sips and small talk, his eyes drifted now and then to the framed photo of Sasha.

Once they finished, they returned to the studio. Misha stretched languidly, then padded over to her gray bed and curled into a tight circle. William settled onto the antique bench.

"Alright, let's do a relaxation session to prepare you for your Piano Zen lesson," said Miss Rosa as she reached for the Tibetan bowl, running her fingers along its rim.

The bowl had always fascinated him—the fine engravings in its metal, the purity of its tone, the way its resonance lingered in the air. But lately, he'd begun to notice something else: a subtle, fleeting sensation of lost time.

Sometimes, when the sound faded, he would surface with faint traces of dream images drifting through his mind—the kind he often jotted down later in his journal.

It reminded him of what often happened at home when he played familiar pieces from memory. Without meaning to, he would slip into autopilot—his fingers gliding effortlessly through the entire piece, yet afterward, he could barely remember playing a single note. As if the music had flowed through him but bypassed thought entirely.

He had always found that a little eerie. If he couldn't recall playing the notes… who was?

The gap he felt during the Tibetan bowl was strangely similar—a moment when he wasn't sure if he'd merely closed his eyes too long or drifted somewhere else entirely.

He had never mentioned it to Miss Rosa. How would he even begin to describe it? The more he tried to form it into words, the more absurd it sounded. But maybe there was something more to it.

"Close your eyes," she said softly, her voice interrupting his thoughts. "Feel the weight of your body on the bench. Soften your mind; let your breathing slow."

William exhaled, allowing himself to settle into the familiar mindful state.

As Rosa struck the bowl, the sound swelled, sending ripples through the air. He thought he felt a vibration in the bench, but it was so subtle, he dismissed it. Instead, he focused on the tone of the bowl, his awareness narrowing to the steady hum vibrating inside him.

With each breath, the world around him faded. The vibrations intensified, radiating up from the bench, until it felt like he was floating in a sea of sound. His awareness of the room, the bench—even his own body— dissolved into the resonance of the bowl.

The tone deepened, stretching outward, wrapping around him. The edges of the world began to blur.

Then, suddenly, the sound vanished.

Water soaked through his clothes. A sharp, musty scent of damp earth filled his nose.

William's eyes snapped open. He was sitting on a wooden bench along a lonely, rain-soaked path. Rain pelted down through a dense canopy of branches.

Miss Rosa's studio had vanished.

# Chapter Twenty-Eight

## *The Treehouse of Ning Jing*

The downpour drenched him to the bone. Wiping the rain from his eyes, he scanned his surroundings. A dense forest stretched in every direction, unfamiliar and shadowed beneath a storm-darkened sky.

There wasn't time to panic. He needed to find shelter. William hesitated, unsure whether to follow the path to the right or left, until a familiar voice called down to him.

"Will... what are you doing down there? You're getting soaked! C'mon up."

He squinted up through the sheets of rain. Densho, the White-Tufted Marmoset, was perched high in a sprawling treehouse, mostly hidden by thick foliage. As William's eyes adjusted, he took in more of the structure: a winding staircase curled around the trunks of four massive trees, connecting three distinct levels of the treehouse. Wooden platforms extended from each tier, sheltered beneath sloping Dutch gable roofs, their wooden tiles slick with rain.

He had no idea how he'd ended up in the middle of a rainforest, but there was no time to figure it out. Head down, he bolted toward the stairs and began to climb. Glimpses of rooms flashed past as he sprinted up the spiraling staircase to the top.

Rain hammered the rooftop as he reached the highest tier, where Densho stood in the doorway beside a three-toed sloth whose calm gaze met his through the rain.

Densho leapt up onto a small bronze bell mounted beside the door. The bell gave a cheerful ring that echoed through the treehouse before Densho landed lightly on the railing, tail flicking.

"Will, this is my good friend, Ning Jing. I've told her all about you."

The sloth's eyes widened in concern. "Greetings! Oh my goodness, you're getting soaked! Please, come inside and dry off."

As he stepped inside, William noticed Ning Jing's attire: a fandango-pink tang suit adorned with pale-gray embroidery, rope loops fastening the front to delicate buttons along the left. She exuded a quiet serenity; her velvety, light-brown fur was neatly brushed, the white of her face contrasting with a dark nose and deep-brown circles that swept outward along her cheeks, accentuating her calm, knowing expression.

She turned to Densho. "Would you be so kind as to fetch a towel from the linen closet?"

"Of course!" Densho scampered across the room and returned moments later, offering William a towel.

She bowed slowly. "I am so happy to make your acquaintance, William. Please, make yourself at home."

Rain drummed steadily on the roof, filling the space with a rhythmic pulse. The treehouse opened before him in a single airy sweep: vaulted ceilings, wide windows framing the green canopy and the mist-filled valley below. Four immense trunks rose straight through the floor and ceiling, anchoring the dwelling in living wood.

The black-walnut floors gleamed beneath pendant globes that cast pools of amber light. Upholstered chairs and low tables softened the space with warmth and texture. In one corner, a curious device glowed with gentle heat, though it burned no fuel and hummed with no power line. Beside it stood an inviting chair, flanked by bookshelves. Across the room, a small kitchenette held rows of jars and tidy cupboards.

William tousled his damp hair with the towel, marveling at the space. "I've never seen a three-story treehouse before."

Ning Jing's eyes twinkled. "This has been our home and sanctuary for many years. We're all quite partial to life in the treetops—well, most of us, that is." She chuckled. "Ukumari struggles a bit with the stairs."

Just then, a loud snort erupted from across the room.

William turned to see a rather portly bear sprawled across a futon mattress near the far wall, snoring heavily, surrounded by mango pits.

Densho bounded over and leapt onto the bear's belly. "Ukumari, wake up! Will's here! C'mon, rise and shine!"

Ukumari cracked one eye open, regarded Densho with sleepy indifference, then let out a deep yawn, rolled onto his side, and promptly resumed snoring.

"Ukumari is a sweet fellow," Ning Jing said, "but he has a little trouble waking up." She turned to William. "I was just about to make some tea. Would you like some? It's a special blend, one that helps to soften and relax the mind."

"Yes, please," William said.

As Ning Jing moved to the kitchenette, William noticed the neatly arranged shelves lined with jars, each filled with tea leaves, spices, and dried herbs. A small warming plate glowed softly beneath a steaming teapot. With practiced grace, she selected ingredients, adding precise pinches to the pot. Every movement was fluid and unhurried, like a choreographed ritual.

Suddenly, a brilliant flash of color burst from the shadows, and a majestic bird leapt into flight, skating beneath the vaulted ceiling with breathtaking fluidity.

It was the most striking creature he'd ever seen — shimmering gold-green iridescence flowed across its feathers, while its spiky crest glowed with emerald-hued plumes. The deep red of its lower breast and belly caught the light in bold contrast, and its long, twin tail-streamers trailed behind like living silk.

It began to sing. The melody was rich and sweet, almost hypnotic. As the notes filled the air, its feathers pulsed with a luminous glow.

The bird circled the room several times, each loop catching the light and throwing shifting hues across the walls. Then it settled on a slender branch protruding from one of the tree trunks, wings folding in a silent flourish.

Densho bounded up a nearby branch and reached out a paw. "Will, this is Quetzal!"

William bowed slightly. "Pleased to meet you, Quetzal."

With a graceful sweep of her wings, Quetzal bowed in return, releasing a soft cascade of notes that set her feathers aglow.

Densho grinned. "She says she's excited to finally meet you too, Will!"

Ning Jing approached. "Her full name is *Pharomachrus mocinno*, but her kind are more commonly called the Resplendent Quetzal."

"She prefers just, Quetzal," Densho piped in.

The bird's iridescent plumage reminded William of the illuminated koi in the Smiling Pond. Spellbound by her beauty, he was unable to look away. For a long moment, he simply stared at her.

Quetzal tilted her head, her feathers ruffling with a soft flutter. Densho gave her a side glance, then raised a furry brow. William blinked, suddenly aware of the silence stretching between them. Thankfully, Ning Jing came to his rescue.

"The tea is ready," she announced.

She carried a tray adorned with a large teapot, four teacups, and a bowl of dates, figs, and nuts. William noticed how her claws moved with surprising dexterity, more like nimble fingers than rigid claws.

Ning Jing placed the tray on the table near the windows, then gave a small gesture, inviting everyone over.

Densho hopped up onto the table and wrapped his paws around his favorite teacup, the one etched with an infinity symbol.

Quetzal fluttered to a small perch beside the table, where a tiny bowl of tea awaited her.

William pulled up a sturdy chair, one clearly built with human guests in mind.

Ning Jing surveyed the table with playful curiosity. "Hmm," she mused. "It feels as though we are missing someone. Now, who could that be?"

As if in response, a loud snore rumbled from the corner.

Ning Jing chuckled. "Ah… yes. Monsieur Ukumari! *Que ferons-nous?*" She gave Densho a knowing wink before raising a claw in the air. "Ah *oui*— mangos!" Then she glided back to the kitchenette and retrieved a few ripe ones from a basket on the counter.

William, Densho, and Quetzal sipped their tea, watching as Ning Jing peeled and sliced the mango with practiced ease. The sweet, fruity aroma filled the treehouse.

Across the room, Ukumari stirred. A low grunt escaped his throat. His nose twitched, nostrils flaring as he snorted the air. Eyes still shut, he licked his snout lazily with a long tongue, then let out a contented sigh.

With considerable effort, the stout, spectacled bear rocked himself upright on the futon and lumbered across the room in a slow, groggy waddle. He plopped down onto a massive tree stump, clearly his designated seat, and smacked his lips a few more times before cracking open one eye.

His deep, baritone voice rumbled, "We havin' mangos?"

Ning Jing suppressed a laugh as she carried a large bowl of freshly cut mango to the table. Ukumari's eyes lit up. Without hesitation, he speared a chunk with one of his claws and tossed it into his mouth. Then another. And another. His movements settled into an unbroken rhythm—stab, toss, chew, repeat.

Everyone at the table watched in amused silence.

Mid-stab, Ukumari froze. Slowly, he lifted his head from the bowl and stared at William. His paw hovered mid-air, a chunk of mango skewered on the tip of his claw—aimed squarely in William's direction.

Ukumari narrowed his eyes. "Who's that guy?"

Ning Jing chuckled softly. "This is William," she said patiently. "You remember? Densho's friend from the Smiling Pond? He's come to visit."

Ukumari's expression softened as realization dawned. "Oh... yeah! The nice kid Densho talks about all the time." He gave a toothy grin.

Ning Jing turned to William. "William, this is Ukumari. He's a spectacled bear."

Now that Ukumari was in the light, William took in his impressive appearance. His thick, black fur was speckled with patches of beige and wisps of white and ginger, particularly around his face and chest. Dark markings encircled his eyes, resembling a pair of spectacles, though, to William, they looked more like a superhero's mask.

Ukumari extended his massive paw toward William. "Pleased to meet you, my good fellow! You're all Densho talks about these days!"

William reached out, needing both hands to grasp the bear's enormous paw—only to feel something sticky. Mango pulp clung to his fingers.

Ning Jing handed him a napkin. "Ukumari, where are your table manners?"

Ukumari let out a sheepish laugh. "Oops! Forgot to pop that piece in my mouth first."

William managed a grin. "Oh... uh... no problem."

Everyone around the table chuckled. As the laughter faded, a peaceful stillness settled over the room. The steady drumming of rain filled the quiet spaces between voices.

"So, William," Ning Jing said, "how did you find yourself on the bench by our treehouse in the middle of such a heavy rain shower?"

William furrowed his brow, trying to remember how he'd gotten there, but the memory was hazy. He reached for his basalt stone to focus his thoughts, only to find his pocket empty.

"Well, I was studying the Water Element. Learning how water moves— how it flows without resistance, like playing the piano. Touching the keys like raindrops on a pond. And then... somehow, I ended up here."

Ning Jing's eyes twinkled with recognition. "Ah, of course. If you've been studying the Water Element, then I suspect you're meant to see Master Lan Su."

Densho's tail twitched excitedly. "That makes perfect sense! Lan Su is a Master of the Water Element, and her Piano Zen studio's at the Garden of the Awakening Orchid. You should have a lesson with her." He tapped his paws together, thinking. "But, Will, her home's near the foot of the Pahada Mountains. Looks like you got a little off track again—just like last time."

"You're right," William said, shaking his head. "I must've ended up in the wrong place again."

Ukumari popped another mango into his mouth and waved a paw toward the window. "Ah, no problem, Will. Once the rain lets up, I've got a boat we can take down the river. It flows right past the Garden of the Awakening Orchid. Shouldn't take us too long."

"That would be great," William said. "Thank you."

"So, William," Ning said as she poured more tea. "I've heard that your Element training has been progressing quite well."

"I guess so," William said, shrugging his shoulders.

Densho piped in, "Guess so? Will, your Element abilities are amazing!" He turned to the group, eyes wide. "Master Shinichi showed him the nekkara martial art, and in no time, he was sparring like a natural. Then, during an Air Element exercise, he nearly floated right out of the Ubar rotunda."

Densho shook his head. "We haven't seen someone take to the Elements this easily since Florestan came through here..."

The moment the name left his mouth, he froze. His nose twitched. "Eh... you know... um... well, n-never mind." His voice trailed off, and he shrank down, hopping off the table to a chair.

Quetzal gave an abrupt squawk. Her feathers flared as she took flight and vanished through an open window into the rain.

A heavy silence fell over the room. Densho hung his head, his tail drooping.

Ning Jing approached and gently smoothed the fur on Densho's head. "Oh, it's all right, Densho. Quetzal will always be sensitive about all that. You needn't worry. She's not mad at you."

A crease formed between William's brows. He turned to Ning Jing. "Every time Florestan's name comes up, something shifts—the way everyone reacts." He tightened his grip on his teacup. "What happened?"

Before she could reply, a low vibration began to pulse through the room. The sound deepened, building in waves until the teacups rattled on the table. Everyone looked around, startled.

"Will," Densho said. "I think it's coming from your... backpack."

# Chapter Twenty-Nine

## *Florestan*

Wide-eyed, William unzipped his backpack. Inside, the Piano Zen Book seemed alive with energy. A faint glow pulsed along its edges. He set it on the table, and the moment he did, the pages flipped open on their own, as if caught in a strong wind. Sparks of light hovered over the open book.

A hushed gasp filled the room.

The pages slowed, then stopped on one suffused with soft, golden light. For an instant, it was blank—then a luminous symbol appeared, looping gracefully across the page.

Densho peered over his shoulder. "It's the infinity symbol, Will! I've got one of those on my teacup."

Ukumari leaned in and snorted. "Yeah, but why is it showing up here?"

William shrugged. "I'm not sure."

Just then, the image lifted off the page and began to float—looping and folding in on itself like a silent hologram. A few soft *oohs* and *ahs* rippled around the table.

"That is very… unusual," Ning Jing said. "I wonder—can you ask the book to clarify what it means?"

Before William could even form the question, the pages flipped again in a blur, settling on another one, faintly illuminated. New words emerged, fading into view as if written by an invisible hand.

William read aloud, *"'To know more, you must use the Dream Dorje. Soften your mind. Slow your thoughts. Then let the pendant guide you.'"*

He reached under his shirt and pulled out the dorje. Threads of colored light flickered across his face, and a soft, resonant tone hummed through his fingertips.

"That object seems to be the key," Densho said.

As if in response, the book shuddered and flipped to a new page, where another glowing inscription appeared. William traced the words as he spoke, *"'The Dream Dorje is more than an object. It is a bridge. One that can take you deeper into the currents of time.'"*

Ukumari shifted, his fur bristling. "I don't like the sound of this, Will. A bridge… to where, exactly?"

The book responded, its pages flipping once more.

*To the past. To what came before.*

Ning Jing's expression darkened. "Your dorje appears to be a kind of portal, William. I suspect that you're the only one who can use it this way." She exhaled softly. "You—and all of us here—are protected in the Whispering Woods by the vibrations Master Wu Wei created. They form a veil of invisibility, shielding us from the shadowy forces that move between worlds. But if you step beyond the veil, I can't say what you'll find—or what will happen."

Ukumari crossed his massive arms. "Great. Yeah, nothing ever goes wrong when ancient artifacts start glowing and giving instructions. So, do we have a plan to help Will, or are we just letting magic jewelry call the shots here?"

Densho's tail flicked anxiously. "Yeah, Will, I don't know. I'd feel a lot better if you could take Nasim—or one of us."

A shiver ran down William's spine. His pulse quickened. Doubt pressed in, but he exhaled and steadied himself.

"I don't know why, but I feel like I'm supposed to do this."

The book's final instruction appeared in radiant script.

*Close your eyes.*

*Hold the dorje. It is your anchor, your key to return.*

*Breathe deeply.*

*Step beyond the veil.*

*The past calls to you.*

William took a slow, deep breath, then gripped the dorje. He glanced at everyone in the room. His eyes then lingered on Densho, who gave him a small, encouraging nod. With that, William let his eyelids fall shut.

Immediately, the sense of the room faded.

The sounds of the treehouse—Ukumari's nervous breathing, Densho's fidgeting, the patter of rain on the roof—slipped away. William felt weightless, adrift on an unseen current.

On the inner screen of his mind, a shimmering, blue infinity symbol appeared. A pulse of energy surged from the dorje in his hand, expanding outward in radiant waves. The world fractured—like rippling glass.

A voice emerged—low and resonant. Unfamiliar.

*"The Dream Dorje is bound to the fluid nature of the Water Element. Time, like water, moves in currents, ripples in the fabric of space. Step beyond the veil, and you can drift along the time stream, slipping past the boundaries of past and present.*

*"But be warned: Memories from such places rarely stay whole. When you wake, details of the experience fade like mist in the sun. The deeper the vision, the more it dissolves upon waking. Still, your heart will remember what your mind forgets."*

William felt himself pulled—not in a direction he could name but along a force beyond gravity, beyond space. He couldn't explain it, not really. But the sensation was real, like riding light itself—no sensation of movement, yet a feeling of expanding outward, dissolving into the flow of time.

A vast, incandescent ribbon of energy stretched before him, curving through the fabric of space and time. But it wasn't just light—it was something deeper, something alive. A river of memory, a current of choices, echoes of the past reverberating through eternity.

Colors beyond earthly sight pulsed through it—ultraviolet gold, infrared violet, cascading bands of sound and light woven together in perfect harmony.

A whisper surfaced in his mind.

*"Time is not a straight line but a shifting probability wave. Past, present, and future do not simply follow one another; they coexist, layered, intertwined."*

And now, he was riding that current. Before he could stop himself, he reached out. The moment his fingers brushed the ribbon, the world gave way and he plunged backward.

William opened his eyes to a city bathed in golden light. He stood on a balcony overlooking the kingdom of Zarashad, the most enlightened realm on the continent of Ulandia. He wasn't sure how he knew it—only that he did.

Nestled at its heart, the capital city of Zarashad was a breathtaking metropolis: white limestone pyramids, stepped terraces, and golden temples carved into violet-hued hills. Opalescent towers rose in elegant symmetry. Wide avenues stretched below, alive with music, color and motion. The streets bustled with scholars and artisans, Element students honing their craft in open-air courtyards. The air itself—thick with energy—hummed with an ancient vibration.

As William took in the city, the same voice emerged like a current in his mind.

*"The Four Elements were not tools for power, nor were they meant to be wielded for display. They were a path, a way of knowing oneself and the world. In Zarashad, people did not command the Elements; they listened to them, learned from them. The Elements revealed one's strengths and limitations, their harmony shaping both the land and those who walked it."*

The illuminated city faded away, and William found himself once again riding the curving wave of time like a small boat adrift on a cosmic ocean.

He reached for the ribbon of light, and as his fingers touched it, the scene shifted into a cavernous shaft buried deep beneath a mountain.

The voice continued as William floated like an ethereal spirit in the darkness.

*"Not all in Ulandia sought wisdom. In the shadowed, outcast kingdom of Keshmara, miners delved deep into dormant volcanoes, searching for gems and metals. What they found instead was something far more mysterious: lustrous, black, obsidian stone, laced with reddish fire.*

*"The miners, once disheartened by their fruitless search for riches, fell under the spell of the stone's strange radiance and the unsettling power that seemed to stir within it. Yet its gift was not universal. Some who touched it felt nothing, while others experienced a strange ability for fleeting tricks, colored smoke, flashes of light, brief illusions.*

*"For a gifted few, however, the stone unlocked something deeper, phenomena beyond reason: levitation, invisibility, bursts of unnatural strength... even miracles.*

*"Emboldened, the prospectors abandoned their hunt for common riches and began harvesting the trace amounts of the stone they could find.*

*"And so, a mysterious order of wizards emerged from the shadowed realm of Keshmara. Wielding the stone's power secretly woven into sequined gloves, they appeared in the courts of Ulandia's rulers, cloaked in mystery."*

The echo of the dark mine faded and the ribbon of time spiraled again as the vision shifted. William found himself floating, an observer inside a hushed concert hall, filled with an eager audience. A polished, white, concert grand piano sat in the center of the stage.

A moment later, a young Florestan strode confidently into the spotlight. His left hand was clad in a white sequined glove, its fingers exposed. He wore a crimson cape fastened at the collar. With a theatrical flourish, he extended his arms, and a sudden wind swept through the auditorium. The cape billowed behind him, snapping like a sail, drawing gasps from the crowd. As if obeying his silent command, the cape detached itself and fluttered to the floor, falling behind him.

Florestan sat and began to play. The music was dazzling—technically perfect, impossibly fast, breathtaking in precision. Each note rang like a crystal bell, cascading through the hall in a blaze of brilliance. A reddish aura radiated around the piano like heatwaves.

Then, without warning, Florestan and his magic piano began to rise. The audience gasped as he levitated above the stage, fingers still flying across the keys. The applause was thunderous.

Yet the longer William watched, the more unease crept in. For all its brilliance, the music left no lasting imprint; it stirred no memory, no ache, no joy in his heart.

Then, like the fading of a dream, the stage lights dimmed, the roar of the crowd dissolved, and the vision shifted once again.

A breeze swept across the grand square of Zarashad. A lone figure stood at its center, surrounded by a crowd. He wore a pristine, dark-red cloak, the fabric rippling softly in the wind, its hood drawn low, shielding his face.

William didn't need to see it. He already knew.

*Florestan.*

It was later—after he vanished from the world of music and returned, transformed. People still whispered in awe; memories of his dazzling concerts lingered. But now, new stories spread—not of music but of magic. Florestan had become something else: a wizard. And his abilities, they said, far surpassed those of his peers.

He lifted his left hand—no longer clad in the white, sequined glove so common among the Wizards of Keshmara. Bare, it seemed to summon the obedience of the Four Elements.

Stone and soil shifted. Flowers bloomed. Wind curled around him. Water flowed wherever he willed.

At first, the people admired him.

Then they worshiped him.

Time folded once more.

William drifted farther along the time track, now at the edge of the Whispering Woods—an unseen observer to the scene unfolding below.

A hush fell over the gathered crowd, their eyes fixed on Florestan as he knelt beside a dying fawn. Its breath was shallow, an arrow buried deep in its side.

But Florestan didn't reach for herbs or poultices. He raised his left hand and called upon the Fire Element—a volatile art, seldom used on living creatures without consequence.

The crowd, unaware of the black obsidian stone hidden in his cloak, watched as flickers of dark amber light played across the fawn's still form. A low hum threaded through the trees—subtle at first, then swelling.

The fawn shuddered. Its body tensed, then went unnaturally still.

For a moment, nothing. Then a final pulse—deep, resonant, almost imperceptible.

The fawn gasped. Its eyes snapped open, strangely bright. Disoriented, it sprang to its feet and vanished into the woods.

At first, silence. Then murmurs of disbelief.

Florestan had defied death itself—though the act left him momentarily and blissfully incapacitated.

In the seasons that followed, he continued to perform wonders, each more astonishing than the last. At first, the people marveled. He had emerged from nowhere, a mystery from the dark outcast lands of Keshmara.

But as the years passed, amazement gave way to unease—first in Zarashad, then across the many realms of Ulandia.

Schemes and alliances formed in secret. Court wizards were summoned, consulted, even mobilized. But Florestan pressed on, unconcerned, driven to push further.

More sick and dying animals were brought to him, and with each restoration, his confidence swelled. Healing had an unexpected side effect: the creatures changed. They moved with heightened awareness, their instincts sharpened, their gaze more focused—almost human.

It was instant evolution, miraculous… otherworldly.

A white-tufted marmoset, a spectacled bear, a three-toed sloth—one by one, Florestan healed and transformed them, expanding their consciousness beyond the natural bounds of their kind.

Each wonder left his left hand trembling, his expression euphoric, his body frail.

And then…

A pair of resplendent quetzals in a cage: stunning birds with no visible ailment. William could tell immediately that Florestan was entranced, intoxicated by their beauty.

An uncontrollable urge overtook him. In a fevered, delirious state, he evolved the first one. Her feathers ignited with color; her voice grew musical, flute-like, though still unable to speak.

Then he turned to Nasim, a sister nearly identical—until the moment Florestan pushed further.

Merging all Four Elements into her being, light exploded around her—a force too strong, too wild to control. When it faded, her body was gone. Nasim, the resplendent quetzal, had vanished.

Her sister's cry pierced the forest, the notes trembling with grief.

Florestan staggered back, the process ravaging his body. In an instant, his face withered by decades—eyes blazing with a hunger that no power born of black obsidian could ever sate.

The vision shifted once more. William floated above the luminous ribbon of energy—vast and iridescent, like a living current. As his hand brushed against it again, he was pulled forward, plunging ahead on the time track.

Zarashad.

The city still stood—but a shadow of its former self, a civilization slipping into its own dark age.

The gleaming towers were dull, their once-vibrant murals chipped and faded. The open-air courtyards where students once trained in the Elements sat empty, overgrown with vines. The fountains, once flowing with nourishing water, now stood dry. The music that had once floated through the streets—gone.

The people remained, but they had changed. Gone was the eagerness in their eyes, the quiet strength in their posture. Instead, they waited, loitering in shaded alleys, peering expectantly toward the grand square where Florestan would appear, weaving miracles before their eyes: food, water, small displays of wonder, but the true draw as always… the healings.

And then time pulled him forward once more. William tumbled ahead on the time track, and the vision darkened further.

Evolved predators stalked the streets—creatures once ordinary, now terrifyingly intelligent. Golden eagles with cruel, knowing eyes. A tiger with dark, gleaming stripes. A massive grizzly bear: hulking and aware, ruling the wilds with unmatched ferocity.

Fear gripped the city. People hurried along the alleys and backstreets. Doors slammed shut. They had no power to resist.

And at the heart of it all stood a figure in a tattered, dark-red cloak. A black helmet covered his head, its design reminiscent of the ancient warriors of Keshmara. Worn, dented, cracked, its angular form concealed his face. His arms were folded across his chest. On his left hand, a black, sequined glove.

And then… darkness swallowed everything.

A jolt surged through William. He gasped, fingers releasing the dorje as he snapped fully awake in the treehouse.

The familiar sounds of the room rushed in—the quiet patter of rain, the creak of the wooden beams. His tea, still steaming, sat untouched on the table. His heart pounded, his breath shallow as his mind scrambled to process something that was already slipping away.

William bolted upright, startling Densho, who leapt into the air. "Will, what's wrong?" His tail puffed with alarm.

Ukumari placed a heavy paw on William's shoulder. "Yeah, you just shut your eyes for, like, two seconds, then you gasped like you had the wind knocked out of you. What happened?"

William shook his head, as if trying to clear a foggy haze from his mind.

Ning Jing studied him. "What did you see?"

He swallowed hard. "I'm not sure. So much seemed to happen all at once—and yet I can't recall the details."

He rubbed his hands over his face, trying to catch the fragments. "I think I went back—back to the kingdom of Zarashad. A time before everything changed. Florestan was there." William's thoughts reeled. Images flickered at the edges of his memory. "I saw predators… a tiger."

A silence fell over the room as the animals exchanged worried looks.

Densho's tail stiffened. "That's probably Typhon the tiger."

"A huge, brown bear and a crocodile," William added.

Ukumari's shoulders tensed. "That's Gorgon the grizzly," he murmured, "and Cerberus the crocodile."

William turned to Ning Jing. "Florestan had this stone. He used it to do things—magical things. And it was like I saw his whole life flash before my eyes… but so much happened, I can't remember the details."

She hesitated, choosing her words carefully. "It sounds as though the dorje showed you his past—memories imprinted on the current of time. The stone you saw may be the source of his power. But be careful, William. Florestan has mastered many of the secrets of the Elements—especially Air— which allows him to move freely within the mental realms."

She walked to the window, watching as the last mist of rain faded into the valley. "Thankfully, we are protected here in the Whispering Woods." Then she turned and met William's gaze. "Now might be a good time to journey to the Garden of the Awakening Orchid to meet Master Lan Su. You may find answers to what you can't remember from your dream."

Ning Jing glanced outside. "Perfect. The rain has stopped. You all best hurry along. I'll stay here and tidy up."

"You're not coming?" William asked.

Ning Jing chuckled, waving him off. "Oh no. I live life in the slow lane. It's mindful and enjoyable but not much help on an adventure like this. Ukumari and Densho will help guide you down the river."

Ukumari grinned, tossing a few more pieces of mango into his mouth. Densho had already vaulted onto the window ledge, waiting impatiently.

William slipped the Piano Zen book into his backpack and slung it over his shoulder.

He turned to Ning Jing and bowed.

She bowed in return. "Safe travels, all of you."

# Chapter Thirty

## *Life is But a Dream*

With their spirits lifted, the trio made their descent from the treehouse. The wooden steps creaked gently beneath William's feet, still slick with lingering moisture. Ukumari moved cautiously, gripping the rail with his large paws, his bulk swaying slightly with each turn.

Densho skipped the stairs altogether, leaping nimbly from branch to branch before landing on a wide stone. He began tapping his fingers, waiting impatiently for the others to catch up.

"Guys, we're never going to get there at this rate," he called up. "Will, too bad we can't use your book as a sail again. But Ukumari's not exactly built for flight. He's more of an Earth Element kind of guy, if you know what I mean."

Ukumari paused mid-step, gave Densho a pointed look and a snort, then continued downward, carefully navigating the twists and turns.

They set off down a winding path, past dew-laced ferns and moss-covered stones—the same trail where William had been caught in the earlier downpour. Sunlight filtered between the tree branches, catching on droplets clinging to the leaves and scattering soft, magical sparkles through the forest.

Up ahead, nestled beside a cluster of reeds, a weathered, blue rowboat bobbed at the edge of an old, wooden dock. The current surged from the heavy rain, its rhythmic gurgling filling the air.

"We call this river the Harmony Stream," Densho said as they reached the bank. "Something about its voice always makes us break into song whenever we ride it."

Ukumari gave the rushing current a wary glance. "Good thing we're going *with* the flow today. I'd hate to paddle upstream right now."

The spectacled bear then gestured for William to step into the boat. Across the stern, the name *Djembe* was painted in elegant calligraphy. William raised an eyebrow. "Did you paint that? It's beautiful handwriting."

Ukumari caught the look and grinned. "Ah, yeah—no. That's Amara's handiwork. I tried painting it myself once, but it didn't go so well." He held up his big paw and clumsily wiggled his claws.

"Wow, that's an understatement," Densho interjected. "Amara told him she'd need the Rosetta Stone to decipher his handwriting. That's why she offered to do it for him."

Unfazed, Ukumari continued, "I told her I wanted to name my boat Djembe."

William tilted his head. "Don't you already have a djembe? Did you name that one too?"

Ukumari lifted his snout. "Yes, I did. *Mango*, if you must know."

Densho held up three fingers, ticking them off. "Yeah, Will—here's Ukumari's life in a nutshell: mangos, sleeping, and djembe drumming."

William chuckled as he and Densho climbed into the blue rowboat. Ukumari untied the mooring rope, then hopped in behind them. With a strong push of his paddle, the boat slipped free, into the fast-flowing stream.

Ukumari rowed with surprising finesse. His oars were customized with looped handles to fit his paws, and each stroke cut cleanly through the water. For all his love of naps and mangos, the spectacled bear was undeniably strong.

William softened his ears. There was something in the tone of the Harmony Stream—soft and clear, like the world itself was humming. And as if on cue, Densho and Ukumari burst into a song they liked to call "Life is But a Dream."

*Row, row, row your boat*
*Gently down the stream*
*Merrily, merrily, merrily, merrily*
*Life is but a dream*

William chimed in, and their voices rose above the rushing water as they sang the song several times, rocking the boat back and forth with merry abandon.

William raised a hand. "Hey... guys, I know this in French. Have you ever tried it in French before?"

Densho and Ukumari exchanged a look and shook their heads.

"It's easy," William said. "I'll teach you."

*Rame, rame, rame ton bateau*
*Doucement sur le ruisseau*
*Heureusement, heureusement, heureusement, heureusement*
*La vie n'est qu'un rêve*

To William's surprise, his friends picked it up quickly. Soon, all three were belting out the French lyrics at the top of their lungs, their laughter drifting along with the current.

"Hey, Will, buddy, that was fun!" Ukumari said after several renditions in French. "What other languages do you know?"

William paused, shrugging his shoulders. "Hmm… I'm not sure. Let me think." He looked into the sky above, searching his memory. It was now a clear blue, with only a few whisps of white clouds. Ukumari and Densho waited eagerly, clearly enjoying the new twist on an old favorite.

William stroked his chin. "*Deutsch, ja… auf Deutsch.*"

"*Deutsch?*" Densho and Ukumari echoed.

"Oh—sorry. German. It's another language," William said.

He began:

*Ruder, ruder, ruder dein Boot*
*Sanft den Fluss hinab*
*Fröhlich, fröhlich, fröhlich, fröhlich*
*Das Leben ist ein Traum*

Densho and Ukumari nodded enthusiastically, and soon they were all singing the German version together over and over.

The game continued as William added new languages.

Next was Italian:

*Rema, rema, rema la tua barca*
*Dolcemente giù per il ruscello*
*Allegro, allegro, allegro, allegro*
*La vita è solo un sogno*

"Keep going, Will!" Densho exclaimed.

William tapped his lips with his index finger, then his eyes lit up. Without thinking, he began to sing in Japanese.

*Kogeyo kogeyo booto o*
*Yasashiku kawa o kudarou*
*Tanoshiku tanoshiku tanoshiku tanoshiku*
*Jinsei wa tada no yume*

Then, mid-verse, a brilliant countermelody soared above them—a voice as bright and quick as a piccolo. The trio fell silent, all eyes turning skyward.

A blur of green, red, and gold feathers streaked down toward them.

"Quetzal!" they all cried, throwing their arms up and shouting, "Hooray!"

The bird dove, rolling gracefully, her iridescent tail feathers streaming behind her like liquid turquoise. She skimmed just above their heads, her wings slicing through the air—her movements an aerial ballet.

"Hey-hey, guys!" Densho shouted. "Now that Quetzal's here, do one more, Will!"

"Hmm…" William said, pondering. "Um… how about Arabic?"

"Oh, yeah. That's a good one, Will," Ukumari said. "Amara taught it to us—she learned it at the Palace of Ubar."

And, without missing a beat, they all sang out together, voices lifted in joyful unison, with Quetzal weaving in a perfect harmony above.

*Jadhdhif, jadhdhif, jadhdhif qaribak*
*Bilutf ʿala al-jadwal*
*Bifarah, bifarah, bifarah, bifarah*
*Al-hayat laysat siwa hulm*

They sang, laughed, and swayed—almost capsizing the rowboat a few times. Soon, a wooden dock appeared on the riverbank, jutting out from the edge of the forest, and the singing came to a pause.

William blinked. "Wait—are we there already?"

"Oh no," Densho said. "Ukumari lives here. He's just grabbing his djembe for a jam session at the Awakening Orchid."

Ukumari gave a nod. "Yep."

*Jam session?* William wondered. Ukumari didn't exactly strike him as the musical type. It was hard to picture the lumbering bear, who could barely hold a paintbrush, keeping time on a drum with real musicians.

The bear eased the boat in until it bumped softly against the dock. Densho bounded out and looped the boat's rope around a worn post. With a motion of his big paw, Ukumari led them up a wooden staircase and onto a winding path into the dense forest.

The walk was brief. They followed a narrow trail beneath a canopy of mango trees until it opened into a sun-dappled clearing bordered by gentle rolling hills. Tucked into the slope of one of the mounds was Ukumari's home. A round wooden door and a small, circular window framed in river stones gave it a rustic charm—exactly the kind of house William imagined a bear, or hobbit, might build if given the chance.

Ukumari lumbered up to the door. "Give me a minute, guys. I'll be right back." He stepped inside and quickly shut the door behind him.

"Aww, I was hoping to go inside," William said. "I'm curious what a bear's home looks like."

Densho leaned in, lowering his voice. "Believe me, you don't wanna know."

William shrugged and found a tree stump to sit on. Quetzal glided over and perched on a nearby branch.

From inside the house came a loud ruckus—thumping, crashing, an occasional grumble. William and Densho exchanged amused glances. Finally, the commotion settled, and Ukumari emerged victorious, djembe in paw.

A wide stump stood just outside, perfectly positioned. Ukumari plopped down, balanced the djembe on one paw, and gave it a few impressive spins, like a rock drummer twirling a stick. At just the right angle, he locked it between his legs, then, with a flick of his paw, he launched into a rhythm.

At first, the beat was steady and deliberate. Then it grew, layering into intricate patterns of sound. Ukumari's claws moved like nimble fingers, rolling across the drumhead with precision. His paws struck the rim, the sides, even tapping accents on the wooden frame. The rhythm surged with energy, blending deep, resonant thumps with sharp, syncopated slaps. Then, without missing a beat, he lifted the djembe, spun it several times in midair, and caught it, resuming the groove in perfect time.

The vibrancy of the rhythm gripped William. He could feel it in his chest. Ukumari played like the drum was part of him—not just performing but pouring joy into every beat.

Densho could no longer hold back. With a delighted whoop, he sprang from a tree branch and landed in the clearing. He began to move, his body pulsing with the beat, carried by the intoxicating groove. Twitching footwork flowed into fluid breakdancing moves, each motion sharp and electrifying. Then he launched into the air—flipping and twisting, catching impossible hang time before landing in perfect sync with a drum break.

Ukumari's solo built toward an impressive finale, a climactic roll across the rim of the drum, punctuated by a deep, resonant slap from his powerful paw. As if rehearsed, Densho nailed a quadruple twist, landing flawlessly as the final beat echoed into the trees.

William jumped to his feet, clapping and cheering. Quetzal let out a jubilant, high-pitched trill.

Ukumari stood, closed his eyes, and took as deep a bow as his belly would allow. Then he gestured toward Densho, who responded with a nimble triple backflip, landing in a dramatic pose, arms flared wide.

"That was amazing," William said. "Where'd you learn to drum like that?"

The spectacled bear slung the drum over his shoulder and hesitated. "Strange story, for sure," Ukumari said. "After I was healed—when I was on death's door—something changed. I started to evolve. I felt out of rhythm inside; everything in my head was louder, more tangled than it used to be. You know, back when I was just a bear."

He ran a paw over the drumhead. "Master Shinichi said it happens to those who walk between worlds. I was still a bear but also something more, closer to… human. But it wasn't until he placed this drum in my paws that I finally began to feel steady. Drumming gave me a way to flow with the currents inside me instead of against them. At first, I played to feel whole. And then…" He grinned. "I got really good at it."

Ukumari flipped the djembe onto his belly. "I took to drumming like…" He tapped out a quick rhythmic pattern and chuckled. "…like a monkey to a banana."

He nudged William in the ribs.

Densho crossed his arms. "Ha! If you must know, Will, if given a choice, I actually prefer avocado toast."

Quetzal let out a quick, urgent trill, cutting through the banter.

Densho's ears twitched. He nodded. "Yeah, you're right, Quetzal. We've got to get Will to the Awakening Orchid."

Ukumari slung the djembe over his shoulder. "Good call. Let's get back to the boat and shove off."

A few minutes later, they were gliding once more along Harmony Stream, its gentle curves drawing them deeper into the heart of the forest. The sunlight that had broken through earlier began to fade, and a soft mist gathered over the water, thin at first, then thickening until it blanketed the stream in a veil.

"Is it going to rain again?" William asked, squinting at the shifting haze.

"No," Densho replied. "This is just a sign we're getting close to the Garden of the Awakening Orchid. When it's not raining, the garden is usually wrapped in mist. It's part of the atmosphere there."

The boat rounded a sharp bend, revealing an elegant, blue-and-white moon bridge arching high above the water. Its exaggerated curve looked almost too steep to climb.

Just then, a single shaft of sunlight pierced the fog—as if summoned by the river itself—striking the mist that hovered over the stream. The particles of moisture caught the light and shimmered like silver dust suspended in the air.

For a brief moment, the bridge cast a perfect reflection on the water below—forming a circle, whole and unbroken.

The magical scene elicited a soft gasp from everyone in the boat. Then, just as quickly, the mist closed in again, and the circle disappeared.

Everyone glanced at each other in stunned silence.

"Well, that's never happened before," Ukumari murmured.

"Yeah, and so fast, too," Densho added. "If you guys hadn't been here, I might have thought I imagined it."

"*Miroir*," William whispered.

Densho tilted his head. "Huh? What's that mean, Will?"

"It's French," he said softly. "It means mirror."

As they all pondered the image of the moon bridge, a soft, cool breeze drifted through the mist—gentle, familiar.

"It's Nasim," Densho said.

Quetzal let out a rapturous melody, her piccolo-like voice soaring as she launched into the sky. Spiraling upward, she met her wind spirit sister in midair—their reunion a swirl of color and motion.

Ukumari guided the rowboat to a small dock at the base of the moon bridge, bringing them safely ashore. Ahead, the path continued, only reachable by climbing over the bridge's high arc. In the distance, a high, narrow waterfall cascaded from a towering cliff, its mist forming a veil of silver.

"That's Shooting Star Falls," Densho said, pointing. "It's fed by snowmelt from Mt. Parthena and flows straight into the Garden of the Awakening Orchid."

"Um… w-what?" William asked. "I see the waterfall, but where's the Awakening Orchid?"

Densho gestured with his paw. "Just up there, along the path beyond the bridge. It's right there. You don't see it?"

William glanced around, puzzled. "No… I don't see anything."

# Chapter Thirty-One

## *The Garden of the Awakening Orchid*

William squinted into the thickening mist. Only trees, stones, and the gentle flow of the stream met his gaze. No garden. No home. Just wilderness.

Densho stood beside him, tail twitching with unease. He stole a glance at William. "So... you still can't see it?"

"No... I'm sorry."

Densho scratched behind his ears, then looked up. "Nasim, can you help Will?"

Disappointment settled over William's thoughts. Just like the other Element schools, the Garden of the Awakening Orchid was hidden. He still hadn't learned to see with inner vision. As doubt began to seep in, Nasim's presence caressed his face—like a breeze through tall grass, gently brushing his hair to one side.

A suggestion surfaced in his thoughts.

*Soften your gaze.*

Her voice wasn't made of words—it was an intuitive transmission, like a candle being lit inside his mind.

His eyes relaxed, his vision softening into a gentle blur.

But something else stirred—subtler, harder to grasp.

*Focus on the space behind your eyes.*

The phrase made little sense, but William tried. As he did, a quietude rose within him. His breath deepened. His thoughts slowed. Awareness shifted. The world around him didn't change… but something within him did.

And then—he saw it.

The Garden of the Awakening Orchid slowly materialized before his eyes. Details sharpened—delicate blossoms, an arched entryway, the sweeping lines of Lan Su's home. A thrill ran through him, and goosebumps rose along his arms.

"Oh my gosh! I see it, Densho!" William gasped.

Densho whooped and spun in a joyful circle. "You did it, Will!"

Nasim had guided him, but she hadn't revealed the garden. She'd simply shown him how to find it himself. With his vision clear, he could see that the entire sanctuary lay on a higher plane, overlooking the Harmony Stream. A white wall, etched with intricate geometric designs, encircled the grounds. Beyond it, dark-gray terracotta rooftops peeked over the edge—curved silhouettes, serene and ancient against the sky.

To reach it, they still had to cross over the moon bridge. Its narrow, steeply pitched steps were no challenge for Densho, who scampered over with ease. William, however, took his time, gripping the railing as he carefully made his way across.

Ukumari had the hardest time of all. Pressing his belly against the railing, he turned sideways, gripping the edge with both paws as he edged his way up and down the bridge like a bear-sized crab.

Densho stifled laughter as the Ukumari finally arrived on the east bank, out of breath. "It would have been *so* much easier if they just built the dock on this side of the river," he grumbled.

"My dear Ukumari, that would defeat the purpose of the journey over the moon bridge," Densho said with a wink. "It reflects the challenge of going from one state of consciousness to another."

The bear huffed. "Easy for you to say, monkey. It's no challenge for you to scamper across."

"Ah, but not all challenges are physical. Maybe my challenge isn't the bridge but what happens after I cross it?"

Ukumari narrowed his eyes. "*Touché*, my marmoset friend. *Touché*. I may soon endeavor to help you experience a few more of those challenges, up close and personal."

The two exchanged a playful bow.

Quetzal dusted the heads of her two animal friends, encouraging them to drop their shenanigans and keep moving.

The group began the final ascent, following a narrow stone path of mossy-covered steps that wound upward. At the entrance, an archway adorned with golden Chinese characters welcomed them. Densho leapt onto William's shoulder and whispered, "It says *Peace and Tranquility*."

As William stepped through the gateway, he immediately felt the impact of the words as a deep sense of peace washed over him. The beauty of the inner garden wasn't just visual, it shifted the rhythm of his thoughts, making them softer, more fluid.

At the center of the Garden of the Awakening Orchid lay the Pond of Cosmic Reflection—a mirror-still expanse dotted with lily pads and lotus flowers. Along its banks, elegant pavilions and houses nestled among silk trees, bamboo groves, and vibrant, flowering shrubs. Beneath the surface, Koi fish glided through the water, their bright colors glimmering with each movement, while the songs of unseen birds drifted through the air.

The architecture echoed the Ming Dynasty, with rooftops of curved, green-gray clay tiles resting atop dark, wooden columns. Ornate ridges and upturned eaves crowned each pavilion, their corners adorned with carved dragons—mouths open in silent dialogue with the heavens. Intricate latticework framed the windows and doors, their patterns casting delicate shadows across the pathways.

On the eastern wall, a towering rock formation rose, crowned by the Shooting Star waterfall as it cascaded gracefully into the Pond of Cosmic Reflection.

William gazed across the pond and felt something stir within him. It reminded him of the Smiling Pond from the Whispering Woods, yet the feeling here was different. The Pond of Cosmic Reflection exuded a quiet depth, expanding his awareness in a way that felt effortless and natural.

They all stood in silence, each lost in their own thoughts. A koi splashed as it snatched food from the surface, sending ripples across the pond. The moment stretched until a sudden musical trill broke the silence.

Quetzal swooped down and perched on the terrace railing, her voice rising in a lilting melody. It seemed to announce the arrival of Master Lan Su, who stepped gracefully from the nearby Pavilion of Serenity.

Densho and Ukumari bounded forward to embrace her. William hung back—observing.

She looked no older than thirty. Her long, dark-brown hair was tied in a ponytail, a blue ribbon trailing over her shoulder. Her white robe was cinched at the waist with a flowing, blue, satin sash.

She greeted them warmly, then turned to William. "Welcome to the Garden of the Awakening Orchid, William. I have heard many wonderful things about you. Come inside, all of you, and enjoy some refreshments."

She led them through the main hall of the Pavilion of Serenity and up a staircase to the second floor, where a large, round table awaited with various seats arranged around it. Ukumari found a perfectly sized stump, settling in with a satisfied grunt.

Open windows overlooked the pond and surrounding gardens, letting in the soft scents of jasmine and Chinese silk tree blossoms. Sunlight filtered through carved wooden columns, their intricate patterns drawing the eye upward to the dark crossbeams above. Several attendants moved quietly through the room, serving hot tea and delicate desserts, while in the corner, a student plucked a tranquil melody on a Chinese zither—the notes mingling with the soft murmur of the waterfall outside.

As they sipped fragrant oolong tea and sampled Chinese mooncakes filled with lightly sweetened lotus paste, Lan Su turned her attention to her animal guests. She asked Densho and Ukumari how they were faring and whether they'd faced any recent challenges. From what William could gather, his companions no longer visited the Awakening Orchid as often as they once had; perhaps because they no longer needed to—not in the same way.

Just then, a side door creaked open, and a familiar fragrance drifted into the room. Ukumari, still facing forward, twitched his nose—once, twice— his beady eyes lighting up with instant recognition. Without turning, he broke into a wide grin and bellowed, "Amara!"

He tried to leap up from his wooden stump, but his paw caught the edge, sending him tumbling forward. Rather than faceplanting, the portly bear rolled into a surprisingly graceful somersault and popped back onto his feet. He bounded over to Amara and wrapped her in a massive hug, nearly knocking her over as he rose onto his hind legs.

Amara laughed as she wobbled to stay upright. "Nice tumble-and-roll there, Ukumari! And how is my favorite bear doing?"

"Much better now that you're here!" he replied, beaming.

She stroked his thick fur, giving his big neck a hearty scratch.

Densho launched into the air, floated across the room, then scrambled up Ukumari's back, planting himself atop the bear's head.

Amara caressed the white-tufted marmoset's cheeks. "And how's little Densho this fine day?"

Rather than answer, he just nuzzled into her palm.

Amara led them back to the table. "Hello, William. What a pleasant surprise."

"Nice to see you again, Amara," William said. "Do you help out here like you do at the Palace of Ubar?"

"Now and then," she replied. "I was visiting a few musicians and decided to stay for a calligraphy class. I couldn't resist. And you never know when Ukumari will rope me into another one of his… creative projects."

The spectacled bear lifted his drum. "Yeah, that reminds me. You still need to write *Mango* on my djembe."

"Yes, yes. Of course, Ukumari, I'd love to."

"Amara," Master Lan Su said. "Would you mind keeping our animal friends company while I spend a bit of time with William?"

"Sure." She turned to Densho and Ukumari. "C'mon, guys, let's see if we can find some musicians in the courtyard to jam with."

Ukumari grabbed his djembe. "Oh yeah, let's groove!" Densho did a double backflip, and in a whirlwind of energy, the trio bounded out the door together.

# Chapter Thirty-Two

## *Moving Like a Three-Toed Sloth*

Once the others had gone, Lan Su led William down the stairs to the first floor of the Pavilion of Serenity. Stepping outside through a side door, they entered a shaded path, hidden beneath the canopy of tropical trees and surrounded by lush ferns, flowering shrubs, and delicate vines weaving through the landscape.

The path itself was a mosaic of small, cut stones—some off-white, others deep gray—arranged in a checkerboard pattern. Along its edges, the stones curved and undulated in contrast to the rigid squares at its center.

Lan Su gestured toward the design. "The contrast between structure and movement is intentional. The sharp lines of the stones balance the flowing curves of the path, just as the structured pavilions of the Awakening Orchid are softened by the natural forms of trees, water, and rock. This principle of balance is also reflected in the Four Elements—Earth and Air complement each other, as do Water and Fire."

She slowed her steps and turned to William. "Look closely at the shape of the path. Does it remind you of anything?"

William studied the winding trail, then answered, "It looks like a river flowing through a… jungle."

"Exactly. Now, slow your steps and soften your gaze. As you do, imagine yourself as a boat drifting down a stream."

William followed her guidance, picturing himself as a boat gliding along a river's current. For a moment, he imagined he could hear the gentle rise and fall of Ravel's *"Une barque sur l'océan"*—not as a melody, exactly, but as a sensation, a memory of motion embedded in sound.

They continued in silence, moving with the rhythm of the winding path. As the trees parted, they stepped into a clearing that revealed the broad expanse of the Pond of Cosmic Reflection. Its waters mirrored the sky, the pavilions, and the quivering leaves.

Lan Su paused at the edge of the clearing, her eyes on the water. "In the worlds of time and space, the flow is always present. Everything is in motion. And you can place your awareness on the flow quite easily, simply by slowing down your movements."

She lifted an arm, moving it in an unhurried, fluid motion. Her voice slowed to match the gesture. "When you deliberately slow your movements, your mind and your thoughts follow. Everything softens. You become fully present and aware."

William closely watched as Lan Su's arm traced the air like water.

"Come, let us try something," she said, gesturing toward a stone bench in a clearing near the pond.

William followed, and she motioned for him to sit.

"For this practice," Lan Su said, "think of your friend Ning Jing—the three-toed sloth. Breathe naturally and soften your mind. Then, as you rise, move in exaggerated slow motion, each movement infused with awareness."

She signaled for him to begin. William rose in slow motion. It felt strange—almost comical—but the deliberate pace demanded more focus than he expected. Every shift in weight, every movement of muscle and bone, drew his attention.

"Feel the earth beneath your feet," Lan Su said gently. "Stay rooted, yet let your mind become light as air. Now, walk—at sloth speed."

William took a painfully slow step forward, grinning at how unnatural it felt.

"Moving like this changes the mind's inner frequency," she said. "It draws you into a deeper field of attention."

As he moved, she added, "Notice each tiny shift—how your weight transfers, how your breath aligns with your pace. Even the blinking of your eyes becomes a part of your presence."

William turned, adjusting carefully to maintain his balance.

"Sloth speed creates a stillness inside," Lan Su said. "It replaces scattered thoughts and distractions with presence. Every step becomes a meditation."

She pointed toward a cluster of flowers at the base of a nearby tree. "Look down, William. See the lavender blooming at your feet? Reach down, pick one, and bring it to your nose."

William bent down slowly, wobbling slightly to maintain balance as he reached for the flower. He plucked a lavender blossom with care, then rose again—deliberately, steadily—and lifted it to his nose. Closing his eyes, he inhaled deeply. The scent filled his senses. Despite his unhurried pace, he felt more alive in the present moment than ever before.

Lan Su placed a gentle hand on his shoulder. "You did beautifully. I truly saw a sloth before me," she said. "Come, let us move to the Moon Locking Pavilion."

He walked beside her in silence, following the winding walkway. As they neared, he took in the Moon Locking Pavilion—a small, open-air structure with an upturned Ming-style roof that extended gracefully over the still water. A zigzag path led the way out to it.

Once they stepped beneath the pavilion's roof, Lan Su continued, "Movements like Ning Jing's—slow and deliberate—are a perfect example of how we apply awareness in Piano Zen. Did you notice how your attention settled on the smallest details of your body?"

William nodded. "My mind didn't wander at all. Moving that slowly made it easier to stay present."

"Exactly," she replied. "At the piano, we use the same approach. Slowing down, truly slowing down, expands your awareness. Every detail in the music becomes clearer—the subtle techniques, the shapes of phrases, the quiet dynamics—all revealing themselves when you move slowly enough not to miss them."

The cloud cover had thickened, and a light rain began to fall, soft at first, then steady. Raindrops dimpled the pond's surface, forming endless ripples. Water began to drip from the corners of the Moon Locking Pavilion's roof, tracing delicate lines through the air.

Master Lan Su extended her hand, letting the thick raindrops splash against her open palm. "The surface of the piano keys," she said, "can be imagined as the surface of a still pond. When you touch them, think of your fingertips as raindrops falling gently onto water. This image can transform your entire approach to piano technique."

"I remember now," William said suddenly. "Master Shinichi said something about the pond—about touching the surface."

Lan Su smiled. "Yes, the *touching the pond* technique. He gave you your first glimpse of how the Water Element applies to piano practice. But only after grounding your body through Earth and opening your mind through Air can you begin to understand Water—how it flows through your playing, note by note."

She turned back toward the pond, her voice gentle, carried by the falling rain. "Flow is just the beginning. Sometimes, when you soften enough to truly listen, the Water Element becomes a bridge—into the quiet beneath your thoughts, where the Fire Element begins to stir. A kind of awareness that stretches between worlds. A place where learning continues, even in silence. Even in sleep."

# Chapter Thirty-Three

## *Beneath the Surface*

A blanket of heavy clouds rested above the Awakening Orchid. Rain tapped lightly on the roof of the Moon Locking Pavilion. Beyond the wooden railings, a ballet of a thousand tiny circles danced across the surface of the Pond of Cosmic Reflection, calming the thoughts that drifted through William's mind.

"Have you ever wondered what lies beneath the surface?" Master Lan Su asked, gazing out across the water.

Still entranced by the shifting ripples on the pond, William blinked slowly. "Beneath the surface? You mean where the koi fish are?"

Lan Su laughed softly. "Yes, they do live happily below the surface, swimming freely. But when it rains like this, the surface is stirred and disrupted. We can't see their world clearly. Not until the rain stops and the pond becomes still again."

She gestured for William to join her on the bench beneath the pavilion roof. "Our mind is like that pond. Thoughts fall like raindrops—some joyful, some anxious, some merely noise. They ripple across the surface and pull our awareness away from what lies deeper. But beneath the surface lies something far more vast—an ocean that remembers what the surface forgets. All we need to do is learn to dive in."

She rose and walked to the wooden railing, gazing out across the Garden of the Awakening Orchid. Something had caught her attention.

She whispered, "William, look over there. Oh, this is lovely and such a rare sight." Bending closer, she pointed. "There, swimming across the pond, is a blue swan."

It was a magnificent bird, as stunning as Quetzal. William marveled at the deep, iridescent blue of her feathers. She glided without effort, as if the pond itself parted willingly to let her pass. There was something mysterious in the way she moved—weightless, dreamlike, belonging to another world, as though she had landed in the Awakening Orchid by mistake.

A ripple of excitement spread through the Pavilion of Serenity. William glanced up and saw visitors crowding the open windows, whispering to one another. Some pointed eagerly toward the elegant bird, beckoning to friends in the commons.

"Notice how smoothly she glides across the water," Lan Su said softly. "Piano Zen students watch her and try to feel that same flow in their playing."

As the blue swan drifted across the pond, William noticed that she barely disturbed the surface—as if she weren't touching the water at all.

"Her smooth movements are a bit deceptive," Lan Su said. "Beneath the surface, her webbed feet move steadily, propelling her forward. It's a perfect example of what we call *effortless effort*. In Piano Zen, a musician's conscious mind plays on the surface, but it is what lies below that generates the flow—allowing technique and expression to merge, until the work disappears into the music."

A light rain continued to fall as William, Lan Su, and the others in the pavilion remained motionless, entranced by the swan's serene presence. But the spell was suddenly broken as Chuán, the wooden boat of the Pond of Cosmic Reflection, appeared from around the bend. Ukumari stood at the stern, poling the boat forward with enthusiasm. Inside, Amara, Densho, and Quetzal were laughing and singing, their boisterous voices echoing through the falling rain. Their cheerful commotion broke the spell, and the blue swan, startled, suddenly took to the air. Her ascent was a vision of grace and power—giant wings unfurled, revealing a dazzling blend of blue and white feathers. Gasps of awe rose from the pavilion as the swan lifted skyward, vanishing into the mist.

Meanwhile, in the wooden boat, Amara was the first to sense that their arrival had disrupted a moment of serenity. Her laughter faded as she hunched her shoulders, flashing an embarrassed, toothy grin toward Lan Su.

"Oops," she mouthed.

Master Lan Su offered a gentle smile, waved off Amara's concern, and motioned her over to the Moon Locking Pavilion.

Amara signaled for Ukumari to steer Chuán toward a rocky platform at the water's edge so she could disembark. As soon as she stepped ashore, Ukumari gave a cheerful wave, completely unaware of the commotion they'd caused, and the crew of Chuán pushed off again, immediately resuming their rowdy singing. Amara made her way up from the water's edge to the shelter of the pavilion, still feeling a bit self-conscious about scaring off the blue swan.

Master Lan Su greeted her warmly. "It looks like you all got caught in the rain while out in Chuán."

"Oh, no," Amara replied, brushing wet strands of hair from her face. "Actually, the rain is what inspired us to take the boat out in the first place. We all wanted to float on the pond in the drizzle. Um, I guess we got a little carried away. I didn't realize how loud we were."

Amara extended her hand beyond the pavilion's shelter, letting raindrops gather on her palm. "I don't see much rain in Ubar, and, well, it's such a joyful experience." She clasped her hands together enthusiastically, sending a splash across Lan Su's face.

Amara gasped. "Oh—sorry!"

"Quite all right," Lan Su said, brushing the droplets from her cheek with her blue sash. "Amara, considering the time, I have a class to lead on the *Touching the Pond* technique. Would you be willing to give William a Piano Zen lesson—perhaps share how the Water Element can guide his practice?"

Amara froze, uncertainty flickering across her face. She swallowed hard. "Um… well… I've only been playing piano for a few years. And William—he's already so gifted with the Elements training. Are you sure there aren't other, more experienced teachers here at the Awakening Orchid you could ask?"

"Oh, Amara, you don't need to be a piano virtuoso to be a good guide at the keyboard. Just listen, encourage, and share your own journey. That is more than enough."

Amara nodded, though she still looked terrified.

"Follow me to the Hall of Celestial Harmony," said Lan Su. "While I teach my class, you two can use my studio for your lesson."

The three of them stepped out from beneath the Moon Locking Pavilion, crossing the zigzag bridge into the misty rain.

# Chapter Thirty-Four

## *Holding a Ball of Energy*

The Hall of Celestial Harmony mirrored the other Ming Dynasty-style pavilions at the Awakening Orchid, but it rose on a grander scale, its red-earth walls crowned with a gleaming, gold roof. At the base of its broad, marble steps, two carved Guardian Lions perched on pedestals: one resting its left paw on a small lion cub, the other with its right paw atop a carved ball. Thick, leaf-patterned gold necklaces adorned their chests, lending a sense of timeless majesty to the entrance.

A strange sense of familiarity tugged at William, as if he had seen this place before, long ago, in a dream or perhaps in a painting. Then it came to him: the painting in Master Shinichi's living room—the same red temple with the gold roof.

He stood still for a moment, awash in the dream memory: Shinichi's sunken hearth, the wabi-sabi teacups, Nasim's breeze through the open window. Off to the side of the steps, a persimmon tree caught his eye. There had been one in the painting too. He reached out and touched one of the hanging fruits, its skin a mottled blend of green and orange.

Lan Su noticed. "You are welcome to take one, William, but it is not quite ripe yet. Let it soften for a few more days first."

"Really? Oh, thank you. I've been curious to try one." He picked one of the fruits from the tree and placed it in his backpack beside his *Piano Zen* book.

As they reached the marble steps leading to the main doors of the temple, a sound—barely perceptible at first—filled the air: a celestial choir, voices layered in endless harmony. The golden roof radiated a subtle luminescence, mingling with the curtain of rain. He took a slow breath, feeling the resonance settle into his chest, and glanced at Amara, who met his gaze with a smile and a knowing nod.

Once inside, Lan Su departed, and Amara led William upstairs to the Master's Piano Zen studio. Two grand pianos stood side by side, their polished surfaces catching a gentle sheen in the dim light. The air carried a faint trace of lotus blossom incense, blending with the rain-scented breeze drifting in from the garden. The walls displayed artwork depicting the Four Elements, and the far side of the room was lined with large, sliding doors. Amara moved to pivot them open, revealing the misty view beyond and allowing the soft rumble of Shooting Star Falls to flow into the space.

A wooden deck extended from the studio, meeting the edge of a rain-laced infinity pool—each droplet sending ripples across the surface.

"If it weren't so overcast, you'd see the Pahada Mountains from here," Amara said, gesturing toward the horizon. "On clear days, which are pretty rare around here, the mountains reflect in the pool so clearly, it's hard to tell where the land ends and the water begins."

She motioned for William to take a seat at one of the pianos. Then, hesitating, she let out a nervous giggle, clearly uncertain about how to begin.

Sensing her hesitation, William decided to break the ice. "So… do Piano Zen students always practice in slow motion? Like, you know… a sloth?"

Amara blinked, caught off guard, then burst out laughing. "Oh—sorry," she said between giggles, covering her mouth. "It's just… now I can't stop picturing Ning Jing trying to play the piano." She cleared her throat, shaking her head. "Anyway, to answer your question—no, not always. Piano Zen students can play fast and with power when needed. But the foundation, the part that makes that possible, comes from practicing slowly with the Four Elements in mind."

She gathered herself, settling into her role as a teacher. "Slow-motion practice in Piano Zen is an artform of its own. It helps you develop precision, power, and expression through relaxation. Then, when the tempo increases, everything flows effortlessly."

William nodded as Amara continued, her confidence growing. "Even at slow speeds, combining the Four Elements can be challenging. But trying to build those skills at fast speeds? That's nearly impossible. The truth is, most piano students rush through their practice, building tension instead of awareness. That's why so many struggle—mentally, emotionally, and physically."

"That's what Master Lan Su said," William noted.

Amara laughed. "Whew! Good to know I was paying attention in my Piano Zen lessons!" She leaned on the piano. "The funny thing is, once you experience slow-motion practice, you actually start to love it. It's calming—almost meditative. Your awareness expands, and the music starts to feel alive—like it's breathing through you."

She paused mid-thought, then grinned. "Wait, before we dive in, I've got something fun to show you." She clasped her hands together and gave them a tight squeeze, eyes dancing. "Tell me, have you ever tried an exercise to feel your own inner energy?"

William tilted his head. "Hmm... inner energy. Let me think. Sometimes I feel this tingling sensation, usually when something unexpected or strange happens. I can't really explain it, but it feels kind of... supernatural."

"Exactly," Amara said, her eyes lighting up. "That's the Fire Element. What some call *prana*, *chi*, or the *life force*. It's the spark that animates everything. When you slow down, breathe deeply, and move with awareness, that energy awakens and begins to flow."

"Is it like the feeling I got when I opened the Piano Zen book for the first time?" William asked. "I remember a tingling sensation all over."

Amara rubbed her chin. "I've never thought of that before... but sure. Books carry the creative imprint of their author's energy. When you truly connect with one, it can stir something deep inside. I've been told the piano is the same. When you unlock the Pythagorean Code, you awaken its true power—pure expression."

"Have you unlocked the Code?" William asked.

"Me? No... not yet. But the inner-energy exercise I'm about to show you helps open the way."

Just then, the Dream Dorje vibrated softly against his chest. William reached into his backpack and placed the Piano Zen book gently on the piano lid.

"Is this the book you mentioned?" Amara asked.

"Uh-huh."

To their astonishment, the book flipped open on its own. The pages fluttered faster and faster until they stopped abruptly on a single spread. Slowly, words began to appear—forming on the paper as if written in invisible ink.

**Holding the Energy Ball**

William blinked. "What does that mean?"

Amara leaned over to look. "Oh wow, William. Cool book! Where did you get this? And how does it *know* about the energy ball?"

"I'm not sure," he said, scratching the side of his head. "I just always carry it in my backpack. Usually, I have to ask it something first—then it flips to a page with some kind of answer. So… what does *Holding the Energy Ball* mean?"

"Well, your book is remarkably perceptive. That's actually a technique I learned from Master Wu Wei, and it's one of my favorites. Want me to guide you through it? It's an exercise to help you feel the Fire Element—your inner energy."

"Yes, please. Sounds exciting."

"All right. Sit at the edge of the piano bench, feet flat on the floor, and let your arms dangle by your sides."

She waited for him to adjust. "Now, imagine you're flicking water droplets off your fingers. Not just once, vigorously, like this." She gave her hands a rapid shake, wrists loose, fingers snapping by her sides. "Do this about thirty times."

William mimicked her, flicking his fingers briskly at his sides as if shaking off invisible droplets. Outside, the soft *pat-pat* of rain drifted through the open doors.

"Good. Keep going, you're waking up the energy in your hands."

When he finished, he let his arms rest. "My fingers feel tingly," he said, flexing them.

"That's a very good sign," Amara said. "Your fire energy is beginning to stir."

She raised her hands and held them in front of her chest, a hand's-width apart. "Now imagine you're holding a small, weightless ball. Like this. Fingertips almost touching."

William copied her shape.

"Close your eyes," she whispered. "Draw a deep breath into your belly."

He inhaled slowly, shoulders melting.

"As you exhale through your nose, place the tip of your tongue on the roof of your mouth, just behind your teeth. Let the breath out slowly and with control, creating a gentle, ocean wave sound in the back of your throat."

William followed her lead, exhaling as instructed, feeling the breath reverberate at the back of his throat.

"Good," she whispered. "Now bring your attention to the space between your palms—fingers extended, almost touching. You might feel a subtle pressure—like two magnets with the same pole, gently repelling each other."

William's brow softened.

"Do you feel something?" she asked.

He nodded. "Yes… like there's a cushion of energy between my palms, gently keeping my fingers apart."

"That's the Fire Element," Amara said. "Your life force. It's an inner energy always flowing through you—but when you slow down, you can begin to feel it. And one day, perhaps even guide it."

She lowered her voice. "Now… keep your eyes closed. Focus your attention on your energy ball. With each exhale, imagine you're inflating it slightly. Picture a beach ball, and let your hands gently drift apart, just a little more with each breath. Let it grow, while staying aware of the tingling sensation… the gentle pressure between your palms."

William exhaled slowly, sensing the energy ball expanding with each breath—growing lighter, larger, almost buoyant between his palms.

"Feels like I'm holding a large ball now," he said.

Amara smiled. "Excellent, William. You're beginning to feel your Fire Element. This is just a starter exercise. When you meet Master Wu Wei, you'll learn much more—he knows far more secrets about the Fire Element than I do. I'm sure you'll meet him some—uh… William…?"

She paused midsentence. William still had his eyes closed, breathing slowly, palms cupped in concentration.

"Um… William, how are you doing that?"

"Doing what?"

"Open your eyes," Amara said.

As he did, a light-blue orb shimmered between his palms, softly pulsing like a glowing moon, humming with a quiet, radiant tone.

His eyes widened. "Wh—what is that?"

"How did you do that, Will?"

"I—I don't know. I just did what you said. I imagined an energy ball."

As soon as he spoke, the orb flickered, then vanished into thin air.

Amara clutched her cheeks. "That was incredible! You were manifesting the Light and Sound. I've never seen a student do something like that—only the Element Masters."

William shook his head in disbelief. Without Amara there, he might've thought he'd only imagined it.

"Was that… the Fifth Element?" he asked quietly.

"I don't know," she said, still staring at his hands. "I'm not that far along in my training. But I'm so excited for you, Will."

A hush settled between them as they both gazed at the space where the energy ball had hovered moments before.

"We should ah…. probably begin your piano lesson, right?"

William nodded, still a bit dazed.

"Oh! Almost forgot—the Tibetan bowl." She glanced around the studio. "Give me a minute. I need to track down Master Lan Su's bowl. A student might've borrowed it."

Amara exited the studio and didn't return immediately.

William sat patiently on the piano bench and brought his hands together again, trying to summon the humming blue orb—but nothing appeared. The silence that followed made him question whether it had truly happened or if he had somehow only dreamed it.

After more time had passed, he opened the lid of the piano he sat at. Pressing the sustain pedal, he began to lightly improvise on the black keys, letting the tones linger in the air as his eyes wandered around the studio.

Eventually, his gaze settled on the persimmon resting in his open backpack.

He stopped playing. He had never tried persimmon before. *How bad could it be?* he wondered. He picked it up, turned it in his hands, then— giving in to impulse—took a bite.

Bitterness surged in his mouth: dry, chalky—a jolt like static on the tongue. His face twisted at the taste.

At that moment, Amara returned with the Tibetan bowl. She saw the look on his face and stopped. "Will, what's wrong?"

Embarrassed, he forced himself to swallow rather than spit it out. Almost instantly, his vision blurred. The floor beneath him seemed to dissolve, and a wave of dizziness washed over him.

Amara rushed toward him, but her image was already fading.

Outside, the sound of rain began to twist and warp, bending into a strange, scratchy interference—like someone spinning an old radio dial just past the edge of clarity.

The frequencies curled through his ears, sharp and dissonant. William winced, his body tensing, folding inward.

Then—suddenly—it stopped.

In its place was an unnatural silence.

William opened his eyes. The studio was gone. He now sat on a crumbling, moss-covered wooden bench in the middle of a dense, overgrown jungle, the air eerily still.

# Chapter Thirty-Five

## *A Shadow Between Worlds*

He got to his feet. The air was heavy and wet. Not a sound—no birds sang. No music stirred the air. The light was dim, the atmosphere thick and stale. The ground beneath him felt uneven. He didn't know how he had gotten here. Had he somehow wandered beyond the boundaries of the Garden of the Awakening Orchid? Where was Shooting Star Falls or the Pahada Mountains? A heavy humidity clung to his skin as he turned slowly beneath the tangled canopy of green.

His memory wavered: Amara's voice, a room with two pianos. A glowing ball of light between his hands. But why couldn't he remember clearly? However it had happened, he was deep in some unfamiliar jungle, and he had no idea how to get back.

Just then, a figure emerged from the hazy edges of his vision—a tall man with a disarming smile on his face. His cloak, a deep crimson, appeared tattered at first, etched with intricate but faded patterns. The hood concealed most of his face, but what little William could see was unsettling: a gaunt, weathered countenance, marked by old scars and the faint glint from multiple piercings.

William tensed—but as the man stepped forward out of the thick jungle shadows, everything seemed to shift. The cloak now looked almost regal, its red and gold fabric catching the dim light. He lowered his hood to reveal an elegant, distinguished-looking man in late middle age, with sharp gray eyes and a shock of silver-white streaking through his hair.

In his spell-like state, William told himself his eyes had simply played tricks on him—distorting the man's appearance in the jungle shadows.

"Ah… young William," the man said, his voice smooth as silk, almost hypnotic. "I've heard such intriguing things. They say you have a rare talent—a gift with the Four Elements."

William blinked hard, trying to clear his thoughts. The taste of unripe persimmon still clung to his tongue—dry and astringent. He felt like he should recognize the man, but nothing surfaced.

"I'm sorry… do I know you?"

The man stepped closer. A dim phosphorescent glow illuminated the air around him, wavering like a candle near the end of its wick.

"I'm someone who can help you unlock the secrets you're aching to understand," the man said, his tone velvet smooth. "The Four Elements? A primer. Child's play, really. True mastery lies in powers that bend reality itself. Knowledge vast enough to reshape worlds and offer salvation to the desperate, wherever they may dwell."

There was something in his voice that made William's eyes feel heavy, his thoughts sluggish.

"Those of us who carry such gifts," the man went on, "well, we have a duty, don't you think? To use them. To lift others, as we once longed to be lifted."

"I'm… I'm not sure I understand," William said. "W-what are you talking about?"

The stranger's eyes gleamed. "That you have a real gift, my friend. You just need a way to channel it."

He grinned, as if the answer were obvious. "The Four Elements? Merely the foundation. With the right guidance, your abilities could reshape everything—from the world around you to the world within."

He paused. "Forgive me. I've had the advantage. I know quite a bit about you, though you don't know me."

He offered a graceful bow. "My name is Florestan."

William recognized the name. He was certain he'd heard it before, maybe from Densho? Or Nasim? The memory floated, just out of reach. But his thoughts were quickly detoured when he sensed movement—several sets of eyes watching from the edge of the clearing. One by one, the shapes stepped forward, emerging from the darkness.

A menacing crocodile slithered into view, its thick tail undulating through the underbrush as it waddled around Florestan's legs. Moments later, a massive grizzly bear lumbered into the clearing, followed by a sleek tiger whose eyes met William's, just for a moment, before shifting away.

Startled and tense, William froze. But the animals made no move toward him. Instead, they circled around Florestan, and in that moment, William understood: they weren't wild predators. They were with him.

"William," Florestan said smoothly, "allow me to introduce my friends. This is Typhon the Tiger."

Typhon's golden eyes glinted in the dim light. His voice carried a low growl beneath it. "Hello, William. I've been dying to meet the boy everyone whispers about."

"And over here is Gorgon the Grizzly Bear," Florestan continued. "He might seem a bit fearsome at first, but he's really quite friendly."

Gorgon rumbled with laughter—deep, gravelly, a little too loud. "Oh yes. Just a big ol' teddy bear... once you get past all the claws, right?" His grin was wide, teeth flashing like ivory blades.

"Now, down here," Florestan said with pride. "This is Cerberus the Crocodile. He was one of the first animals I healed. He was quite sick and near death. I helped him evolve. Unfortunately... eh... he never learned to speak."

Cerberus opened his jaws, releasing a long, low hiss that curled through the clearing like steam from a vent. Florestan gave a soft chuckle, as if sharing an inside joke. "Ah... I'll tell him, Cerberus." He turned to William. "He says he's very pleased to meet the one who stirs the Elements."

Typhon sauntered over and rubbed himself affectionately against Florestan's shoulder, his massive striped frame brushing close to William as he passed. A guttural purr vibrated from his chest—low and bone deep, like a distant engine idling.

Gorgon sat heavily nearby, watching with unblinking eyes. Florestan reached up to pat the grizzly's massive head. The bear leaned into the touch, eyes half-lidded in what looked like contentment.

Florestan then clasped his hands behind his back and stepped forward, leaving the animals behind. His tone softened, almost confessional.

"When I was a child—alone, unwanted, with no father or mother— I spent hours in the dark, imagining what it would be like to have real superpowers. Powers that could shape the world—not pretend, not make-believe. Even then, I knew such things weren't real. They lived only in the realm of my dreams." He paused, his eyes distant. "But I couldn't accept that. So, I sat alone for hours on end, praying—no, pleading—for the chance to wield something greater. And I made a vow: If such power were ever granted to me, I would use it not for myself but for something higher. For humanity and for the unseen universes beyond."

Florestan looked up into the dark canopy of lush, tangled branches overhead. He paused and took a deep breath.

"Out of the darkness of those many hours of prayers, I was given a gift. It happened the first time I wrapped my hand around the black obsidian— the Wizard's Stone. Its flame was the answer to my prayers."

William furrowed his brow at the term. "What is a… uh… Wizard's Stone?"

"Well, they're exceedingly rare," Florestan said. "Drawn from the deepest mines of Keshmara—where I am from. To most, the stone is useless. Even among Keshmarians, only one with mastery of the Four Elements—and certain rare gifts—can unlock its true magic. And I, once just a child, alone in the darkness, became the alchemist who unlocked the secrets of its hidden fire."

As he spoke, William noticed the predators, so vivid and menacing a moment ago, slipping back into the darkness of the jungle, as if absorbed by the forest itself.

Florestan reached into a pocket of his red cloak and withdrew an irregular-shaped, glossy, black stone. He placed it gently in William's hand.

It was icy to the touch and surprisingly heavy for its size. From within its dark surface, a faint crimson glow flickered—like a flame trapped inside.

Florestan watched with quiet satisfaction as William's eyes widened, drawn to the shifting flame inside the stone.

As he rubbed it between his fingers, a strange energy stirred—subtle at first, then rushing upward through his arm. With it came an unexpected confidence that quickly flooded his thoughts. It was exhilarating, as if he were suddenly attuned to the hidden forces behind the Four Elements.

Long haunted by feelings of inadequacy, he felt those doubts dissolve, replaced by a startling certainty: He could shape anything he imagined. His mind swelled with possibility, then quickly began to tip off balance. The raw, intoxicating power of the Wizard's Stone began to scatter his thoughts, like trying to hold a hundred songs in his head at once.

Watching him closely, Florestan said in a low, even tone, "I suggest you slip the stone into your pocket, my friend. Holding it for too long isn't advisable, at least not until you've acclimated to its energy."

William hesitated, then reluctantly dropped the stone into his pocket. Almost at once, his thoughts began to clear. The dizzying rush faded, allowing him to refocus and regain his senses.

"That strong energy you felt," Florestan said, "comes from the flame of the Wizard's Stone. It is a rare type of obsidian—formed from ancient volcanic glass before recorded time. To be a true Wizard's Stone, it must be pure, with no trace of crystal."

He watched William carefully. "To unlock the full power of the black obsidian," he added, "one must first master the Four Elements. You are quite gifted, my friend, but I can see the Fire Element still lies beyond your grasp. I could help you—share my discoveries with you." He paused. "The flame within the Wizard's Stone holds a power unlike anything you can imagine— unpredictable, consuming. Yet with the right alchemy, it can be bound to the Four Elements. And in doing so, it will awaken your imagination—sharpen your intuition."

A surge of curiosity rose in William, countless questions pressing at his lips.

Before he could speak, Florestan's eyes dropped to William's chest, where the outline of something beneath his shirt glimmered faintly. "Ah… what's that around your neck? Some sort of amulet?"

William reached for the pendant, pulling it free. To his surprise, it neither sparkled nor rang with its usual tone.

"It's a magical dorje—at least, I think so," he said, puzzled. "Sometimes it glows and makes a sound."

Florestan tilted his head. "A dorje, you say?" He stepped a little closer, inspecting it with measured fascination. "Yes, I've seen one before, some time ago."

He reached out a finger, stopping just shy of touching it. "Beautiful craftsmanship, yes. But magic?" He offered a dismissive smile. "Perhaps. Certainly nothing like the Wizard's Stone. To me, it looks more like a weight around your neck—something that binds rather than frees you."

Florestan straightened, his expression unreadable. "You have a rare connection to the Wizard's Stone, much like my own. Of course, it takes time to master, and you would need guidance. But if you ever unlocked its full power…"

He let the words fade into the humid air. "Well—let's just say… anything you can imagine might come true."

Before William could respond, a woman's voice echoed through the jungle, piercing the ghostly silence. The sound swelled, borne on a wind that began softly but gathered force—thrashing through the tangled trees, scattering leaves and vines.

The dorje at William's chest ignited, casting ribbons of colored light through the gloom and briefly illuminating the predators still lurking there in the shadows.

Cerberus lifted his snout and hissed toward the rushing wind, then slithered silently back into the dark. Typhon and Gorgon lingered, snarls etched across their faces. But after a tense moment, they too slipped into the dense foliage, growling low as they vanished.

Florestan gave a faint shrug. "My friends get spooked by certain sounds in the jungle. I should go see to them."

He turned to leave, then looked back over his shoulder. "Keep the Wizard's Stone. It's a gift." His voice dropped low. "*Je vous dis adieu pour l'instant*, Little Prince."

The world of the jungle began to dissolve before William's eyes. A soft wind brushed his face as a bright light broke through. Somewhere close by, he heard a woman's voice—familiar, lyrical.

He whispered the name, barely audible. "Nasim?"


"William? William… hello… are you there?"

Miss Rosa's voice held a playful lilt. "You can open your eyes now."

He lifted his gaze slowly, as if waking from a deep sleep.

"You were incredibly quiet there," she said with a laugh. "I think you might have dozed off."

The piano studio came back into focus. The Tibetan bowl's vibrations had faded, yet something lingered—an odd sensation, like waking in the middle of a dream.

As he collected his senses, William felt a strange impulse to reach into his pocket, as though he'd placed something there. But when he checked, he found only the dark basalt stone from his last visit to Beacon Rock.

He ran his fingers over its rough and smooth edges, rolling it between his thumb and forefinger, trying to ground himself—to remember.

*Did I put something else in my pocket?* he wondered. The feeling nagged at him—like hearing a melody but never quite recalling its name. It remained in that void of lost time.

Miss Rosa's voice cut gently through his thoughts. "Now that you've been taking lessons for six months, it's time to begin working on 'Life is

But a Dream',” she said. “It's a perfect piece to use the 'touching the pond' technique—and start feeling that flowing stream in your playing.”

William hesitated as a wave of déjà vu washed over him. The title of the song felt eerily familiar, as if he'd already studied the piece once before.

While Rosa stepped out to brew some tea, he pulled his dream journal from his backpack and quickly scribbled down the fleeting images still drifting at the edge of his memory: a rowboat… the same little monkey as before… a bear with a drum… a sloth in a treehouse.

He closed his eyes, reaching further. There was more—he was sure of it: a Chinese garden… a swan in flight… a ball of energy… and a magical stone in his pocket.

He paused and pulled out his basalt stone again, examining it. Whatever he'd put in his pocket in the dream wasn't basalt.

*It had a flame inside.*

# Fire

# Chapter Thirty-Six

## *Theme and Variations*

When he was younger, William's dreams had always been scary—disjointed and nightmarish. Sometimes, he was chased by wild beasts or a gang of violent men; other times, someone would strike at him with a sword or a spear. One recurring dream took place at sea—aboard wooden ships with sails full of wind. The sky might be calm at first, but the dream always turned: a sudden storm, a fall overboard, the ship vanishing into darkness. He would drift alone in an endless ocean, swallowed by silence, as if the world had forgotten him.

Fortunately, he never saw himself die in his dreams. The moment just before death always jolted him awake, followed by a flood of relief.

When Miss Rosa first suggested he keep a dream journal, he had resisted the idea. Why write down those kinds of experiences? Why relive them?

But after she rang her Tibetan bowl during his first Piano Zen lesson, something changed. The nightmares began to fade. And now, whether the dreams came during the sound of the bowl or in the quiet hours of the night, he often wished for more clarity.

He began to wonder if he drifted off each time Rosa rang the bowl. As the final vibrations faded, a rush of dream-paintings would surface—memories, fragments, it seemed, from another world. They would vanish quickly unless he paused to capture them, jotting down notes in the dream journal he always kept in his backpack.

He would transfer the fragments of notes into his journal, then review them at home and try to add more details, things he remembered—images, impressions, and moments etched in color and sensation, like paintings in his mind. But the story behind each one remained elusive.

Often, the next morning, he would wake with new dream scenes waiting—never quite the same as before yet undeniably connected. They reminded him of "Theme and Variations," like in his music books: a simple melody introduced once, then revisited again and again—each time reshaped, expanded, transformed into something both familiar and new.

There were always pianos in his dreams—antique models, glossy black grands, white ones etched with gold, glowing ones, even impossibly strange, magical ones. They reminded him of *Sparky's Magic Piano*, the old story he used to listen to with his dad. But unlike Sparky's tale, the magic in William's dreams didn't live in the piano alone—it flowed from the player too.

Other images returned again and again: a talking monkey, a bear and a drum, a breeze that seemed to whisper secrets. He sketched out rough drawings when he could—scenes, characters, landscapes. Snapshots from a dreamworld just out of reach. Placeholders for what felt like time-bending adventures.

This flurry of dream journaling went on for a full year. Then, gradually, the dreams grew quiet. He stopped remembering them—and with nothing left to record, he eventually set the journal aside and turned his focus more fully to his piano studies.

It happened so subtly—the fading of dream memory—that he didn't notice at first. There was no single event that explained it. Still, looking back, he sensed a kind of turning point after the time of the Wildwood Trail hike.

He remembered how Miss Rosa had begun mentioning the strange pilgrimage more often as the date approached. She never said what they might find or why it mattered. But her tone was light, almost playful—like she was keeping something hidden. William didn't press. Still, the mystery of the Wildwood Trail stayed with him, quietly tugging at his thoughts. It wasn't just any trail but a hidden path that wound through the private forest on the Prescott Estate. According to Rosa, its secrets were reserved for students who had completed a full year of study.

Then, one afternoon, she said simply, "Be ready next week. It's time for our hike on the Wildwood Trail."

But for what, he wondered—a lesson? A test? He wasn't sure.

With the hike still a week away, curiosity got the better of William. Rosa wouldn't give him answers but maybe Montgomery would. So, he decided to wander down to the Marrakech West Bazaar. If anyone could shed light on the Wildwood Trail, it was the professor.

Over the past year, they'd grown close. Between the professor's performances at Marrakech, they'd talk about music, the town, and life. Montgomery always had a story to share, each one more fascinating than the last. William often helped him set up and tear down for his shows. He'd even recently joined the School of Blues—a community program Montgomery ran to teach local kids how to play blues and jam together.

The day he decided to head to the bazaar, Nightingale was simmering from a late-summer heatwave. The air was dry and hot, sidewalks radiating intense temperatures. For a moment, he considered waiting for a cooler day, but if Montgomery was out there performing in the sun, he figured he could show up too.

As he neared the Gateway of the Moors, a familiar voice cut through the hum of the market. The sound pulled William forward. He quickened his pace, weaving through the crowd until he found an open spot on the concrete steps off to the side. From there, he could see the Professor at his usual post—guitar in hand, eyes half-closed as he lost himself in the music. The crowd swayed with him, already caught up in the rhythm.

The Professor had just launched into a familiar tune—the unmistakable opening chords of *Love is All There Is*. His fingers moved fluidly over the guitar strings, sliding into a gentle, bluesy intro. A cheer rippled through the crowd— loyal listeners who had braved the heat, drawn by the Professor's magnetic presence. It was one of his best-known songs, a folk-rock ballad laced with his signature blues, and the moment those opening chords rang out, people perked up with recognition. A few voices began to hum along before the first verse.

### Love is All There Is
*I sometimes think of where we live; is it*
*Safe for children fit*
*Is heaven here and in your soul*
*And is there room for all in it*

Montgomery's voice, deep and weathered, rolled over the crowd, rich with a kind of lived-in wisdom.

*I lost myself in letting go*
*And got back more than I ever wish*
*For your eyes I see myself*
*And know again I'm innocent*

*Love is all there is*
*Love is all there is*
*Love is all there'll ever be*
A few hands lifted, couples swayed, shoulders brushing. The chorus took on a life of its own, voices overlapping, filling the space. William felt the music settle into his chest.

*I carried guns and I prayed for war*
*Cried for help then I shut the door*
*Died alone of bitterness*
*Wanting only you to kiss*
The guitar hummed beneath his voice, a steady pulse carrying the words. William watched as the crowd fell into rhythm, some nodding along, others murmuring the lyrics under their breath.

*Wrap my arms around this world*
*Believe in things I knew absurd*
*Like God and light and selfish dreams*
*I danced with all my enemies*
Montgomery's foot tapped the beat, his guitar laced with a hint of grit. He played effortlessly, the rhythm pulling the crowd deeper into his repeating chorus.

*Love is all there is*
*Love is all there is*
*Love is all there'll ever be*
The Professor's voice lifted, strong and unshaken.
*Been a man, woman, child*
*I've lied, I cried, you know I tried*
*To find inside what must be best*
*And not become what I detest*
*Claim my victories as defeats*
*Climb up a mountain and then retreat*
*Struggle in, the eye of the storm*
*I need someone to keep me warm*
The crowd swelled with him, some singing full-voiced, others just letting the words roll over them.

*The air was pure and the grass was green*
*The wind blew, laughin' through fields*
*And the rain dripped down upon our skin*
*The sun warmed both our bodies*

*And I was you and you were me*
*And there was no difference in between*

*I fought with demons and I sang with saints*
*Soared like an eagle with no restraints*
*A shark in desperate waters clingin' to his teeth*
*A coward in a cave with only dark beneath*

Montgomery's voice got quiet, more hushed and intimate. Drawing the crowd into the delicate lyrics.

*Now I open up to all there is*
*To find an answer in the mist*
*A world beyond these fragile forms*
*Where all there is, is happiness*

People closed their eyes as they sang, some with tears, some with smiles stretched across their faces. The guitar softened, the final chorus swelling, voices rising in waves. Montgomery leaned back slightly, letting the crowd take over the chorus.

*Love is all there is*
*Love is all there is*
*Love is all there'll ever be*

The Professor repeated the refrain, his voice blending with the swelling chorus of the crowd. Arms wrapped around shoulders, hands joined, and voices lifted together in a shared moment of song—blissfully oblivious to the day's searing heat.

When the final note faded, the crowd erupted in applause. Montgomery gave a few playful bows. He then looked over in William's direction, a big grin spreading across his face as he tipped his hat to him.

The applause gradually died down, the crowd still basking in the afterglow of the song. Montgomery adjusted the strap of his guitar and leaned into the microphone.

"Alright, folks, let's keep this train rolling. This next one is called 'End of All My Dreams'."

He strummed the first chord—

*CRACK!* A sharp pop rang out from the nearby generator. The amplifiers sputtered, then cut out completely.

Confusion rippled through the crowd as the speakers fell silent. Montgomery strummed again, but only the quiet, unplugged twang of his guitar filled the air.

Then, the entire power grid in the square shut down. Stalls flickered dark, fans stopped spinning, and the hum of electricity vanished. A few murmurs rose from the audience, uncertain laughter mixed in. Montgomery pushed up his fedora and gave a theatrical shrug, hands raised in a what-can-you-do gesture. The crowd responded with a ripple of good-natured chuckles, then began to disperse—some shaking their heads, others lingering in hopes the power might return.

William watched as Montgomery exchanged a few words with the sound crew, but it was clear—the show was over. Disappointing, maybe. But it gave him a chance to talk to the Professor, perhaps even get some answers about the Wildwood Trail.

William lingered by the entrance of the Gateway, waiting. When the Professor finally turned and spotted him, he lifted a hand in greeting, his face lighting up.

"Well, look who braved the heat! Good to see you, Will. How are you?"

"I'm doing great! I'm glad to see you, too," William said.

"I guess *Love Is All There Is* was a little too powerful today," Montgomery said with a laugh. "It's like it blew out the whole system." He dabbed his forehead with a handkerchief. "No telling when they'll get it running again."

He shook his head. "Whew, it's a scorcher today. But... it looks like I've got the afternoon off now. You free for a bit? I'd love to catch up—hear how your Piano Zen lessons are coming along."

"Sure! That would be great."

"Okay, help me pack up the gear, and we'll head to Sweet Muejanat. Maybe Hadiya is working today."

They packed the Professor's gear—guitars and harmonica in their cases, cables coiled, mics stashed—then set off through the winding paths of Marrakech West.

A year ago, William had felt like an outsider navigating the maze of food carts and artisan stalls. But now he knew the route by heart. As they walked, he waved and nodded back as vendors and craftspeople greeted him by name. They passed the bustling main thoroughfares and slipped into the quieter back alleys of the bazaar. Here, conversations unfolded in their native tongues, the scent of slow-roasting spices and fresh bread thick in the air. William had come to love these hidden corners, where the best food and art were found, but only if one was willing to get lost along the way.

As they rounded a bend, the sweet aroma of rosewater, toasted almonds, and warm honey drifted toward them. The familiar cart came into view—

Sweet Muejanat, with its turquoise and cobalt arabesques and faded saffron-striped awning, where copper lanterns hung from slender chains, rocking faintly in the warm air.

"*As-salaam alaykum*, Professor!"

"*Wa alaykum as-salaam*, Hadiya!"

"*Kaifa haluk, Ustadh?*"

"Very well, thank you," the Professor replied.

Hadiya's smile widened as she turned to William. "Hey, Will." She checked her watch, eyebrows lifting. "You two are early. What time's your set today, Professor?"

"Already played my first set. William was there. But then the generator gave out—guess the music was too much for it," Montgomery said, chuckling.

"Spoken like a true rockstar," Hadiya grinned. "Alright, what can I get for the two of you?"

"It's a hot one today, Hadiya," said Professor Montgomery. "How about two double servings of *bastani sonnati?*"

"Ooh, nice choice! Good thing *our* generator's working, or we'd be serving melted *bastani* today. Want it between wafers?"

Montgomery considered, then shook his head. "Tempting but better make it cups. We've got a walk ahead of us. Heading down to the Makah River."

Hadiya opened the freezer and began scooping.

William glanced over. "What did you order?"

"Oh, you'll love it, Will. It's Persian ice cream—vanilla, saffron, pistachios, salep, even frozen chunks of cream. A sweet, icy delight on a day like this," Montgomery said, handing over the cash and dropping a generous tip in Hadiya's jar.

"Thank you, Hadiya. *Ma'a as-salama.*"

"You're very welcome, Professor. *Ma'a as-salama.*"

# Chapter Thirty-Seven

## *The Light That Remains*

William and Professor Montgomery made their way down to the Makah River. Fortunately, a bench was free beneath a broad tree, offering welcome shade from the burning sun.

As they sat, the professor grinned. "Wait till you try that Persian ice cream—one of my all-time favorites."

William took a bite and lit up. "Mmm… it's really good! So sweet. I've never tasted anything quite like it."

"Yes, I love it," Montgomery said. "Strangely enough, it reminds me of some of the desserts I had at the Samaritan Temple. As I recall, your mother catered a few of the community gatherings there. I could tell she had a real gift in the kitchen. It wasn't until later that I learned the chef was Phillip Emerson's wife."

William nodded. "Yeah—my mom said she met my dad at the Culinary Institute of Nightingale. They invited Firehouse Companies to free gourmet meals cooked by the students."

"Ah, that explains it," Montgomery said. "I wondered how they might have met."

William smiled faintly. It was still hard to square the idea of her as a chef with the mom he knew. He was used to seeing her come home exhausted, often too tired to cook anything beyond simple meals. The image of her in a professional kitchen, creating culinary masterpieces, was a side of her he'd only heard about but never really known.

They savored their *bastani* while gazing at the gently flowing Makah River. Nearby, the Lady of Light copper sculpture glistened beneath the relentless sun. The heat pressed down—dry and still. With so little breeze, it felt like the world had paused.

William remembered a similar summer day years ago—his mother standing at the kitchen window, drying dishes and staring out at the same kind of hot, windless afternoon. She had murmured, almost to herself, *"It was a day like this... when the Fisher King fire started."*

The comment had caught him off guard. She never spoke of that day—not ever. Even then, William sensed it wasn't a memory to be touched.

So, he went looking for answers on his own, searching the *Nightingale Observer* archives at the public library. According to the reports, two teenagers playing with fireworks had started the blaze. Within hours, the fire had raged out of control, drawing in every available firefighting crew across the Pacific Northwest.

His father, Phillip Emerson, had still been an active firefighter at the time. Years earlier, he'd served as a smoke-jumper, but he had stepped away from that duty after William was born.

The articles described how the Fisher King fire spread with terrifying speed, consuming beloved hiking trails, old-growth forests, and entire neighborhoods. Wildlife scattered in all directions; their habitats reduced to smoldering ash.

One report told how Phillip was called to lead a veteran smoke-jumper crew in a final, desperate attempt to save a family trapped in their home, already surrounded by flames. MAFFS-equipped Lockheed C-130s were dispatched to drop fire retardant, carving a potential escape route from Angel Crest Ridge down to the Rogue River. Phillip, the articles noted, was the only firefighter on scene with extensive experience in both wildland and residential operations.

Another article described how Phillip and his crew had parachuted in and reached the house—but it had already been ablaze. Smoke poured from the shattered windows as the team raced to evacuate the mother and her children. The scene, as William had imagined it many times while reading and rereading the reports, must have been chaos—a tangle of panicked cries, choking smoke, and roaring flames.

Then came the moment everything shifted. One firefighter later recounted the event:

*"We saw the propane tank on the side of the house engulfed in flames. A knowing look passed between us. For a second, time froze. The fire, the mother's pleading—everything became a distant echo. Phillip had already hooked up his oxygen. He had his ax in hand and signaled for us to move out of the area.*

*As we pulled the mother away, he shouted, 'I'll find the child!' Then he was gone, disappearing into the burning house.*

*Minutes later, the propane tank exploded. The house vanished in the blast. We had no choice but to run. The fire was closing in."*

When the fire finally relented, rescue crews found Phillip's body in the basement. He had shielded the little girl in his arms, curled around her even in death.

The image stayed with William. Details of the events blurred together—part newspaper, part imagination—but always an emptiness.

He traced the ridges of his father's Master Samaritan ring beneath his shirt and stared out across the slow-moving river.

Professor Montgomery took note of the extended silence. "Ah… don't wait too long with your *bastani* there, Will. It'll melt fast on a day like this."

The words brought him back. He blinked and looked down at his bowl, watching the sweet saffron ice cream slowly melt in the summer heat.

The Professor took off his jacket and wiped his brow. Even in the shade, the heat was oppressive. In the plaza nearby, the main fountain's jets threw columns of water into the air, offering a welcome respite. Children ran through the mist, shrieking in delight, while their parents stood around the edges, occasionally extending their hands to catch some of the cool spray.

He finished the last spoonful of ice cream. "Will, I'm glad we finally got a chance to talk again. Good thing the power went out. It gave us a moment to sit down." He smiled. "So, tell me—how are your piano lessons going with Maestra Rosa Carreño?"

"I've learned so much," William said, taking in a deep breath. "I'm coming up on my first year with her, and she's taking me on a special hike. I think it's some kind of initiation—all her students do it after the first year. The trail's on the Prescott estate, but Miss Rosa's been kind of secretive about it."

"Ah… yes," Montgomery sighed. "The old Wildwood Trail."

"You know about it?" William's eyes shot up. "What do you think she wants to show me?"

Montgomery waved off the question. "Oh, now, that would ruin the fun, Will. Rosa should be the one." He smirked. "But I'll be curious to hear what you think of the ravine. That was always my favorite part."

William stood, gathering their empty bowls, spoons, and napkins. As he walked to the nearby trash bin, he glanced up at the copper statue and the ever-present flame in her lamp. It burned steadily, untouched by wind—which was rare; there was almost always a breeze off the river.

When he returned, he said, "You know, it's strange."

"What's that?"

"Well, I was looking at the statue's flame, and it got me thinking. If the treehouse fire never happened, then maybe Miss Rosa wouldn't have studied Piano Zen with Eleanor Prescott, and if she never studied it, then she wouldn't be teaching me. It's like… things had to happen exactly the way they did, or none of this would exist. I wouldn't have become friends with you, either."

Montgomery turned slightly toward William. "Yes, it's amazing how a fire like that can change the course of events. It's often hard to say for certain if a tragic event is ultimately a bad thing or a good thing. It all depends on perspective." He adjusted his gold-rimmed sunglasses, and as he did, they caught sunlight filtering through the tree overhead.

Finally, a gust of wind rolled through, bringing a cooling breeze off the river. William felt it sweep across his face like a gentle hand, softening the day's relentless heat. He closed his eyes, inhaling deeply as the air shifted. Somewhere in the bazaar, an oud was strummed, its bright tones weaving around the lively pulse of a doumbek drum.

# Chapter Thirty-Eight

## *The Lady of Light*

The Professor's phone rang, a bright trill cutting through the sound of street musicians and murmuring voices. He pulled it from his pocket and answered. As he listened, his brow furrowed.

"Pardon me a moment, Will. I need to take this call."

"Oh, sure," William said, rising from the bench and drifting toward the towering copper sculpture. He wandered slowly around its massive base, wondering how Camille Claudel had managed it. He tilted his head back, taking it in—the sheer size of it always stunned him. He could almost see her hands moving over the copper, breathing life into the metal itself. And then there was that photograph he saw a year ago in the Rodin book—Madeleine Monnier at the piano, Claudel leaning on its curved edge.

Montgomery finished his phone call and slipped his phone back into his pocket. "Sorry for the interruption, Will. The new *Corps of Discovery* exhibit is being installed in the Samaritan Museum—it's all about Nightingale's *Spirit of Lewis and Clark Expo* from 1912. There are a lot of moving pieces to put in place, and they keep calling with questions."

"That's okay. I was just standing here admiring the statue."

"Ah, yes—*La Dame de la Lumière*. Beautiful, isn't she?" Montgomery leaned on his cane.

"I've always wondered about her. How did she end up in Nightingale?"

"It's quite a story, Will—and really, a small miracle that it happened at all."

"What do you mean?"

"Well, at the time, Camille Claudel had been in an institution for seven years."

William blinked. "An institution? I'm not sure what you mean—what kind of place is that?"

"It was a psychiatric hospital," Montgomery said quietly. "Her family put her there after her father died."

"Why... why would they do that?"

Montgomery took a slow breath. "Sometimes people who feel things deeply—artists, dreamers—can seem strange to the rest of the world. In her time, there wasn't much understanding of the mind. What might be called extreme sadness or anxiety today was often labeled *madness*. Once her father was gone, her brother made the decision. And that was that."

William looked up at the copper figure, her flame held steady in the still air. "So, she was trapped there? For the rest of her life?"

"Yes," Montgomery said softly. "But even from that place, she found a way to keep creating. The hospital staff believed in her. They gave her space, tools, a workshop of her own. And it was there, in the quiet, that she had a dream."

"What kind of... dream?"

"Of the woman with the lamp. Claudel woke one day and began sketching immediately, as if the dream were guiding her hands. That vision became this statue. R.C. Prescott learned of it, commissioned her to build it, and she gathered a few trusted artisans to help her bring it to life. It was built in secret, far from the world that had forgotten her."

"But I don't... I mean... how did Prescott learn about her dream in the institution?" William hesitated. "Wait—does Madeleine Monnier have something to do with this?"

"Oh, most definitely. Camille was friends with Madeleine. She sent the sketch in a letter, and Madeleine showed it to Prescott."

William stared out at the Makah River. "So, she made her masterpiece while everyone thought she was broken."

Montgomery adjusted his sunglasses, thoughtful. "Yes. I think the dream came to her in what mystics call the dark night of the Soul—a place where there seems no end, no light."

"So, the statue was her light in the darkness... for Camille, I mean?"

"And for us too, Will. You see, the world had barely begun to heal from the war—cities in ruin, famine spreading, millions dead across Europe—

when the Spanish flu of 1918 swept through, over fifty million gone in total. Among them, his mother and sisters."

He paused. "And then, not long after… his wife."

"Madeleine Monnier?" William asked. "That's why he commissioned the statue?"

"Yes. He hoped Madeleine might have lived to see it completed."

William's gaze lifted to the flame in her lamp, burning against the blue sky. "But she never saw it, did she?"

"No," Montgomery said. "She never did."

For a long moment, neither of them spoke.

Montgomery's phone rang again. He sighed, rubbing his forehead before answering. "Hello? …No, I can't make that decision remotely… just hold tight until I get there."

He snapped his phone shut. "Sorry, Will. There's an issue at the Samaritan Temple I need to handle." He hesitated, tapping his cane lightly against the pavement. "Want to come along and go inside the temple, maybe see the exhibit?"

Will nodded enthusiastically. "Oh yes, I would love to. But I would need to let my mom know where I was going."

Montgomery handed William his phone so he could ask.

"Mais oui, mon chéri," his mother said. "I think it's a wonderful opportunity. I'll pick you up there in an hour."

A few minutes later, the taxi the professor called pulled up, and they both climbed in. The city slipped past the cab windows in a blur of brick façades and tree-lined boulevards. When the car turned a corner, the golden ziggurat of the Samaritan Temple came into view.

# Chapter Thirty-Nine

## *Inner Sojourn*

William and the Professor climbed the long procession of steps leading to the grand entrance of the Samaritan Temple. The sheer scale of the building never failed to captivate him. He had passed it countless times—its golden tiers bright in the afternoon sun or luminous against the indigo of night, but now, after all these years, he was finally stepping inside.

As they crossed the threshold, a rush of cool air enveloped him, carrying the faint mineral scent of wet stone. Inside, the temple felt grander than he had ever imagined, alive with a sacred presence that quickened his pulse. At the center of the great hall, a waterfall of light and water descended from a wide, circular opening in the vaulted ceiling. Known as the *Celestial Veil*, the sculpture never ceased—pouring down in a perfect cylinder, as if the heavens themselves were spilling into the temple. Golden light streamed from a hidden skylight above, striking the cascade and turning it into a living prism, an ever-shifting halo of droplets and mist.

The water struck a vast, black-stone basin below, sending ripples outward toward the edges, where visitors could walk around the structure. Every sound— every footstep—seemed to hum in harmony with the soft roar of falling water. William stood motionless, transfixed by the spectacle of motion and light.

A gentle tap of Montgomery's cane echoed off the polished floor, pulling William's gaze from the Celestial Veil. "Will, I need to meet with a few people. Let me take you to Memorial Concert Hall. There's a grand piano on stage, and if you like, you can practice on it. Just remove the covering and open the lid. It's not usually allowed, but if anyone comes in, just tell them I said it was okay."

The Professor led him up the wide staircase, their footsteps echoing through the vast corridors. Soon, they came upon the double doors of the Memorial Concert Hall. Inside, it was completely dark. William couldn't see his hand in front of his face.

"Hang on, Will. Don't want you tumbling down the stairs."

Montgomery's feet shuffled beside him. A flick, then another, and the concert hall lights hummed to life, flooding the room with a warm glow.

William drew a quick breath as the space revealed itself—a stunning, intimate auditorium modeled after a Greek amphitheater. Near the entrance, Doric columns framed the upper tier, while rows of ascending seats curved in a semi-circle around the stage.

At the center of the stage, waiting in the quiet of the empty hall, stood a massive concert grand piano.

"Have fun," Montgomery said before departing.

William paused at the top of the steps, his heart thudding with anticipation. The instrument's size was staggering—larger than any he had ever seen. Slowly, he descended toward it, hesitating before lifting a corner of the heavy, leather covering. Beneath, the piano's polished burr walnut caught the stage lights, its dark ribbons of wood grain flowing like waves.

Carefully, he removed the cover and stepped back to take in the instrument. Its finish reminded him of the antique music boxes at Marrakech West—the same swirling wood grain, the same warm, golden sheen.

His fingers trembled slightly as he lifted the fallboard. The name on the key lid caught his eye—*Bösendorfer*. It had to be the Imperial Grand he'd read about, renowned for its responsive touch and deep, resonant tone. But standing there before it on the stage felt like something else entirely.

He let his hand glide along the polished wood and glanced down the keyboard, noticing a small, wooden cover at the far left.

*A box?*

Curious, he lifted it. Beneath, a hidden surprise revealed itself—an extra set of piano keys, their colors inverted: black where white should be, white where black should be.

"Cool," he murmured, tracing a fingertip over the smooth, inverted keys. For a moment, he considered playing—then paused. His gaze traveled the full length of the Imperial Grand, and a sudden impulse took hold. He rose, slid his hands beneath the piano lid, and with some effort lifted the heavy weight, propping it open until the stick locked into place.

Inside, an intricate leaf design was sculpted into the heavy metal frame, its metallic surface catching the light like fire. The Bösendorfer wasn't just an instrument—it felt alive. William wondered if Cristofori could have imagined his creation evolving into something like this.

He began with a few pieces from memory, then let his hands drift into improvisation, testing the Bösendorfer's touch and responsiveness.

Now and then, he glanced around, half-expecting someone to walk in, but the auditorium stayed silent—his only audience the solitude of the grand hall.

He drew in a slow breath and centered himself, recalling his Piano Zen training. Resting his hands on his thighs, palms upturned, he closed his eyes. Awareness shifted to the contact points of his body—the steady weight of the bench beneath him, the grounding press of his feet on the floor. Each inhale and exhale carried a gentle flow of energy, and with it, his mind began to settle into stillness.

A warmth spread through his hands, making them feel lighter—tingling with a mysterious energy. When he opened his eyes, a calm sense of purpose filled him.

He placed his hands on the keys and began "Inner Sojourn," the Piano Zen piece he had been refining for weeks. Tonight, alone in the grand hall, he let go of thoughts of correctness and surrendered wholly to the music.

The opening chords resonated through the concert hall, their sheer depth startling him. It was as if a great bronze bell had been struck, sending vibrations through the air, humming through his skin. A shiver ran down his spine.

With his mind light as air, he pressed forward. "Inner Sojourn" had always felt like ocean waves rolling toward shore, so he let that image guide him, flowing from phrase to phrase like water carried by the tide.

And then—it happened.

Something inside him unlocked. Ideas surged faster than thought, notes cascading like a rushing current. His fingers responded intuitively, shaping phrases with natural rubato, lingering in delicate moments before surging ahead. Each note vibrated with nuance—his touch refined, his expression effortless.

It was like catching a wave on a surfboard—he had to stay loose, balanced, attuned to the energy moving through him. Thinking too hard, trying to control it, would only break the connection.

The experience was exhilarating, overwhelming. He wasn't just playing—he was inside the music, carried by a power rising from deep within. The piano seemed alive beneath his hands, its rich, resonant tone breathing his emotions into sound with unforced grace.

For the first time, he caught a glimpse of what it might feel like to be Rosa Carreño or Madeleine Monnier—totally immersed, completely free. This wasn't just playing the piano, it was something else entirely. The Bösendorfer wasn't merely an instrument; it was an extension of his thoughts, his breath, his being. Every phrase, every note felt alive, as if the music had been waiting for him to awaken it.

As he played the final low note of "Inner Sojourn," a bittersweet ache settled in his chest. The moment felt too fleeting, too private. Shy as he was about performing, a longing stirred within him—he wished someone else had witnessed it.

The last note faded into silence, and William sat motionless.

And then—

A slow, steady clap echoed from the back of the auditorium.

"Bravo, Will! Bravo!"

William's head jerked up, startled. Standing in the shadows of the upper tier was Professor Montgomery, grinning from ear to ear.

"Oh, thank you," William said, shifting on the bench.

Montgomery walked down the steps, shaking his head in amazement. "I can't believe you're playing like that after only a year with Rosa. You've got something special going there, Will."

He ran his hand along the Bösendorfer's polished wood. "You know, she played this very piano years ago—right on this stage."

"She did?"

"Brought the house down. Chopin, Ravel, Gershwin." Montgomery's expression softened. "There was something else, something I've never shared with anyone. Every note she played seemed alive with... light. When Rosa performed, I saw an entire spectrum of colors—something I had never experienced before. The whole auditorium sparkled like a living kaleidoscope." He tapped the piano's edge lightly. "And the strange thing is, I saw that same symphony of colors just now while you were playing."

Montgomery clapped him gently on the back. "Come on, let's head back to the lobby before it gets too late."

# Chapter Forty

## *Echoes of the Expo*

They stepped back into the temple's grand lobby. Threads of light from the Celestial Veil wove through the falling water, filling the air with a soft mist. William stood listening to its steady fall, feeling the cool droplets brush his face, until, after a while, he forgot all about the heat outside.

A woman in a charcoal suit approached. "Mr. Montgomery, they need you in the exhibit hall. We're finalizing the text for several panels on Lewis Hayden Montgomery and would like you to review them before they go to print."

"Of course," Montgomery said, rising. He turned to William. "I'll need to get back to work, but you have a choice. You can wait here or come along and take a sneak peek at the new exhibit. It's still a week from opening, but you're welcome to look around."

"Sure," William said, standing. "I've got a few minutes before she gets here."

He followed Montgomery down a corridor to a special wing marked by a grand banner stretched across the entrance:

The 1912 Spirit of Lewis and Clark Exposition — A Commemoration of Exploration, Innovation, and Unity

Montgomery exchanged a few words with the woman in the suit before disappearing with her into a side hallway. William stepped into the dimly lit lobby of the exhibit.

At the center of the room, beneath a halo of soft light, a glass case drew his attention. He moved closer. Resting on a velvet pedestal was a rare, leather-bound volume—one he instantly recognized from Shelley's rare book room.

He leaned in to read the placard:

*History of the Expedition Under the Command of Captains Lewis & Clark... Performed During the Years 1804–5–6. Published in 1814. On loan from M.W. Shelley Bookstore for the duration of the exhibit.*

Something across the room caught his eye—a large, illuminated display stretched along the far wall. As William approached, a thrill of excitement rose in him. The placard read:

*Original scale model of the Spirit of Lewis and Clark World's Exposition of 1912, designed by Lewis Hayden Montgomery, Chief Architect and Planner.*

William had often wondered what it might have been like to walk those grounds in 1912—surrounded by wonders from every corner of the world. He stepped closer. The intricate replica revealed a city that no longer existed: gleaming towers, sweeping gardens, and pavilions rising in ornate detail—China, Japan, Persia, Egypt, France—all rendered in ornate miniature. The Makah River wound through the center, its bridges spanning from Nightingale's east side to its west.

The placard next to it read:

*From Frontier to World Stage: The 1912 Spirit of Lewis and Clark Exposition fused global cultures with cutting-edge technology, placing Nightingale on the international map. Once known primarily for timber, quarries, and mining, the city briefly transformed into a hub of art, innovation, and progress. For one summer, visitors from every continent walked these grounds, experiencing a glimpse of the future shaped by exploration and unity.*

*The Gateway of the Moors: Most Expo buildings were never meant to last. Constructed of wood and reinforced with light metal supports, their grand façades were crafted from staff—a mixture of burlap fiber and plaster shaped to resemble stone and marble. Within months of the exhibit's close, planned demolition erased the structures, many already showing signs of decay.*

*The Gateway of the Moors stood apart: built from enduring Imperial Heights limestone. Funded personally by R.C. Prescott, the monumental arch was designed to remain long after the fairgrounds had vanished, a lasting symbol of cultural exchange.*

William studied the replica, his gaze tracing miniature esplanades and towers. He turned as Montgomery's footsteps approached behind him.

"Professor Montgomery, this replica is amazing. I've seen pictures of it, but I didn't know there was an actual model."

"Yes," Montgomery said, smiling. "My grandfather designed and drafted it. He later donated it to the Samaritan Temple."

"I have a question, though," William said. "Where's the Lady of Light statue? Shouldn't it be near the Gateway of the Moors?"

"Ah... remember, Will—that wasn't installed until 1923, years after the Expo."

Just then, Montgomery's phone buzzed, and he pulled it from his pocket. "Hello?... Ah, yes, he's right here... Of course, we'll meet you outside... Au revoir, Aimée."

He slipped the phone away and smiled. "Well, Will, it seems our little adventure is over for today. Your mother's just a few minutes away."

Together, they left the Temple of the Ancient Mystic Order of Samaritans, descending the long flight of steps and onto the bustling sidewalk. The streets were alive—businesspeople in crisp suits, tourists snapping photos, buses hissing to a stop. From down the block, the pounding of a construction site echoed between high-rises.

A familiar white Trailblazer pulled to the curb.

Montgomery clasped William's hand with both of his own. "It's been my pleasure, Will. I've no doubt you'll enjoy your hike along the Wildwood Trail with Rosa next week. Let me know what you think of the ravine—and stay safe, my friend. They're calling for high winds and possible thunderstorms. You wouldn't want to be caught on Imperial Heights in a storm like that."

William blinked. "Right... I almost forgot. The Wildwood Trail—that's next week."

As the Trailblazer merged into traffic, William rested his head against the window, watching the blur of passing cars. Beyond the city, the dark line of Imperial Heights rose against the sky—where the Wildwood Trail and its hidden ravine waited.

# Chapter Forty-One

## *To Build a Fire*

The storm broke just as they reached the Gate Lodge, breathless. Rosa pushed the door shut against the wind as thunder rolled through the valley; gusts howled through the towering sequoias, their branches bowing beneath torrents of rain. A jagged bolt of lightning streaked across the sky, illuminating the trees for a split second before a deep clap of thunder shook the earth beneath their feet.

William peeled off his soaked hoodie while Rosa removed her drenched shawl, hanging both on the hooks near the door.

"My word!" Rosa said, brushing damp strands of hair from her forehead. "Did you notice how quickly the temperature dropped? It's given me quite a chill." She eased herself into a chair with a small groan as she removed her shoes. The hurried walk back to the lodge had clearly been a strain on her knees.

"William, could you start a fire for us? Are you comfortable doing that? It would go well with a hot cup of tea."

"Um… sure," William said.

Rosa glanced toward the window, shivering slightly. "I've still got wood left from last winter. Never thought we'd need a fire this time of year, but this storm dropped the temperature fast."

Rosa looked at her clock on the shelf. "We still have time. Your mother isn't due to arrive for a little while. I'm going to change out of these wet clothes and dry my hair. I'll be back in a moment. If you need help with the fire, just call out."

William nodded slowly, glancing at the hearth. He'd once studied how to build a proper fire but had never managed to make it work.

Kneeling beside Rosa's fireplace, he remembered the camping trip with his mother a few years ago—their one and only attempt together, a disaster from the start. He'd volunteered to build the campfire, but the wood had been too wet to burn. The garage-sale tent his mother had proudly found turned out to have no stakes, and worst of all, she'd forgotten their cooking utensils. By nightfall, they gave up and traded the campsite for a roadside motel.

Back then, kneeling at the campsite firepit, William had felt like the doomed protagonist in Jack London's *To Build a Fire*—cold, clumsy, fumbling helplessly against the elements. He could still remember the sting of sulfur on his fingers as he struck match after match, burning through the entire book without ever getting a flame to catch.

Fortunately, Rosa had everything laid out perfectly—dry tinder, slender sticks of kindling, and larger logs stacked nearby. William built a small log-cabin frame, arranging tinder in the center with narrow gaps for air to flow. It was the same method he'd tried at the campsite with his mother.

Once the frame was ready, he glanced around for a matchbook or lighter but saw nothing. As he stood to call out to Rosa, his eyes caught on a small blue dish on the redwood mantel above the hearth—a single match resting inside.

*Only one match?* He grinned, liking the challenge.

He struck it against the hearth and lowered the flame to the tinder. It caught almost instantly, curling into bright embers that licked hungrily at the kindling. For a moment, he feared it would sputter out, but the flame leapt higher, engulfing the cabin of sticks with surprising ease. Soon, heat radiated from the budding fire. William added a few larger logs, coaxing the flames upward.

The warmth from the fireplace felt good—strange, considering that just a week ago, the sun had been relentless, baking Marrakech West. Now, high in Imperial Heights, the air had turned sharp and cool. Wind roared through the trees as rain lashed the roof. Another jagged flash of lightning lit the windows, followed by a low roll of thunder that seemed to vibrate through the wooden beams of the lodge.

He wandered to the French doors and peered out at the storm. Rain, running in rivulets down the glass, blurred the world beyond. His thoughts drifted to the journal tucked in his backpack—the notebook where he still scribbled dream fragments he could remember: flashes of light, haunting melodies, animal figures that sometimes matched the illustrations in Miss Rosa's rare Piano Zen book. After a year of lessons, the entries made little sense, yet he kept writing. Lately, his thoughts kept circling back to his quiet obsession with Madeleine Monnier. Somehow, she held the key to a deeper mystery about Piano Zen. The old Prescott Mansion where she'd once lived was nearly ready to reopen as a museum, and he couldn't wait to step inside at last… and maybe find some answers.

Glancing back to the fire, the flames were steady now, and his thoughts drifted to Misha. Where was she? She usually came to greet him. *Probably tucked safely under Rosa's bed*, he thought.

Rosa returned, her hair brushed dry and a fresh shawl draped over her shoulders, carrying a freshly cut purple orchid and a small watering pitcher. "Oh my… you've really got a fire going there," she said. "Lovely. That will take the chill right out of my bones."

She moved to the kintsugi vase on the side table, poured in a trickle of water and carefully placed the flower inside. Stepping back, she let her fingers brush beneath the orchid's petals, as if testing their softness.

William drifted closer, drawn to the vase with its metallic gold veins. "You mentioned once there was a story about this vase," he said. "I've been meaning to ask. I don't think you ever told me."

"Why, yes," Rosa said. "It sat by Madeleine Monnier's bed during her illness."

William's eyes widened. "Wait… this was *her* vase?"

"That's right," Rosa nodded. "Eleanor told me R.C. brought her a fresh flower every morning so it would be the first thing she saw when she woke. As for how it was broken and pieced back together—well, that part of the story's been lost."

Rosa said quietly. "I do the same. Put a fresh flower in it every day, too. It reminds me to be grateful for each new morning. And…" Her hand brushed lightly over the orchid's petals. "I always say a little prayer for Sasha."

A sudden flash of lightning split the sky. A heartbeat later, thunder rolled through the valley, rattling the windows. William flinched, the sharp crack snapping him back to the present moment.

Rosa's eyes fixed on the storm outside. "Lightning is one kind of energy," she said. "But the kind we cultivate in Piano Zen is more subtle—an inner fire, the lifeforce that flows within us."

She started toward the kitchen. "Before we get started, I'll put the kettle on—let's have some tea. There's something I want to talk to you about."

Soon, the scrape of the kettle on the stove and the soft clink of teacups drifted into the room. "How does oolong tea sound? It's a little stronger, but I think you'll like it," she called out from the kitchen.

"That sounds great."

A few minutes later, Rosa returned, gathering her hair and fastening it with a clip. She smiled lightly and nodded toward the piano bench. "The water will take a few minutes. Why don't we get started?"

William slid onto the bench as Rosa lifted the Tibetan bowl from its shelf. Outside, the storm was breaking—lightning flared only now and then, thunder fading into low, distant rolls.

"Hmm…" Rosa said, tilting her head toward the window. "Looks like the worst of it is already moving on. Perfect. Let's do a relaxation session before we have some tea."

She gave him a small nod. "Close your eyes. Rest your hands on your thighs, palms up. We'll move through the Elements—Earth, Air, and Water—before arriving at Fire."

William steadied his breath. After nearly a year of lessons with Rosa, these relaxation sessions had become a quiet ritual—one he enjoyed deeply, often so calming that he sometimes drifted toward sleep.

Rosa's voice stayed steady and calm as she slowly traced the mallet around the edge of the Tibetan bowl, coaxing out its deep, meditative tone.

"Earth," she said. "Feel the weight of your body, your contact points, the steady foundation beneath you. Relax into that awareness."

A brief silence followed.

"Now Air—soften your thoughts, let them drift like a breeze, open and spacious, as your body remains grounded."

Rosa waited. William's mind began to slow down.

"Feel Earth and Air balancing one another." Her voice lowered. "Water— breathe deep into your belly. Draw a wave of energy into you… and release it. Flowing in and out… in and out…"

William sank deeper into the exercise.

"Now," Rosa whispered, "bring your focus to your palms. Notice the tingling. As you concentrate, it grows stronger—like holding weighted balls of energy."

At first, just a faint stirring. Then pulsing warmth spread through his hands.

"Let that inner energy move through you," Rosa continued. "Your feet, your legs, your arms, your chest… your whole being alive with it."

The Tibetan bowl's tone vibrated through the room.

"Your mind is soft, at ease. Awareness, clear and luminous, sparkling as you breathe in… and out."

William felt it—a subtle shift, a living presence stirring inside him.

"Soften your eyes and ears," Rosa murmured. "Awaken to the Sound and Light within."

The tingling sensation deepened, turning to movement, vibration. On the inner screen of his mind, a twinkling blue star appeared, dancing at the edges of awareness.

"Now… listen," Rosa whispered.

His breathing eased while the storm's remnants faded into silence.

And then he heard it.

At first, only a faint shimmer, like distant wind chimes. Then, layered tones, delicate and bright, as if the air itself rang with bells. The sound swelled, surrounding him, filling the space until there was nothing else.

His eyes fluttered open, and the Gate Lodge was gone. The world around him had changed.

# Chapter Forty-Two

## *The Gates of Parthenopolis*

William found himself sitting on a bench beneath the glow of a moonlit night. As with other journeys triggered by the Tibetan bowl, a wave of amnesia washed over him—no memory of how he'd arrived, nor where he had come from.

A low hum stirred against his chest. He reached inside his shirt and drew out the Dream Dorje, its tone singing softly as flecks of light danced across his face. Rising from the bench, he caught his breath. He was perched on a mountainside, dizzyingly high. The moon floated above like a pale lantern, casting a sheen across the view. Far below, a valley stretched into shadowed folds, threaded with a faint glimmer of water. Wisps of cloud drifted lazily past, yet the air felt surprisingly mild for such altitude—cool enough to notice but gentle on his skin.

As he turned to take in more of the view, his gaze lifted upward—and froze. Behind him rose an immense white wall, its sheer height unlike anything he had ever seen. Towering and imposing, it gleamed in the moonlight—pristine, smooth, as if untouched by time.

Had he been awake, he might have wondered how anything so colossal could ever have been built on such a high peak. But dreams seldom pause for reason. Here, the wall's presence felt natural—timeless.

And in the stillness of the night, faint, tinkling bells echoed softly. Their source was unseen, yet something in their sound stirred William's thoughts awake.

*Why does this feel familiar?*

Something vibrated in his backpack. He swung it off, set it beside him on the bench, and unzipped it. The Piano Zen Book shivered in his hands, then flipped itself open. Pages fluttered in a blur before stopping on one that glowed faintly. Words emerged slowly, forming themselves upon the page.

**You have been here before**

The words felt true, yet uncertainty tugged at him. "I don't remember. Are you sure?"

The page went blank, then new letters appeared.

**Yes**

"Hmm, but where is… here?"

The page shimmered, then a single word formed.

**Parthenopolis.**

He closed his eyes, chasing that answer in the deepest recesses of his memory. When he opened them, it struck in a flash. "You're right, this isn't the first time," he murmured. "Parthenopolis, I remember now. It was a bright day, blinding. I stumbled straight into some giant temple inside the city. There was a man there—I talked with him. But I can't remember his name…" He glanced back at the book.

**Wu Wei – Master of the Fire Element**

"That's right! So, I have been here once before."

The pages flipped quickly, halting on new words.

**No. You have been here many times**

"Many?" he breathed. He could recall only one—the light, the temple. And yet here he was again, this time outside the walls, under the moonlit sky.

He stepped to the edge of the overlook. Far below, he spotted the Harmony Stream—the same river he had once rowed along with Densho and Ukumari on their way to the Garden of the Awakening Orchid. From this height, it appeared as a thin, silver thread, winding through the shadowed mountain passes.

As his eyes lifted, something on the horizon seized his attention—a faint, restless aura, tinged in red. The crimson light bent and twisted in the distance.

"What's causing that light?" he asked.

The book flipped to a new page. Letters gathered out of the blankness, coalescing into words.

**That is Ulandia. A vast land of many kingdoms. Often locked in discord. The red you see is their vibration.**

A certainty gripped him. "Is that where… Florestan is?"

**Yes.**

Unease rippled through him as dream-images surfaced: Florestan in his red cloak, a dark, humid jungle… Gorgon… Typhon… Cerberus.

He was about to ask another question, when a faint glow caught his eye. It was coming from his own skin. If it hadn't been so dark, he might have missed it entirely. Slipping the book back into his backpack, he slowly lifted his arms, turning them over. A pale blue light traced along his hands and forearms—subtle yet undeniable. He undulated his arms, watching them leave streaks of blue light trailing through the air. Looking down, he saw his entire body wrapped in a faint blue aura.

He pressed his palms together, noticing how the glow seemed to pulse brighter—gathering into a small sphere of light. For a time, he simply stood there, arms raised slightly, playing with the ball of light between his hands, entranced.

At last, curiosity beckoned him onward. Lowering his arms, he swung on his backpack and turned toward the massive wall. Somewhere ahead, there had to be a way in. His feet found a narrow path running along the wall's edge, and he began to follow it, eyes scanning the large structure for an entrance.

Now and then, figures wandered the outer grounds—moving slowly, as if half-asleep. Dream Walkers, he realized. They drifted near the wall, appearing and fading.

As he passed a stone bench, a light gathered in the air above it. A moment later, a person materialized—blinking, unsteady. They stood, glanced in his direction with unfocused eyes, then drifted away without truly seeing him.

William watched them go. Even here, just outside Parthenopolis, the dream world had its wanderers. But he was alone on this journey.

He continued on.

Rounding a bend, he entered a wide clearing—and stopped. Before him rose a monumental gateway. At ground level stood a pair of immense copper doors, their burnished surfaces shimmering with ancient symbols. Above them, a tower climbed into the sky and vanished into a veil of moonlit mist. Tilting his head back, William drew a deep breath, dwarfed by the scale of it all.

A soft radiance appeared in the distance. William assumed it was only the reflection of moonlight—until it advanced, steady and deliberate. Someone was walking toward him, drawing closer step by step.

He soon made out the figure—robed in white, the fabric shifting gently as it moved. For a moment, the person seemed made of light itself, edges blurred, almost dissolving into the night air. But as they drew closer, the glow softened, revealing more detail: flowing sleeves threaded with gold, a copper-colored sash, and long tasseled ropes swaying with each step.

When the man came near enough for William to see his face, recognition struck—that calm, timeless presence, the voice that had once spoken to him through a haze of unbearable brightness.

It was Master Wu Wei.

"William Longfellow Emerson," he said warmly. "A Wind Spirit watching over the Dream Walkers told me you were outside the walls."

William swallowed, still reeling from the sight. "Hel-hello," he managed.

"Your last visit was unexpected. You arrived before you were ready for the vibrations of Parthenopolis. Most new Dream Travelers arrive at night—darkness softens the city's light and spares their eyes."

Wu Wei motioned to the towering entrance, and together they gazed up at the gates.

William shook his head. "I can't even... it feels impossible that anyone could build something like this."

Wu Wei clasped his hands behind his back. "In Parthenopolis, such marvels are not uncommon. Its inhabitants are mostly Dream Travelers. Guided by intuitive imagination, they manifest wonders—temples, towers of light, creations far beyond the limits of the critical mind, beyond the reach of reason."

He nodded toward the grand city beyond. "Many Dream Walkers are drawn to Parthenopolis as they slumber, though few recall their visits. They drift through it half-aware, gathering only fragments of inspiration. With the quiet help of guides and Wind Spirits, the currents of Light and Sound awaken their creativity—planting seeds in the subconscious that bloom later in waking life."

Wu Wei stepped toward the gates and motioned for William to follow. As they approached, awe welled up inside him. Each massive door appeared to be formed from a single, seamless sheet of copper—no joints, no rivets—as though it had emerged whole from some ancient act of creation.

"Are you ready to open the Gates of Parthenopolis?" Wu Wei asked. "This time as a Dream Traveler—ready to experience the city with truer clarity."

"Open the gates? Me? I... don't understand."

Wu Wei gestured toward a small, modest handle set at shoulder height near the base of the gateway door. The copper handle had darkened with age, polished as if generations of hands had grasped it. It seemed impossibly small, just a speck set against the towering expanse of the gate.

"This is the way," Wu Wei said. "Only you can choose to cross through."

William stared at the handle, then lifted his eyes toward the colossal doors whose weight defied imagination. The challenge of moving them with his bare hand seemed impossible.

Wu Wei's expression remained serene. "Are you ready to take the next step?"

Doubt churned through William's mind. There had to be an easier path to enter. Why did it have to be this way?

"Because this is a challenge you must face alone," Wu Wei said, answering the unspoken question. "Crossing this threshold will not simply move you forward—it will awaken you to your greater purpose."

"The Fifth… Element?" William asked.

Wu Wei lifted an eyebrow, the faintest hint of a smile at the corner of his mouth. "I can only show you the door, William. You must find the way through yourself."

Fear of failure began to swirl in William's mind, clouding his thoughts. Then he felt it—a faint sensation against his leg. Sliding his hand into his pocket, his fingers brushed a jagged, cool surface pulsing with power.

Recognition jolted him, slicing through the fog of his doubts and bringing sudden clarity. Still there. Florestan's gift.

*The Wizard's Stone.*

As his fingers closed around it, a surge of energy leapt up his arm—an electric rush that filled his chest, flooding him with fierce, intoxicating confidence. He pictured it: his right hand gripping the handle, the other clutching the magic stone, forcing the gate open through sheer power.

His breath quickened—until Wu Wei's calm, steady gaze met his own. The master rested a hand on William's shoulder.

"This gate does not answer to strength," Wu Wei said. "Nor to the Four Elements. It yields to a different power."

Something deep inside William stirred. The feeling carried no clear memory—only an intuitive knowing, a truth rising from the depths.

*I've been here before… many times… and failed.*

He loosened his grip and let the stone slide back into his pocket. Drawing a steady breath, he summoned the courage to face what felt impossible. With trembling resolve, he reached for the small metal handle.

# Chapter Forty-Three

## *Into the Abyss*

William's fingers tightened around the handle. The cool metal pressed into his palm. He drew in a breath and pulled hard. Once. Twice. A third time. Every muscle straining.

Nothing. The massive copper doors didn't budge.

Again, he tried—teeth clenched, legs braced—pulling with everything he had. But it was like trying to move a mountain. Stumbling back, chest heaving, he opened his eyes and shook his head. "I… I can't do this."

It was more than the futility of the task. Something lay at the edges of his memory. Deep in his bones, he sensed he'd stood here before, his hand on the same handle, pulling with all his might— and the gates had never moved. Why would it be any different this time?

His hand drifted toward his leg again, fingers twitching as they brushed the jagged edges of the object in his pocket.

A woman's voice floated through his thoughts like a Wind Spirit. Tender at first.

*You have a gift, William.*
*Of course you can do this.*
*Use the flame of the obsidian stone.*
*Open the gates.*

As if guided by her voice, his hand slid deeper into his pocket. The moment his fingers neared the stone, energy surged upward, pouring through his palm like liquid fire. Heat threaded through his veins, climbing into his mind.

For a dizzying instant, William felt certain he could rip the Gates of Parthenopolis wide open with the power of the flame.

The voice deepened, wrapping itself around his thoughts.

*You have failed so many times.*

*Remember…*

*But now you have the stone.*

*You can do the impossible.*

William's left hand froze. He closed his eyes, and in that instant, he slipped deeper into the dream realms—but this was different. It was the place of his childhood nightmares.

Suddenly, he found himself clinging for life, his right hand gripping a small rocky ledge by only the tips of his fingers. A windswept cliff stretched beneath him—thousands of feet straight down into darkness. A gale roared around him, tossing his body violently from side to side as his fingertips fought to hold the precipice.

His grip slipped.

Alone, abandoned, he felt the choice pressing in on him, tears streaming down his face.

*William.*

*Use the stone.*

*You will not come back.*

He let go—releasing his right hand and plunging into the black chasm below. And like in the nightmares of his childhood, he was falling—falling by his own hand this time, toward his own death.

As he fell… his left hand grasped the Dream Dorje.

But this time waking did not rescue him.

He felt his body strike the rocks below, shattered, broken. Like a small boat swallowed by a violent ocean, he was hit—hard.

A force ripped through him to his very core.

And then everything dropped away.

There was no light. No sound. Nothing.

A wave of fear rose up—raw, primal, stronger than anything he had ever known. His entire being trembled. This wasn't merely his fear of death; it was the terror of vanishing completely, dissolving into the void until even the memory of his existence was erased.

But then... far off in the distance, a pinpoint of light seemed to flicker across the black expanse—a lone star sparkling in the dark void, impossibly far away, separated by what felt like millions of lightyears.

And yet, somehow, with uncertain resolve, he willed himself toward it. He seemed to walk at first, then run. Then he broke free, soaring forward, drawn faster and faster until he was flying at impossible speed, a comet streaking through the blackness, pulled irrevocably toward that tiny spark of light.

And as he drew near, he realized it wasn't a star at all—it was a window. Slowing to a stop, he hovered before it. The surface projected an image he recognized—the photograph from his room, the one of him and his dad on the camping trip.

Compelled beyond thought and reason, he reached out and touched the luminous image and was pulled into it. The world folded inward instantly, like liquid glass, bending, stretching time and space. Colors swirled past in ribbons of light, fragments of memories fluttering alongside—the scent of a campfire, his mother's laughter, the white Trailblazer—the experience of that day caught in the photograph.

Then, with a jolt, his body dropped into a familiar weight, settling into what felt like a saddle. He was a toddler again, riding in his father's backpack. The leather straps creaked softly, and the scent of pine needles rose around him, pulling him deeper into the moment. He was three years old, yet part of him remained quietly aware, an observer floating just beyond time.

His body was perched high on his dad's shoulders, snug in the hiking pack. Nearby, his mother stood smiling—her eyes bright, her dark brown hair not yet touched with gray.

Beside the campsite stood a bright orange tent.

*Of course—the orange tent.*

And there beside it, the white Trailblazer—newer, with camping gear strapped to its roof.

His father turned his head slightly, grinning. "How's the view up there, Sparky?"

William giggled. "Good... good!" In his toddler voice, he squealed, "Daddy go! Daddy go!"

His father chuckled. "Alright, buddy. But let's make a deal. I'll carry you for the first part of the hike, and then we switch on the way back. You carry me. Deal?"

William shook his head. "Uh-uh... uh-uh."

His father staggered in an exaggerated way, knees pretending to buckle. "Aimée, we've got a problem." He twisted sideways with a grunt. "Sparky's growing again." His voice cracked into desperation. "He's way too… heavy!"

He lurched hard to one side, arms windmilling. "Whoa!" He wobbled back, spun in a crooked circle, and teetered wildly until William erupted in a storm of giggles.

His mother reached for her camera, grinning. "Hold it, you two. Let me get a picture."

His father froze mid-spin, flashing a lopsided grin at Aimée. William, patting his dad's head like a drum, never looked over as the shutter clicked.

Lowering the camera, Aimée shook her head with a warm laugh. "Ah, mes chéris… you two are having way too much fun!"

William, watching the memory from outside of time, turned toward his mother. Something in her expression struck him—something unfamiliar. She was radiant, bathed in a soft glow that enfolded her. Joy emanated from her face—unguarded, luminous. And his father stood with quiet strength and kindness.

Tears welled in his eyes. For a heartbeat, the observer slipped fully back into the toddler's body—small arms wrapping around his father's head, clutching him tightly, holding on with all his heart.

Then—slowly—the scent of pine began to fade. The warmth of his father's body, his mother's beaming smile—gone. All of it slipping away, the memory drifting back into the deep recesses of the dream worlds.

A hand rested gently on his shoulder.

"William, open your eyes."

It was Master Wu Wei's voice.

"You found it, my friend—the light in the darkness."

William blinked and drew in a breath. Before him, the massive gateway to Parthenopolis stood ajar. He had parted its towering doors by his own hand, open just wide enough to invite him through. He staggered back, releasing the handle in disbelief.

Wu Wei let out a delighted laugh. "Now do you believe?" he said, sweeping a hand toward the opening. "With love, nothing is impossible. Come—our time is short."

Together, they stepped through the narrow opening.

The Gates of Parthenopolis closed silently behind them.

# Chapter Forty-Four

## *The Court of the Cosmos*

As they passed beyond the gates, night gave way to dawn. The twilight sky glowed anew with an ever-shifting symphony of rose and lavender light.

Parthenopolis unfolded before William like the opening of a vast panorama. To either side, sweeping colonnades curved in perfect symmetry—familiar in shape, like the images he'd once seen of St. Peter's Square, yet transformed by a harmony of styles no single culture could claim. Marble columns carried fluted grooves reminiscent of ancient temples. Farther on, a multitude of glass domes reflected soft bands of morning color.

His gaze followed the arc of the colonnade to where two immense archways, large enough to swallow a cathedral, faced each other across a massive esplanade. Pale onyx columns framed them, veined in soft blue. Between the arches stretched a wide stone path leading to a pair of fountains, where water rose and fell in gentle, rhythmic patterns. From the heart of each fountain rose a slender column of pink quartz. Atop one stood a winged woman with her left hand lifted toward the heavens; atop the other, a winged man mirrored her with his right. Their fingertips hovered in the space between, as though reaching for a world just beyond sight.

A gentle nudge drew William's attention back toward the entrance. The Gates of Parthenopolis had shut behind them, but high above, newly revealed in the morning light, rose the massive tower that the night had kept hidden. Seven luminous tiers climbed into the sky, each lined with arched windows and balconies from which light streamed in steady waves. Jewels set into its stone caught the dawn and scattered it into drifting rainbows. To William, the tower seemed to rise like a stairway, lifting the gaze from earth toward the heavens.

"The ancient Pharos of Parthenopolis," Wu Wei said. "The first of its kind."

William blinked. "Pharos?"

"A lighthouse," Wu Wei replied. "This was the model that seeded every great lighthouse—even those in your world. The Pharos of Alexandria, one of Earth's Seven Wonders, was but a reflection of its design—now lost to time."

Blue waves pulsed from the tower's summit, sweeping outward like distant beacons and fading into the farthest reaches of the universe.

"That light you see," Wu Wei said, "draws visitors here in the dream state. But it emits more than light—it sings. A sound like a choir of strings drifts through the multiverse, calling dreamers. Some arrive with purpose—the Dream Travelers. Others follow the light and music without knowing why—the Dream Walkers—coming and going like tourists lost in a strange city."

Master Wu Wei invited William to walk down the esplanade toward the center of the spacious forum. Lining the sides, elegant white, marble benches offered places for reflection.

After a short walk, Wu Wei motioned for William to sit. William eased onto the cool marble bench, his senses steadying after the spectacle of the illuminated city. Only then did he see the quiet flow of people moving in and out of the surrounding temples.

A faint shimmer of light gathered above the bench beside him, brightening until it shaped itself into a person. They stood slowly, eyes unfocused. William smiled and gave a small wave, but they didn't react.

"They cannot see you, William," Wu Wei said. "You are vibrating at a higher frequency. To them, it is still night."

A guide in a maroon robe appeared and rested a gentle hand on the newcomer's shoulder, leading them toward one of the nearby temples.

"Many of the Dream Walkers you see here," Wu Wei said, "arrive in a mental haze—unaware of how the dream world pulls them here, then shapes their waking state. In truth, they are seeking something: a composer hoping to spark a new symphony, a novelist breaking through writer's block, a scientist chasing a discovery. Others come for inspiration, clarity—answers. A path forward."

"So is this place sort of like a dream… university?" William asked.

Wu Wei laughed. "You could call it that, though we do not hand out formal diplomas. Parthenopolis is more like a vast research library—for inspiration and creativity. Most cannot remember their time here, but they carry their dream insights back with them into the waking world."

William's eyes swept across the Court of the Cosmos. "It does feel familiar," he said. "I get that sensation a lot—where something feels known, but I can't say why."

Master Wu Wei nodded. "When you return, many of your questions will find their answers—perhaps even those about the Fifth Element."

"When I return?" William asked

Before Wu Wei could answer, a piercing sound split the air, sharp and jarring, like an air raid siren. William flinched, gripping the sides of the bench as the Court of the Cosmos trembled around him.

"The Fifth Element?" he pressed. "What is it?"

Wu Wei's voice remained steady, almost amused. "It seems our time is up, William. But I suspect you will return soon."

The wailing sound grew more intense. The grand structures of Parthenopolis began to dissolve—walls, archways, towers—crumbling into nothingness.

The last thing William saw was Wu Wei, standing calm amid the chaos, raising a hand in farewell.

# Chapter Forty-Five

## *When the Time Comes*

William jolted awake, heart pounding. The deafening roar that seemed to shatter Parthenopolis was nothing more than the shrill whistle of Miss Rosa's tea kettle in the next room.

She set the Tibetan bowl on the piano. "Oh dear, excuse me, William," she said, rising from her chair. "I completely forgot about the water on the stove. Let me take care of that and bring us some tea."

As Rosa hurried into the kitchen, William shook his head, trying to steady himself. The interruption had left a strange feeling behind. He must have nodded off, dreaming again, but this one was unusual—an entire city collapsing right in front of his eyes.

The scene reminded him of black-and-white photographs of the demolition of the 1912 Spirit of Lewis and Clark Exposition—its grand, elaborate exhibits brought down by massive cranes, reduced to rubble, all except the Gateway of the Moors.

He pulled his dream journal from his backpack and began jotting down details before they faded. The city he'd seen didn't quite match the Expo. There had been a man in the dream—bald, with a long ponytail trailing down his back, his face familiar in a way William couldn't place. And there had been an entrance, too, framed by enormous metal doors, far larger than the Gateway of the Moors. He was still scribbling notes when Miss Rosa returned with a tray.

"Come sit with me, William. Let's chat."

He capped his pen, slid the journal into his backpack, and rose from the piano bench. Crossing the room, he sank into a plush armchair as she set the tray on the small table between them.

Rosa lifted a porcelain teapot from the tray, its surface painted in soft, impressionistic strokes—cool blues and muted greens blending into the faint suggestion of a woman seated at a piano. The matching teacups carried similar dreamlike scenes: moths circling a pale light, a solitary bird among leafless branches, a small sailboat gliding across shifting water, and a distant valley dotted with bell towers.

"These were Madeleine Monnier's," Rosa said, pouring oolong into William's cup. "Her husband commissioned the set for her. The artist worked in the Belle Époque style—very much in the spirit of the Impressionists she admired."

"This belonged to… Madeleine Monnier?" William asked, his voice catching.

"Oh yes," Rosa said. "It was a cherished gift."

William lifted his cup. The sailboat, painted along its side, leaned into a breeze, its white sail catching a breath of wind against a clear blue sky.

In the quiet that followed, they sipped their tea while the storm outside eased into a steady drizzle and the fire's warmth filled the room. Misha emerged from her hiding place and leapt onto William's lap, purring as she curled against him. He stroked her fur, answering her soft meows with quiet words.

Rosa set down her cup. "William, I'm getting older. My health isn't what it used to be. I teach only a handful of students now, and I stopped taking new ones years ago—until you walked through my door. I had an inner nudge to make an exception for you."

She glanced toward the window, where the rain had softened to a mist. "I need someone to continue the legacy of Piano Zen." She paused, turning back toward him. "And I believe that someone… might be you."

William's grip tightened on his teacup. "Me? But I've only been studying for a little while. I've only finished the first lesson book. I—I can't even…"

Rosa raised a hand to calm him. She walked to the French doors leading to the balcony, watching the rain slip down the glass.

"Yes, of course, you still have much to learn. And this isn't something you have to decide now." She turned back. "The piano will show you what's possible, in its own time."

"I don't…" William rubbed the back of his neck. "Teaching Piano Zen? I'm not that good yet."

Rosa's brow lifted. "Oh, William… you've learned more than you realize. And one day, you'll grow even more by helping someone else."

William hunched his shoulders.

"And I'm not saying you're done with your studies," she added. "Quite the opposite. You must go deeper than ever. But there will come a time when you're ready… and when that time comes, I hope you'll say yes." Rosa took another sip. "I don't want this talk of the future to overshadow what you've accomplished. You completed the first Piano Zen lesson book. That's not easy to do in one year." She set her teacup down. "Come, let's head to the piano and get started."

William took one last sip of tea and gave Misha a scratch behind the ears before moving to the piano bench. The cat stayed curled in his chair, now a warm, cozy nest.

# Chapter Forty-Six

## *Turning the Page*

William sat on the piano bench with the demoiselle cranes carved into its legs and took a slow breath. He opened his Piano Zen lesson book for the last time—the one Rosa had given him at his very first lesson. For months, its familiar illustrations had watched over his practice like quiet companions. How strange, he thought, that the same places and faces from its pages had been showing up in his dreams this past year—the flying monkey, the bear with the drum, the resplendent quetzal. Sometimes it felt as if the book had wandered into his dreams... or his dreams had wandered into the book.

Rosa rubbed her hands together. "Well, you've made it through every piece in the first Piano Zen book. That's a milestone. You're ready to start Book Two. Before we peek at that, are there any songs you'd like to play from Book One?"

"'Ode to Joy'?" William asked.

"Of course."

He turned to the page. The piano arrangement filled the right-hand page, and on the left were the Piano Zen lyrics beside his favorite illustration in the book—an ethereal, winged woman drifting along the margin of the poem. Ode to Joy was the only place that illustration appeared.

He began the piece, quietly humming. When the last chord faded, Rosa leaned gently on the piano lid.

"Very musical, William. And your phrasing was so expressive."

Through the French doors, a soft beam of sunlight broke through the rain clouds as Rosa stroked her chin thoughtfully. "Tell me, what would you think about giving a little informal recital here at the Gate Lodge? All your Book One pieces. Nothing formal—just your mom and a few friends."

William hesitated. "Oh, I don't know. I've… I've never done anything like that. I don't think so, not yet."

"Of course," Rosa said warmly. "Whenever you're ready, just let me know."

Relieved, William turned back to his lesson book and chose "Inner Sojourn." Just as he was about to begin, the studio door opened, and his mother stepped inside.

"Bonjour, Aimée," Rosa said. "Come, sit. We're almost finished. William is about to play 'Inner Sojourn'."

"Bien sûr," his mother replied, settling on the couch. "I love that one." Misha hopped down from the armchair and curled into Aimée's lap, purring as she stroked the cat's cheeks.

"Inner Sojourn" had always been William's favorite piece as well. He loved its flowing, river-like motion but also because it had been composed by Madeleine Monnier. Whenever he played it, he felt the famous pianist reaching through time to communicate with him.

He placed his hands on the keys, grounding himself in Earth through each contact point, welcoming the open mind of Air, letting Water carry the music forward, and calling upon the quiet Fire within to give it voice.

The first chord clusters rang out like a gong. Eyes closed, he let the melody flow as it wished, winding like a mountain stream around polished stones. When the final note faded, he opened his eyes.

Rosa and his mother sat motionless for a moment, as if holding the last traces of the sound. Then they exchanged a glance and broke into applause.

Rosa rose to her feet. "That was beautiful, William, such expressive playing."

"Mon chéri, c'est magnifique!" his mother exclaimed, rising to embrace him.

William grinned, the tingling energy of the piece still alive in his fingertips.

"Aimée, why don't you join me in the kitchen for some tea?" Rosa said. "I'd like to catch up and talk about a few things, if that's all right. William, give us a few minutes. I'm sure Misha would love having you all to herself."

"Okay," he responded.

The two women disappeared into the kitchen, their faint conversation drifting back to him—now and then catching his name mentioned.

Misha leapt up beside him, pressing her head against his arm until he gave her a scratch between the ears.

His Piano Zen lesson book still rested on the music rack. He lifted it carefully and turned the pages one by one—past scales and theory, improvisations and repertoire—each brightened by the whimsical illustrations of the monkey, the bear, and the bird in far-off, dreamlike places. They had been his companions, keeping him company through long hours of practice.

But now he was ready for the next step. Book Two—thicker, more demanding, and with no pictures. A small part of him felt like Christopher Robin leaving the Hundred Acre Wood, knowing it was time to say goodbye to his animal friends.

As he closed the book, his mother returned from the kitchen. He slipped Book One into his backpack and tucked Book Two beside it. They both said goodbye to Miss Rosa and headed home.

Aimée softly hummed a musical phrase from "Inner Sojourn" as the weathered white Trailblazer wound its way down from Imperial Heights along the curves of Madeleine Way.

William sat quietly, eyes on the passing trees.

Then, from out of nowhere, an image flashed in his mind—bright fabric against green pines, a shape from somewhere deep in his memory.

His brow furrowed. "Mom… um…?"

"What is it, Willy?"

"Ah, did we ever own a big… orange tent?"

Aimée's humming stopped. "*Excusez-moi?*"

"A big orange… tent," he repeated.

She glanced at him, an unreadable shift crossing her face. "*Quoi…* wh—where did that come from?"

"I'm not sure. It just popped into my head. Like I could see it—a huge orange tent beside the Trailblazer, only the Trailblazer looked new, not rusted out."

The hum of the tires and the steady sweep of the wiper blades filled the car as a silent moment stretched between them. Near the large Sitka spruce at the end of Madeleine Way, Aimée eased the SUV to a stop.

Her hands stayed on the wheel, eyes fixed ahead. Her voice was quieter, almost careful. "The orange tent… what made you think of that?"

"Do we still have one?" William asked. "I'm just curious."

Aimée's fingers tightened slightly on the wheel. "Yes. But it's been in storage since you were a toddler. You remember it?"

William nodded. "Yeah. When I walked out of the Gate Lodge just now, I saw the Trailblazer next to the pine trees, and this image of the tent just flashed in my mind. It was so clear."

Aimeé's chest tightened.

She had nearly forgotten about the tent herself. Over the years, she had sold off most of Phillip's camping gear, but for reasons she never fully understood, she could never bring herself to part with the orange tent. It had been their companion on so many adventures. A piece of their life before.

A memory surfaced—one of their many camping trips together. Rain drumming against the orange fabric, the soft glow of a lantern flickering inside. She nursed baby William in the quiet warmth of that tent, then later watched Phillip—always playful, always lighthearted—make some quip about how she was in charge of one end of the baby while he managed the other.

Then, without warning, the weight of it all—long buried—came crashing through her. It was as if the tent had been ripped open, unfurling itself.

She turned her face away, toward the side window, pressing a trembling hand to her lips.

"Mom…?"

Her shoulders shook, and tears spilled uncontrollably down her cheeks.

"I'm sorry, Mom. I just remembered it, that's all. I didn't mean to—"

He reached over and put his arm around her. She buried her face in his shoulder, softly sobbing. He tightened his arm around her, unsure what else to do.

They stayed like that for a moment, the car idling beneath a looming spruce, a touch of rain tapping softly against the windshield.

With a deep breath, she pulled back, wiping her eyes and letting out a small, shaky laugh. "Oh, *mon dieu*," she said. "I don't know what came over me."

William returned her smile.

He watched the wipers sweep back and forth across the window in a slow steady rhythm. The synchronized movement played on his thoughts, sparking an idea—a perfect way to shift the mood.

"I was thinking about something Miss Rosa said. You know what, I'd like to put on a little piano recital for you. And maybe a few friends."

His mother wiped away the last of her tears. "Ah… really, *mon chéri?*" She exhaled. "Of course, that sounds like a wonderful idea. Is that something you truly want to do?"

"Yeah," William said, almost surprised at himself. "I wasn't planning to, but now I want to." He glanced out the window. "Last week, Professor Montgomery took me to the Memorial Hall at the Samaritan Temple. I got a chance to play on the grand piano. I'll ask him if I could give my recital there."

His mother arched a brow. "Do they allow that sort of thing? What would it cost?"

"I have no idea," William said, "but I'll ask him. If it's too expensive, I could just play my recital in the Gate Lodge. Miss Rosa already offered it."

"That's good to know," she said, her voice steadier. "Maybe I could bake something for it, one of my old dessert recipes." She put the Trailblazer back in gear, turned off Madeleine Way, and drove toward home.

# Chapter Forty-Seven

## *The Dreamers of Dreams*

William called Professor Montgomery, his first step toward turning the idea of a recital into reality. He left a message to ask if Memorial Hall at the Samaritan Temple might be available.

Several days later, Montgomery's voice greeted him on his phone.

*"I got your message, Will. Memorial Hall is undergoing some remodeling work and won't be available. But I've thought of an alternative that might interest you. Meet me this Saturday at noon—at the Lady of Light."*

William's stomach tightened. Memorial Hall had been the dream—the Bösendorfer Imperial Grand beneath his fingers, the same stage where Miss Rosa once performed. It seemed almost too perfect. How could another stage measure up to that? At least the Professor had another option—one he thought worth teasing.

That Saturday, William headed for the copper statue, curiosity alive with what the Professor might suggest. Montgomery was already there, waiting for him on a bench facing the Makah River.

They greeted each other as William settled in beside him.

"I've been thinking about your recital idea, Will. I mentioned it to Winston over dinner, and the question of another venue came up. He had a great idea."

Before Montgomery could finish, a voice called out, "Monty, William, hello!" Winston McFarland approached, lifting a hand in greeting. He carried an effortless charm in his smile, impeccably dressed as always—a navy double-breasted blazer, a charcoal-and-gray silk scarf draped loosely around his neck, and alligator-patterned gloves tucked neatly into his pocket.

His smile widened as he took William's hand in a firm shake, giving his shoulder a friendly squeeze.

"Ah, Will—nice to see you again, my boy. How are those lessons with Rosa Carreño coming along?"

"I just finished my first Piano Zen book," William said. "Miss Rosa already gave me volume two."

"Splendid. Monty hasn't stopped talking about that performance of yours in Memorial Hall. Said he saw the hall fill with colors—the same way it did when Rosa played. My, my. Impressive. He tells me you've got a rare gift."

William's cheeks warmed. "But I'm just a beginner. Miss Rosa is much more advanced than—"

Montgomery lifted a hand, gently interrupting. "Beginner or not, Will, you play from the heart. That's rarer than you think."

Winston set his hands on his hips. "So, Monty tells me you're looking for a place for your recital?"

"Yes," William said. "It's nothing big. Just a small gathering for my mom and Miss Rosa, maybe a few friends. Rosa said I could use her home if I want."

"Hmm... interesting." Winston glanced at Montgomery, who was wearing a smile that spread slowly across his face.

"Well, you *could* use the Gate Lodge..." Winston let the pause stretch, then added, "but why not go a little further up the road?"

"I'm not sure I follow... 'further up the road'?"

"I'm saying you should give your recital in the music room of the Prescott Mansion."

William blinked, swallowing hard. "The Prescott Mansion? Wait—what?"

"Of course. Why not? My sisters are putting the finishing touches on it before the grand opening. Imagine it, Will—a private tour of the mansion, and then your concert as the finale."

William froze. A chill crawled up his spine. He drew a quick breath. "I... I don't know. Playing a concert in the Prescott Mansion..." He stood speechless.

"Nothing to worry about," Montgomery assured him. "It can be casual if you like. And you can invite whomever you want—your mom, Miss Rosa, any close friends."

Before William could respond, Winston cut in. "Really, Monty? Casual attire in the Prescott Mansion?"

Winston's eyes twinkled. "Tell me, Will, have you ever worn a tux?"

William shook his head. "No."

"Well," Winston said, leaning in conspiratorially, "this might be the perfect occasion—a formal recital in the Prescott Mansion, you in a tux. What do you say, old chap?"

For a second he saw himself inside that mansion, giving the concert in a tuxedo. A rush of excitement caught him by surprise, and before he had time to think it all through, he said, "Yes… let's do it."

Winston grinned. "Excellent. I know the owner of a formal wear shop in the Emerald District. I'll take care of everything. What do you think, Monty? Are you on board with all of this?"

Montgomery dipped his head. "Indubitably, Mr. McFarland."

The two men burst into laughter and launched into playful debate over who would cut the finer figure in formal wear.

When the ribbing faded, Montgomery turned to William. "You see, Will, the McFarland Sisters Company asked for my help with the mansion's restoration. I've shared historical records, photographs, even some of my grandfather's architectural notes. They want visitors to understand the mansion's significance—its place in the legacy of Randolph Cornelius Prescott, from his rise as a business magnate in Nightingale to the philanthropic work that defined his later years."

"And let's not forget the most important detail," Winston added. "There's a grand, oval-shaped music room where you can perform. Very French in style—you'll fit right in wearing your tux, my good fellow. Crystal chandeliers, oak parquet floors, and crown molding. There's even a harp. But the real treasure is the centerpiece: an Érard concert grand piano."

William's eyes widened. "Wait—would that be Madeleine Monnier's piano? Miss Rosa told me about it on our hike."

"Why, yes," Winston said, delighted by the recognition. "Fully restored by a French piano technician." He leaned toward Montgomery and murmured, "Cost a fortune. Had to fly the chap over first class from Paris."

William's pulse quickened. For the past year, he'd devoured every scrap of Madeleine Monnier's history he could find. The thought of playing her piano felt unreal.

"Now, picture this," Winston said. "Before the recital, Monty and I take you and your mother on a private tour of the mansion. You'll be the first official guests of the museum."

William nodded, excitement rising again. "Yes… that sounds great."

"Brilliant! Let's plan for next Tuesday. Check with your mom. The mansion will be empty that evening, just the staff outside finishing the landscaping."

William hesitated, his eyes lifting to the burning flame of the statue's lamp, sparking his imagination. Slowly, a plan began to take shape in his mind.

After a long pause, Montgomery tilted his head. "What's wrong, Will?"

"Actually… you know what?" William said. "I don't want to tell my mom yet. I want to surprise her."

Winston's eyes sparkled with delight. He clapped his hands together. "Well now! Surprise your mother with it all? How delicious. What do you think, Monty?"

Montgomery chuckled. "I think it's a wonderful idea, Will. Consider us in on it. What's your plan?"

William stared at the ground, gathering his thoughts. "I'll tell her it's just for her and Miss Rosa at the Gate Lodge. Keep it simple."

Montgomery gave a small approving nod. "Not bad. But how will you explain the formal dress? That would be unusual for a little recital at your teacher's house."

William furrowed his brow. "You're right." He thought for a moment, then snapped his fingers. "I'll tell her I'm taking her to a fancy restaurant after the performance. That way, she'll have a reason to dress up."

Winston's face lit up. "Ah, excellent. A clever deception! I like it."

"But how would you pay for such an expensive dinner, Will?" Montgomery asked gently.

William hesitated. "Hmm… yeah, I don't have enough money for that… but I'll tell her I earned it helping you set up and take down your equipment all summer."

"Will, I've offered you money every time, and you've declined it."

"Yes… but my mom doesn't know that."

Winston chuckled. "The plot thickens. Very clever, Will."

"So, when my mom and I drive up to Miss Rosa's house and —"

Winston waved a hand at once. "No, no, no, my dear boy—that won't do at all! I wouldn't dream of having your mother drive up for something like this. That is not how one makes an entrance at the Prescott mansion. I'll send a limousine. Leave the transportation to me."

William blinked. "A… limo?"

"Of course!" Winston said, as if it were the most obvious thing in the world.

William shifted, uneasy. "But… uh… how do I explain *that* extra expense without her suspecting anything?"

"You're a bright young man, Will," Winston said, tapping a finger to his temple. "I've no doubt you'll come up with something clever."

William sighed, rubbing the back of his neck. "I guess I'll think of… something."

Winston rested his hand on Montgomery's shoulder. "Oh, this is going to be marvelous. The suspense, the surprise—your mother will be absolutely enchanted!"

Montgomery smirked. "A formal event at the mansion. Hmm… that brings back some memories, doesn't it, Winston?"

"Oh yes. No one entertained like the Prescotts."

Winston glanced at his watch. "I must dash—big plans for the upcoming Blues Festival. But, Will—this recital? It's going to be memorable. I look forward to it."

As Winston strode away, William exhaled, shaking his head in disbelief.

Montgomery rose, adjusting his trilby hat, and unfurled his cane. "Time for me to go as well."

William looked at him, somewhat dazed. "Did this just happen, Professor? Is this… real? The mansion, Monnier's piano? It feels like something out of my dream journal."

Montgomery just smiled and patted his shoulder. "See you next Tuesday, Will."

# Chapter Forty-Eight

## *The Ride Awaits*

William called Miss Rosa to share the secret plan—the one that had quickly snowballed with help from Professor Montgomery and Winston McFarland.

"Oh my, William," she said as soon as he finished. "I'm… surprised. You brushed off my idea of a little recital in my studio, and now you're planning one in the Prescott Mansion?" A soft laugh followed. "But I think it's wonderful. Truly. And this idea of surprising your mother? That's beautiful."

"Really?" William asked, relief loosening his shoulders.

"Of course. It sounds exactly like something Anthony and Winston would dream up—but hearing you take the lead makes me very proud." She paused. "Now then… who's invited?"

"Well… you and my mom, Professor Montgomery, Winston, Hadiya from Sweet Muejanat, and Lina Bauch from Shelley's. A small group. Just enough so I don't get too nervous."

In the days that followed, he carefully selected and ordered his pieces from the Piano Zen lesson book. He would begin with "Life is But a Dream," invite everyone to sing along on "Ode to Joy," and close with "Inner Sojourn."

As he adhered small colored tabs along the page edges, he heard Miss Rosa's steady reminder: no matter how simple the song, make sure it says something. Let every note carry your whole heart.

He tried to hold to that advice, yet he couldn't help wondering where his mind would be once the spotlight was on him. Would he get nervous when he walked into the music room and sat down at Monnier's piano? Would all those hours of practice disappear the instant his fingers touched the keys? With doubt beginning to gather, he opened his dresser drawer and chose not one, as he usually did, but three of his favorite basalt stones, setting them on the desk. They had always helped steady him. Later, he would slip them into the pocket of his tuxedo pants for reassurance.

Fortunately, he had a distraction from his rising performance anxiety—the surprise. Keeping the true location of the recital hidden from his mother was a challenge of its own, and not an easy sell.

Still, he gathered himself and approached her. "So, I talked with Miss Rosa," he began casually. "She said Tuesday night at her home would be fine for the two of us to stop by. I have all my music together."

"*C'est* super, Willy," Aimée said. "Is there anyone else you want me to invite?"

"Ah… no, Mom. I… I might get too nervous. Just you and… um… Miss Rosa."

"*Bien*. Of course."

He paused, searching for courage, then pressed on. "There's something else I want to do. Something, ah… special."

"Special? What do you mean?"

William felt himself tense. He drew a breath. "I want to take you out to eat after the performance."

Her eyes softened. "That's so sweet, *mon chéri*. But I should be the one taking you out. Let me treat you to La Luz Café. It's one of my favorites—very *français*. A little pricey, but we deserve it. I'll call and make a reservation."

"No, Mom," he said quickly. "I—I already made reservations for us at La Dordogne."

Aimée's brows lifted. "Willy, La Dordogne? *Ooh là là…* that place is outrageously expensive…"

"Yeah, but…" William cut in gently. "You told me Grand-mère Giselle used to take you there when you were little. You and Grand-mère are from Sarlat-la-Canéda—I thought maybe it would feel special."

She gave a half-laugh, half-sigh, shaking her head as she set her hands on her hips. Almost thinking aloud, she went on, "Special, perhaps, once upon a time. But that was years ago. These days, they live off their reputation, and that silly *faux décor français*—pfft! You can hardly even call their menu French anymore." She exaggerated the word French with an American twang. "If Grand-mère Giselle still lived here and wanted to treat us, *bien sûr*. But not you, William. *Mon Dieu.* No."

"Please, Mom." His voice cracked, almost pleading. "I want us to dress up, formal, and go out somewhere nice. Just once."

"Absolutely not," she said firmly. "I don't have the money for that, and you certainly don't…"

"I have money," he blurted out. "I've been helping Professor Montgomery all summer—setting up his equipment, taking it down. He paid me a lot… more than he should have, and I've been saving. I wanted… I just want to do something special for you."

A tightness gathered in his throat as he fought back tears.

"Oh, Willy," she whispered, the sharpness draining from her face. "I'm so sorry, *mon chéri…*" She exhaled slowly. "All right. All right. You can take me out for dinner—just not La Dordogne. Any place but there."

He sniffed and nodded quickly. "Okay, La Luz instead. But we have to dress formal."

She raised an eyebrow. "At La Luz? Fine… but people don't usually dress formally there. You can, of course, but that would be a little silly…"

"Well, I've already rented a tuxedo," William confessed.

"*Quoi?*" Aimée pressed a hand to her forehead. "You rented a tuxedo? Why? *Mais enfin*, Willy, it's so expensive. A shirt and tie would be fine for *La Luz.* Just call tomorrow morning and cancel it."

He shook his head, resolve settling in. "No, Mom. Too late. We're going formal. I'm going to play my recital at Miss Rosa's, and then I want to take you out to dinner. That's my plan."

Aimée studied him—the serious set of his jaw, the glimmer of determination in his eyes. He looked so much like Phillip in that moment it made her chest ache. Outlandish, impractical, utterly impossible—but somehow beautiful. She swallowed the lump rising in her throat and nodded.

"Yes, dear. Dinner and a show," she said softly. "That sounds lovely."

William breathed a quiet sigh of relief. At last, the plan was set.


When Tuesday finally arrived, William slipped into his tuxedo, caressing the crisp lapels before tucking a white silk handkerchief into the breast pocket. He studied his reflection in the mirror and almost didn't recognize the boy staring back. For a brief moment, it felt as though he had stepped into another version of himself—a concert pianist, like Madeleine Monnier before a big performance.

Down the hall, his mother emerged from her room, dressed in a stunning black, full-length gown. The sleeveless dress had a scoop neckline adorned with rhinestones that shimmered under the light. A delicate, sheer panel traced along the sides of the gown, giving it an understated sophistication. Her long brown hair had been brushed into loose, polished waves that fell gracefully over her shoulders.

William had never seen her look so elegant. For a moment, he could only stare.

"Wow," he said. "You look…"

"Different?" she said with a playful smirk.

"Incredible," he said.

She laughed. "Well, this is certainly a change from our usual evenings. Shall we get going?"

And then, as if on cue, the doorbell rang.

At first, William barely registered it.

Then panic shot through him. *The limo.* He'd forgotten about the limo. He was supposed to come up with a story for his mother—and now it was too late.

Before he could even pull his thoughts together, his mother was already at the door. She opened it to reveal a chauffeur in a crisp black suit, cap perched neatly on his head.

"Excuse me," the man said. "Is this the Emerson residence?"

"Ah… yes, it is."

"I'm here to escort the Emerson family to the Gate Lodge for a concert, and afterward, dinner at La Luz Café."

Aimée blinked at him, eyebrows lifting high. She turned back into the house.

"William Longfellow Emerson," she called, "come here, *si vous* plait, and explain *what* is going on?"

William peeked around the corner, sheepish. "Um… oh yes. Our ride for tonight. I'm glad it's finally here."

"Our ride…" Aimée repeated slowly. "Did you say?" There was a beat of silence as she tried to process the situation. "Sir, could you give me a moment with my son?"

"Of course, madame. I'll wait outside."

Aimée closed the door and turned toward William.

"I, uh… thought it would be better if we rode in a limo tonight," he said, hunching his shoulders, aiming for casual confidence.

Her eyes narrowed. "William. *Mon Dieu*! What have you done?"

He scrambled. "Don't worry, Mom. I—I borrowed some money from Professor Montgomery to pay for it. I told him I'd keep helping him at Marrakech West the rest of the season. He said it was fine."

"You borrowed money from Monsieur Montgomery to rent a limousine?" Her tone sharpened. "No. No, I'm not buying this. Not one bit, William Emerson. Start explaining what is going on here—"

"Just for today, Mom," he blurted, desperation edging his voice. "Please. No more questions. Just for today, okay? Don't worry. I just wanted tonight to be special. You do so much for me, and I—" His voice faltered. "I just wanted to make it special."

For a long moment they stared at each other. Aimée felt her resistance ebb. She didn't understand how her son had managed all this, but she understood that look. With a quiet breath, she let herself be carried along, the way she once had with another dreamer she'd loved.

"Très bien," she said softly. "We're doing this."

They started toward the door together, but she noticed something. "Willy—your backpack. If you're going to all this trouble, don't forget your music."

William let out a shaky laugh. "Oh! Yeah—almost forgot. My Piano Zen book." He dashed down the hall to grab it.

Aimée steadied herself, straightening her posture. She turned toward the hallway mirror, adjusting a loose curl and smoothing her makeup. Stepping back, she let her weight shift as her figure eased into a model-like pose. Her fingers traced the curve of her waist, and for the first time in years, a sly grin crossed her lips.

The sound of William's footsteps pulled her out of the mirror. He hurried down the hall, slipping his Piano Zen book into his backpack.

Aimée lifted the fine silver chain of her *minaudière* over her shoulder, letting it settle lightly against her hip. She looped her arm through William's, and together they stepped out into the cool evening air.

A dark, polished limousine waited in the driveway, its surface catching the last colors of the setting sun as it stood ready to take them up into the hills of Imperial Heights.

# Chapter Forty-Nine

## *The Wizard's Stone*

Though William now carried himself with confidence at the piano, it hadn't always been that way. Months earlier, a single experience had shaken his faith in everything—his abilities, his progress, even whether he was truly meant for this musical path.

It had been a week much like any other—until winter crashed into Nightingale with sudden ferocity, and everything seemed to unravel at once. A freezing windstorm swept through the city, toppling trees and cutting power. His mother's house was among those left in eerie darkness, silence broken only by the howl of the wind at the windows. Bundled in his coat, William tried to practice for his upcoming piano lesson, but the cold stiffened his fingers. Each note felt sluggish, uncooperative. The ease and flow he'd worked so hard to master deserted him, and with them his fragile confidence. *Maybe Cecil Winwood was right,* he thought. *Maybe piano really isn't my thing.*

Still, something deeper urged him on. Skipping a Piano Zen lesson wasn't an option. He owed that much to Rosa—and to himself.

As they prepared to leave for his lesson, another setback hit—the old Trailblazer wouldn't start. It had never happened before; it always roared to life without trouble. His mother's brow furrowed in disbelief. The battery wasn't that old, so she knew it couldn't be the problem. Still, she searched for a neighbor with jumper cables but had no luck.

She hesitated, weighing whether to keep him home in the bitter weather, but William's persistence won out. With a resigned sigh, she called a cab, knowing how much he cherished his lessons—and his visits with Miss Rosa's cat, Misha.

When the cab finally dropped him at the Gate Lodge, William carefully made his way up the frozen walkway. Miss Rosa greeted him at the door, leaning on a cane.

"My word, William. You actually made it here? Everyone else canceled today."

"Almost didn't. The car wouldn't start, but I convinced my mom to call a cab."

"Oh, I see. I'm surprised any were still running after that storm last night." She sighed, then added, "Please, come in out of the cold."

She shut the door and hobbled beside him.

"Are you okay?" William asked. "What happened?"

"I was shoveling the walkway this morning, just in case any students showed up. Slipped on the ice and twisted my ankle."

"I'm so sorry."

"Oh, don't worry. I'll be fine. Just a little tweak."

"Are you out of power too?" William asked.

"Yes. Went out in the middle of the night. The Gate Lodge was freezing when I woke up." A fire crackled in the hearth, its dry wood popping sharply in the quiet studio. "At least the fireplace still works."

The heat took the edge off the cold but not enough. William kept his coat on, rubbing his hands together. His gaze fell on a small kettle carefully suspended in the flames.

"The water should be boiling by now," Rosa said, nodding toward the hearth. She raised her cane slightly. "Be a dear and fetch it with the oven mitt. I'll set out the cocoa."

William lifted the kettle carefully and carried it into the kitchen. Rosa set two sturdy mugs on the counter. She scooped in the cocoa while he poured the steaming water. The aroma rose up at once, rich and comforting. She handed him a mug, then took her own with her free hand.

"Come," she said, gesturing toward the studio. "Take a seat at the piano. Warm up those fingers a little while the hot chocolate cools, it's still quite hot."

William set his mug on a coaster bearing the image of a lotus blossom. He unzipped his backpack and reached for his Piano Zen book—except it wasn't there. Empty. His stomach dropped. He never forgot his lesson book. Not once.

He cleared his throat, cheeks warming. "Um… Miss Rosa, do you have a spare copy I could use today?"

"Of course. I always keep extra copies on hand."

Shaking it off, he placed his hands on the keys and attempted to run a few scales, but it was no use. His fingers were sluggish, unresponsive. His hands felt stiff, disconnected—as if the piano itself were resisting him. No matter how hard he tried, the notes just wouldn't come together.

Then he noticed something else was missing. Misha hadn't come to greet him. A knot of concern tightened in his chest. The Himalayan cat always greeted him.

"Where's Misha?"

"She isn't feeling well," Rosa said, carefully setting her mug aside. "I took her to the vet yesterday. Nothing serious—probably a little flu bug. She's been curled up on my bed all morning. Maybe she'll come down later." Rosa let out a hearty laugh. "This just feels like one of those days where you wonder if you should've stayed in bed."

William nodded, pressing the hot mug between his palms, trying to drive the chill from his fingers. He tried a sip, but it almost burned his lips.

"Careful—give the cocoa a few more minutes," Rosa said as she hobbled to the shelf to retrieve the Tibetan bowl. But her balance faltered. The heavy vessel slipped from her hands and struck the floor with a loud, jarring clang.

William sprang from the piano bench, scooped it up, and pulled a chair over for her.

"Thank you… I'm okay," Rosa assured him, though she lowered herself into the seat carefully, releasing a deep sigh.

She offered a wry chuckle. "Let's try to get things back on track. We'll start with a short relaxation session. You know the drill: take a seat on the piano bench, close your eyes, and rest your hands on your legs, palms up."

Soon, the steady, resonant hum of the Tibetan bowl filled the room as Rosa traced its rim with the mallet. Usually, the sound grounded him, softening his thoughts. But today, it barely registered. William's mind wouldn't settle. His thoughts darted everywhere—scattered, restless, and out of control.

William's nose wrinkled before his eyes even opened. A sour, rank stench hung in the air, like refuse left to bake too long in the sun. It seeped into his lungs, making him wince. When he finally opened his eyes, he found himself on a bench in a park gone to ruin. Weeds clawed through cracked pavement, branches lay scattered, the grass brittle and brown. Rust spread across the play structures like an infection.

And yet… there was something about this place that felt disturbingly familiar. He had seen it before—though where, he couldn't quite recall. A dream, perhaps?

As he wandered around, parts of the city reminded him of Parthenopolis—but stripped of its brilliance. Here, the marble was cracked, the columns broken, the streets choked with weeds. It was like walking through the bones of the Roman Empire after its fall. The air was thick with neglect, the silence heavy. Once-magnificent structures lay cannibalized, their stones pried loose and repurposed—as if the city itself had been dismantled piece by piece.

And yet something stirred in him—something older than the image of ruins. He had been here before. Not in waking life but in a place between memory and dream—riding a ribbon of light, a current of time, witnessing a city bathed first in glory and then in ruin.

Then it surfaced—Ning Jing's treehouse, the Dream Dorje in his hand, the current pulling him through history. The Kingdom of Zarashad in Ulandia. Yes, now he remembered. But this time, it wasn't a vision. He was standing in it.

A piercing screech split the stillness. William's head snapped upward. Two dark shadows wheeled above, circling in the gray sky. He recognized them instantly—Phobos and Deimos, the golden eagles.

A chill ran down his spine, his stomach knotting. He slipped beneath the cover of a ruined building. The eagles circled once overhead before finally drifting away.

There were people present but they moved like shadows, shuffling forward with bent backs, their eyes cast down as though afraid to meet the light. Now and then, a hollow face turned toward him—cheekbones sharp, mouths slack, expressions emptied of life. The air itself seemed to mourn.

A large temple loomed before him, its columns weathered and strained, bearing the weight of ages. The structure reminded him of the Praetorium in Parthenopolis, though this one was drained of majesty, its stones pale and weary.

From the darkness beneath the temple's portico, a figure emerged, the folds of a deep red cloak dragging across the stone like spilled wine—Florestan. Beneath the hood, his shadowed face appeared aged, pocked, worn.

As he stepped into the light, Florestan stared in disbelief at the sight of William before him. He froze, as though struggling to reconcile what he was seeing. Then, with a swift recovery, his lips curved into a smile that didn't reach his eyes.

He pushed back his hood. The vision shifted—gone was the damaged face William had glimpsed. In its place stood a vibrant, distinguished man, features sharp, his bearing unnervingly poised, almost regal.

But William trusted his eyes this time.

From the darkness behind Florestan came the sound of shuffling. He angled his head sharply to one side and thrust up his right hand. His voice rasped like gravel as he barked, "Wait." Then, "Well now." Florestan's voice faltered before smoothing into silken tones. "The Little Prince himself. You've lost your way, n'est-ce pas? What an… unexpected pleasure this is."

He paced a few steps, his cloak caressing the rubble of marble. "I confess, when my eagles brought word of your arrival, I thought they were mistaken." A hoarse chuckle escaped through his words. "But here you are. My, my— what to do?" Florestan stroked his chin, eyes narrowing as he studied William's face. "You've caught me at a disadvantage, I must admit. That's a rare thing indeed. Had I known you were coming, I might have arranged a… warmer welcome. Cleared the streets, set things in order."

He made a gracious gesture. "Still—what a gift. To have you delivered to me like this, here of all places. Zarashad." He pressed his right hand to his chest, bowing slightly. "I can't even begin to tell you how grateful I am."

William caught it then—a twitch in Florestan's left hand, sharp and involuntary.

With a faint tilt of his head, Florestan summoned them. From the dark mouth of the temple came Typhon the Tiger, Cerberus the Crocodile, and Gorgon the Grizzly.

Florestan gestured toward them. "You remember my animal friends."

Gorgon and Typhon stared hard at William, unblinking, while Cerberus opened his snout with a raspy hiss.

Florestan lifted his right forearm, and a golden eagle descended, landing in perfect silence. "This is Deimos," he said. "He has exceptionally keen eyesight—he's the one who alerted me to your presence."

Deimos let out a piercing shriek, making William recoil. A moment later, a second golden eagle swept down, alighting on a nearby weathered statue— perching on the outstretched sword of a general astride his battle horse.

"Ah, yes," Florestan said with a graceful motion toward the newcomer, "and this is his twin brother, Phobos."

Phobos gave no acknowledgment—not even a glance in William's direction.

"My friends," Florestan murmured, "pay your respects to our visitor."

The eagles stayed rigid, eyes fixed elsewhere.

Florestan shrugged. "Forgive their demeanor—being a friend of Nasim and all." His smile thinned. "What she did to their father, Ares, was quite a pity. He was also… my favorite." Florestan motioned toward the other predators. "Truth is, all of us here have our issues with that Wind Spirit. Certainly no fault of yours, though. Alas—bygones. Please, come inside the temple. Rest your weary bones a while. I have some secrets I wish to share… things you may find interesting."

William's eyes moved across the square of Zarashad. He had seen this place before—in a time-travel vision. But other fragments with Florestan drifted up as well: the wounded demoiselle crane, the jungle meeting, the wizard's stone. All of it converging here.

Fear crept in, tightening around his thoughts. His gaze snapped back to Florestan—who was staring at him, stone cold, expressionless. Then, with unnerving ease, Florestan's face softened into a smile, his voice dripping into a musical lilt. "Don't worry. I won't keep you long."

William's eyes shifted nervously from beast to beast. He felt the tension building in the predators, like a piano wire wound too tight, ready to snap. He weighed his options. Running away was impossible; any sudden move would spark their instinct to hunt, no matter how much control Florestan appeared to have over them. All he could do now was play along—buy time, and hope for an escape.

At the top of the temple's steps, Florestan extended his right hand in invitation, his left twitching faintly at his side. William forced himself upward, into the darkness of the portico. The predators followed close behind, their bulk so near he could feel the hot dampness of their breath against his back.

Inside, William slowed his pace. Dim light seeped through unseen apertures near the ceiling, a pale wash of daylight revealing the sheer scale of the hall. His footsteps echoed off the stone, sharp in the stillness. Murals, once bright with life, now clung to the walls in faded shreds of color. Cracks ran like veins through the columns, as if the very bones of the temple were breaking. The mosaics beneath his feet lay in fragments, their beauty scattered like ashes, patterns lost to time. The air hung thick with dust and the faint breath of incense.

Phobos slipped into the shadows of an archway while Deimos swooped over William's head, the rush of his wings brushing his hair and forcing him to duck. Deimos rose and perched high in a vacant alcove where a statue once stood, his sharp gaze fixed below. He let out another piercing shriek, the sound amplified by the cavernous walls.

Typhon rumbled a growl deep in his throat. "Deimos wants to know if you brought your little flying monkey with you."

The crocodile slithered by, jaws parting in a hiss aimed at William.

Gorgon pressed closer, bumping into William hard enough to knock him over. He grumbled, "Cerebus thinks it's hiding in your backpack." Then the grizzly smirked. "Come to think of it, where's that mango-eating friend of yours? Soft as a teddy bear, that one."

Florestan's eyes narrowed on the predators, his jaw tightening. His voice cut through the growls and hisses. "My friends, enough. I need to speak with William—alone."

The predators didn't move. Gorgon pressed a massive claw onto William's backpack, the weight nearly toppling him over. "We want to see what's in his bag first."

Florestan flared, shooting an intense look at Gorgon. "I said… I need to talk with William. Alone."

Gorgon's head turned slowly toward Florestan. The grizzly dragged his tongue across his snout and rumbled, "Alright. We'll let you two have some… private time."

The three predators lumbered toward the exit.

Florestan looked upward and barked, "You two as well!"

From the alcoves, the golden eagles dove in a blur, wings slashing the air. William ducked as they flew past, talons grazing close before they streaked out through the temple columns, into the sepia-tinged light.

"My apologies, William," Florestan offered lightly. "Their manners leave much to be desired. I've been trying to give their social graces a little polish. But they are predators, after all. One can only expect so much."

With the animals gone, a wave of relief washed over William. But the reprieve was shallow. Florestan's eyes still pinned him, sharp and unblinking, and William knew the real danger hadn't lessened—it had only narrowed to a single opponent. He tried to steady his thoughts, searching for some advantage.

Then it struck him—the black obsidian stone. Was it still in his pocket? Waiting for Florestan's gaze to drift, he brushed his hand lightly against his pant leg. Yes. Still there. But what use was it? He'd never tried to wield its power; even touching it left his head swimming. For now, his only move was to listen… and wait.

"So, my friend, where do you hail from?" Florestan asked, his tone warmer. "I know most of the kingdoms in Ulandia, yet I cannot place your origin. Still, there's no mistaking it. You have the look of a Dream Traveler in training."

The question jolted William. How he'd arrived here—or from where he came—wasn't clear. "The Whispering Woods," he offered cautiously, though he wasn't sure it was true.

"Ah…" Florestan nodded. "The Hidden Forest, I see. A remote part of the Kingdom of Nemoris. Interesting. I'd never have guessed."

His eyes searched William's face, probing. "But maybe you really don't know for sure, do you, Dream Traveler?" he said, stroking his chin. "The currents between worlds can be quite disorienting."

Florestan drifted around him. "I'd help you untangle all of this, you know, but it appears your dear friend Nasim has wrapped a clever little shield around your mind to guard it from prying eyes. A clever trick. But of course, the tighter the seal, the harder it is for her to keep track of you. From the looks of things," he said, rubbing his chin, "I doubt anyone knows you're here."

Florestan's left hand twitched more rapidly. With a swift motion, he clasped his hands behind his back.

"If you are curious," he continued, "I hail from the Kingdom of Keshmara—our rivals call it the black sheep of the Seven Realms. Jealousy, mostly, for it was in Keshmara that the black obsidian was first drawn from the earth—the stone that smoldered with fire. Like the very shard I placed in your hand. Tell me, have you experimented with its magic yet?"

"Oh," William said, feigning surprise, "you mean… the Wizard's Stone?"

He reached into his pocket, his fingers brushing against the cool, angular volcanic glass. As he lifted it into his palm, a deep reddish glow flickered inside. As before, holding the stone sent a surge of energy through his body, leaving him lightheaded.

Florestan's eyes fixed on the obsidian, his lids half-lowered, lips parting as he drew in a slow breath, as if savoring an intoxicating aroma. "Yes… the flame of the obsidian. You are fortunate, my friend—more than you know. It only burns like that for those who can awaken its power."

For a long moment, Florestan stared at the smoldering red flame. Then his voice softened, almost as if speaking to himself.

"I was just a child when I first touched it. Deep within the mountains of Keshmara. An orphan—the smallest among a band of orphaned youths sent to the mines. In Keshmara, orphans learn darkness quickly. We were sent to seek the rare stone that held fire inside. And on the slim chance where fortune revealed a seam, we marked it, leaving the men to claim the delicate, precious gem.

"That day, the air had thickened with odorless gas. One by one, our lamps sputtered, then died. We were swallowed by blackness so absolute I couldn't see my own hands. The others panicked, fumbling in vain with their lamps. Some wailed, calling for mothers they had never known.

"But in that madness, I saw it. Buried beneath layers of rock… a faint, ever so faint, trace of ember-red light. I cried out, but they jeered at me for my foolishness, hallucinating in the face of certain death. Still—I knew what I had seen, and what it meant.

"I searched for my hammer and, in utter darkness, crawled to the cave wall. I struck, blow after blow, breaking away pieces of stone. The closer I came, the more I felt it calling to me. With each layer stripped away, the light grew stronger. Soon, the others saw it too.

"At last, with one final swing, the rock gave way, and the cave released a chunk of the black obsidian. I had heard the stories of the stone with fire inside—every child in Keshmara had—but legends are different in the telling. And many had died searching for it.

"When I wrapped my hand around the stone, the darkness split. A flame, crimson red and fierce, burst forth. The cavern blazed with light so sudden, the others shielded their eyes, blinded by its brilliance. But my eyes needed no adjustment. As they covered their faces and clung to one another in a chain, I carried the light before us, leading the way out of the mine. It saved us all from certain death."

For a moment, his eyes glazed. The strained smile slipped, and when he spoke again, it was not to William but to some imagined witness.

"And there I was… a child with the stone burning in my hand, lighting the path. The Orphan-Master knew what I had done—what I was. Even in Keshmara, such power with the stone was rare. Years of practice were meant to unlock what came to me at once, almost without trying."

His voice lowered. "The orphans, even the ones I called friends, were beaten and sent back into the dark. But I was not. They plucked me from the mines and carried me to the schools, where the secrets of the stone are guarded jealously. No one in Keshmara shares them. All know better.

"Artists of the Stone, we called ourselves. But to everyone else? Wizards of Keshmara—forever wandering the Seven Realms, displaying our arts for their amusement. A certain prestige, yes, but to the rest of Ulandia, still only Keshmarians. And I—an orphan above all.

"In time, I mastered the stone, and then turned my study to the Four Elements—a sophisticated discipline that held little interest in the backwaters of Keshmara. Yet I proved just as gifted there; a natural. And my great secret, the thing no master had ever taught or even conceived, was this: the alchemy of binding the Four Elements and the stone together. That is the Fifth Element."

He blinked hard, shaking himself free. His eyes found William again—more focused now.

"Look at me… rambling on. My apologies. Enough of *my* past. Tell me all about your experience with the stone, my young friend. What did you feel? What magic stirred when it burned in your hand? I must know."

William shook his head. "Um…I haven't really… tried it."

Florestan's smile vanished. "Surely you jest. You've held the stone—you carry the same gift as I. No one touches its fire without tasting it."

"I—I haven't. Honest. I've only held it a few times, and it just makes me dizzy. Like it's doing now."

"Ah… yes. Of course." Florestan raised a hand, his expression shifting as if he had suddenly recalled an obvious detail. "Forgive me. I got ahead of myself."

His eyes narrowed in amusement. Turning away, he moved with a measured step toward a shadowed alcove. His fingers lingered on a shelf before finding what he sought: a metal box, its surface dulled with a greenish patina. He carried it back, as though cradling a relic, and set it before William. With care, he eased open the lid. Inside, nestled on black velvet, lay a white, sequined glove for the left hand. Its surface casting an otherworldly sheen.

"In Keshmara, this is called a Nullsweave," Florestan said.

William tried to focus on the glove, but the stone in his hand scattered his thoughts.

"To most, the black obsidian is only a curiosity, a glossy rock with a faint red ember. But in the hands of one who can master both the stone and the Four Elements—as I have, and perhaps you might—it becomes something else entirely. Power beyond imagining."

William swayed, close to passing out.

Florestan raised his eyebrows, gesturing toward the stone in William's hand. "Best give that to me. I'll show you how to wield its power without the unfortunate side effects."

William hesitated. The stone felt like his only hope of escape, yet its energy was unbearable. His knees buckled, and at last, he surrendered it, letting it fall into Florestan's grasp.

Florestan rolled the stone in his palm, testing its weight, his fingers lingering with reverence. "I made mistakes with the flame," he said softly. "It nearly destroyed me. But you… you don't have to suffer as I did. I can spare you that fate. I can show you how to master it, without the pain."

From his cloak he withdrew another shard of obsidian—thinner, polished to a mirror shine—and slid it into a hidden pocket in the white sequined glove. He extended the glove with a ceremonial grace, as though offering a gift rather than a command.

William froze. Florestan noticed.

"Don't worry. The Nullsweave is harmless. Forged in remote regions of Keshmara, its purpose is simple—to temper the stone's more unpleasant side effects."

Florestan looked down at the glove in his hand.

"I wore one myself, once. It softened the power—made the magic presentable. Palatable. I could levitate a piano, conjure marvels, and the crowds applauded."

He waved a hand dismissively. "But such parlor tricks grew tiresome. I soon realized I had no need of restraint—only the stone."

His eyes closed, nostrils flaring as though drinking in remembered adoration. "The first time I cast aside the Nullsweave… that was when I tasted the flame itself—its rapture. Intoxicating. Mind-altering."

While he lingered in that memory, William searched for any path of escape, scanning the shadowed vaults and columns, buying time. That was when he saw it—half-buried in sepia light near the far wall. A piano. Its reddish varnish was dulled beneath dust, several ivory teeth missing and its bench broken. The sight struck him with eerie recognition. He had seen this piano in a vision once. Florestan's piano—the one that had once risen before cheering crowds.

Florestan's eyes opened. He gave the Nullsweave to William, who cautiously slid the glove onto his left hand.

"Don't feel bad," Florestan said. "All Artists of the Stone in Keshmara wear it. But I'll show you how to build tolerance—to wield the stone without such crutches. To taste its exquisite rapture."

The moment the Nullsweave tightened around his hand, William felt the stone's power surge. The sequins shimmered, the fabric humming faintly.

Florestan leaned forward, disbelief sharpening his features. "I've never seen the glove do that before." His voice dropped. "Fascinating."

William said nothing. The power coursed through him—yet this time there was no dizziness, no nausea. Only control.

Florestan hesitated, his gaze fixed on the shimmer of the glove. For a moment, he seemed unsure—then he straightened, scanning the temple floor for a suitable test.

"Now that you can focus, let's try something simple. A basic merging of obsidian flame with Earth and Air. Lift an object and hold it suspended."

His eyes lit on a toppled marble statue. "Ah… perfect. Come." He beckoned William toward it. The figure sprawled in ruin across the floor, its head snapped off and lying just a few feet away. Florestan gestured, voice hushed but insistent.

"Fix your thoughts on the head. See it rise into the air."

William studied the face of the statue and the fragments of its body scattered around it. Then he looked upward to the loft above and realized it had once stood in the alcove where Deimos had perched moments earlier.

"What statue is this?" William asked.

Florestan blinked. "W-what?"

"The statue. Who is it?"

Florestan glanced at the broken face and shrugged. "Eh… by the looks of it, I'd say… Aphrodite." He flicked the question away with a sharp gesture. "It doesn't matter. You'll only lose focus." A thread of irritation rose in his voice. "Just raise the statue's head."

"But why is she on the floor?" William pressed.

"Obviously because it fell from above. Most likely Deimos knocked it down because he wanted the spot for his perch. Now, please, my young friend—focus."

William knelt and cradled the head in his hands. He examined the beauty of her features, the serenity of her expression. For a long moment, he simply gazed into her eyes.

"What are you… doing? You don't need to touch it to make it rise." Florestan's voice grew sharp, impatient. "Just command the obsidian to shape the Elements. Be firm."

William glanced back. Florestan's left hand twitched harder now, the intervals quickening with his frustration.

"Do it, boy. Raise her head!"

William rose, swallowing hard. His eyes fluttered shut. Shaking, he extended his gloved hand toward the marble fragments. In his mind's eye, the statue took form, and with it came a weight of sorrow. The Dream Dorje stirred beneath his shirt. In an instant, a time-portal opened, and he saw a vision of a half-blind sculptor, old and frail, pouring love into his masterpiece while young apprentices guided his hands.

From the marble block, his cherished Aphrodite emerged—her delicate face first, then the soft chiton flowing from one shoulder. The folds gathered at her waist in an elegant sash. One hand rested over her heart, the other cradling a small dove.

Then the vision shifted: the sculptor collapsing, his heart failing before the work was done. His apprentices completing the master's dream, workers raising Aphrodite high into her alcove.

The vision ended, and William snapped back into his body. Standing before the broken statue, he took a deep breath. Then, instinctively, he flicked his left wrist counterclockwise. All the marble fragments lifted, hovering as though obeying his thoughts. Another flick, and they began to rotate, slowly at first, then tightening into a white-gray cyclone, spinning faster, faster.

"Amazing," Florestan breathed, watching the churning mass.

A cloud of dust formed, engulfing the twirling fragments.

When it cleared, Aphrodite stood again—restored, yet transformed with kintsugi. Golden seams traced every fracture in the statue, veins of light shimmering along her marble skin.

Florestan staggered back, stunned. He dropped onto a nearby bench, bracing himself.

William then raised his left hand, and Aphrodite rose with it, higher and higher, until she reached her former alcove above. With slow precision, he opened his palm, guiding her gently into place. She settled on her pedestal, whole once more.

Florestan stared up at Aphrodite, wild-eyed.

"That was… impressive. You are a Master Artist of the Stone—already surpassing most Keshmarian wizards." His gaze snapped to William. "Tell me. I must know. Did you taste the rapture? The flavor of the flame?"

William lowered his eyes to the floor with the broken mosaic. "No."

Florestan's brow knotted. "No rapture? That's… unusual. But no matter. In time you will. You'll experience intoxicating wonders, beyond anything you could imagine. I've created innumerable formulas using the flame of the stone and the Four Elements. And I'll show you all of them. Perhaps you'll even invent your own. The possibilities are endless…"

But William was no longer listening. He crossed the floor to where the broken piano slumped in a shaft of dusty light. He stretched out his left arm again, spreading his fingers inside the Nullsweave. With a flick of his wrist, the instrument rose, bench and all, hovering. He opened his hand further, and from deep within the heart of its frame, a spark ignited—white, sharp as flint striking steel.

"I've seen enough to believe," Florestan said, his voice slightly impatient. "No need for more tricks, my son. This is child's play compared to what I can show you…"

William ignored him. A sudden blaze rushed through the hollow body of the piano. It streamed through the frame and keys, each piano string, every fissure seared with burning light. The radiance burst outward, filling the temple, flooding alcoves and cracks with illumination.

Florestan shielded his eyes. The piano's faded red veneer shifted, as if sanded away, until the whole instrument sparkled with a glossy white finish. William exhaled, lowering his hand. The piano descended, settling gently onto the floor.

Florestan's lips curved in a wry smile. "Well now. Yes, again… I'm impressed. You already had me with the statue. But that flourish with the piano…" He chuckled. "A performance worthy of me, though I can't say I care for the new color."

He moved with sudden purpose, striding to a copper box on a nearby shelf. From it he drew another glove—black, with a muted obsidian sheen.

"Nevertheless, you've passed every test," Florestan said. "There's only one step left. Give me the amulet around your neck. That is why you felt no rapture. It will only hinder your training." He extended his hand. "Just give it to me. That is all you need to do."

William hesitated… then shook his head. "That's okay. I don't need the secrets of the Wizard's Stone. I wouldn't know what to do with them anyway. Um… I think I should be going."

"No, I think not," Florestan said as he slid his hand into the black glove. His tone hardened. "Last chance. Don't be foolish, boy. It's simple. Give me the Dream Dorje."

William's eyes darted to the entrance of the temple.

"I can see it in your face, Little Prince. Wondering how to twist the stone to your advantage." Florestan sighed. "I had hoped for so much more. I thought one taste of its flame would bind us—master and apprentice, shaping the laws of the universe together. But I see it's no use. You cling to their relic instead of embracing the real alchemy I can share with you."

William raised his left arm, aiming the glove at Florestan.

Florestan cast him a sidelong glance.

"You should know, this glove I wear is no common Nullsweave. I forged it myself, actually—woven entirely from the black obsidian. It nullifies things… but only the power of my rivals." He clicked his tongue. "Alas, I had hoped you'd surrender the dorje willingly. What sweet poetry that would have been—the Element Masters' anointed prince, abandoning their legacy to stand beside me. But… so be it."

His voice thinned into a chilling calm.

"Your journey in the dream world ends here, my friend. And poor Nasim, your dream guardian, failing so miserably. How will she feel when your remains are scattered across the desert?"

He snapped his fingers twice. From the shadows, the predators slunk back into the temple. Deimos flapped to his favorite perch, but Aphrodite's restored form startled him. Thrashing his wings, he veered to another spot.

William could wait no longer. He thrust out the Nullsweave, willing himself to fly from the temple—too fast for even the eagles to follow.

But nothing happened.

His chest tightened. Desperate, he shut his eyes, stretched out his left arm, and poured every shred of will into the stone.

*Fly!*

But when he looked again, the temple was still there.

Nothing.

Only Florestan's smirk.

"Ah… you should never have let me don the black glove. Consider it a compliment, though. I haven't needed it against an enemy for a very long time. Although I'd relish the honor myself," Florestan continued, bowing his head in exaggerated courtesy, "I cannot deny my animal friends the pleasure of tearing you apart."

Typhon padded forward, and Florestan stroked the tiger's massive head. The beast's eyes narrowed, a low growl rumbling from its throat. He lifted his hand, sheathed in the Nullsweave. Phobos swooped down, talons curling around it, wings churning the air.

"You know," Florestan said, surveying the circling predators. "I think you were making them all a little… jealous."

Cerebus dragged his bulk across the marble, scales rasping like sandpaper, while Gorgon lumbered behind William, sealing off his escape.

Florestan's grin widened. "They wanted to rush things, of course. But I advised against it."

He leaned toward William, as if sharing a secret. "I told them to go slowly. You know… mindfully. That way, they'll savor the experience more deeply."

He chuckled, exchanging a glance with Gorgon, who flashed his teeth. "Alas—students always want to play too fast. I fear they may ignore my instructions." He sighed, then waved his hand. "*Au revoir*, Little Prince."

Florestan snapped his fingers, and the signal cracked like a whip. The predators sprang.

William recoiled, ripping the Nullsweave from his hand. The obsidian stone clattered across the marble floor. Bracing for impact, he closed his eyes, clutching the Dream Dorje against his chest.

Then…

Time stopped.

William opened his eyes.

The predators hung in mid-pounce—claws outstretched, talons frozen, snarls and fangs suspended in the air. His chest heaved relief, heart hammering against his ribs. He stepped sideways clear of their path. Florestan too stood motionless—except for his eyes, which tracked William with unnerving clarity.

William remembered the words on the card that came with the Dream Dorje: *It will help you navigate the dream worlds*

He shut his eyes, gripped it tight. A single word flashed in his mind.

*Nightingale*

Instantly, the temple dissolved. Distance unspooled between him and Zarashad. William drew a breath, almost relieved—when something cold clamped onto his ankle.

He looked down. A bony hand had risen from the abyss. Florestan's face emerged—cracked, pitted, yellow-toothed. His sneer curling like a venomous snake.

"I'm not finished with you."

Then, as darkness swallowed all, the grip released.

William's eyes snapped open.

Rosa sat across from him, the Tibetan bowl in her hands, its sound now only a faint tone in the air. His heart pounded, a sheen of sweat dampening his forehead.

The sight of a bony hand clutching his ankle came to mind. Had he drifted off and dreamt it? The image made him shudder. *Not sure I want to put that in my dream journal.*

Rosa set the bowl aside. "The hot cocoa should be safe to drink now."

He lifted the mug from its coaster. The warmth seeped into his fingers, pulling him back into his body, back into the room. He glanced over at Miss Rosa. She was gazing into the fire, sipping her cocoa, lost in thoughts she never seemed quite ready to share.

# Chapter Fifty

## *The Prescott Mansion*

The limousine climbed into the hills of Imperial Heights, William and his mother side-by-side. Through the window, the city stretched out below, glowing against a sky painted in pinks and violets as the sun slipped toward the horizon. The memory of that winter lesson—the icy roads, his shaken confidence, the crackling fire—was like a faint shadow in the rearview mirror.

The limo rounded the bend and slowed in front of the Gate Lodge. The chauffeur stepped out, opened Aimée's door, and held it patiently. William caught her arm just as she started to rise—face solemn, trying to feign worry.

"Mom… I've changed my mind. I don't want to perform the recital at the Gate Lodge after all."

Aimée froze. "W-what? Willy, what are you saying? Miss Rosa is expecting us—everything's been arranged."

William shook his head gravely. "No. I just can't play there tonight. I'm sorry. Driver, could we go, please?"

"William," she whispered, stunned. "*Mon Dieu.* I don't even have my phone to call her. This is not like you—"

He turned to the window to hide his grin.

Robert, receiving the cue, closed the door and eased the limo forward, not back toward the road but up to the black iron gates of the Prescott Mansion. As they approached, the gates parted automatically, gold scrollwork gleaming as they opened.

Aimée's head snapped up. "William? Where are we…?"

He only shrugged, unable to contain his grin.

The car began its slow ascent, the city falling away behind them in a mosaic of violet dusk and glittering lights.

Her breath caught. "C'est… le manoir? We're going to the manor? But how—?"

And then it appeared fully.

The Prescott Mansion.

The château rose before them in full French Renaissance splendor, pale stone blocks stacked with mathematical precision. Twin towers framed the façade, steep slate-grey cones rising above dormered windows and sculpted pilasters. Carved stone brackets supported long balconies draped in ivy, softening the geometry with green. From the great central window, warm light spilled outward, revealing the elegant arc of a grand piano within.

"Willy, is this where you're giving your piano concert?"

He nodded eagerly, taking secret delight in her astonishment.

The car coasted beneath the *porte cochère* and came to a gentle stop. Robert then circled around and opened the door. Ahead stood the mansion's entrance: twin doors of dark oak, each paneled with carved *fleurs-de-lis*, the hinges overlaid in wrought-iron flourishes.

The wooden doors swung open, revealing Winston McFarland, dressed in a crisp white tuxedo jacket with black pants and a black bow tie. "Good evening, Emerson family," he said warmly, his eyes twinkling as they settled on William. "Ah, the man of the hour has arrived! Madeleine Monnier's grand piano awaits you in the music room."

With a theatrical flourish, he swept his arm toward the foyer. "Entrez, s'il vous plaît."

Aimée pressed a hand to her chest, nodding with breathless wonder as she and William stepped into the mansion's elaborately decorated vestibule. Above them, a coffered ceiling was adorned with rosette finishes and intricate leaf-and-dart molding.

As they moved deeper into the main floor, they stopped in awe at the majestic staircase rising before them between two stately columns. The grand marble staircase featured elaborate bronze railings topped with a polished eucalyptus wood veneer. It flowed down from the upper floor like a mountain stream—cascading ivory-white marble with ribbons of gold, anchoring the mansion's architectural heart.

Aimée gasped at the sight.

William drifted into the main hall, wide-eyed, turning slowly beneath the vaulted ceiling, drinking in each detail unfolding around him like a fairytale.

Dr. Anthony Burns Montgomery entered the hall, guided by his white cane. He wore a gray, notched-lapel tuxedo with a matching vest and silk tie, a white handkerchief neatly tucked into his breast pocket. "Bonsoir, Aimée. C'est un vrai plaisir de vous revoir."

Aimée blinked. "Professor Montgomery…" she corrected herself with a soft smile, "I'm sorry, Anthony. How did my little boy pull all of this off?"

"The truth is, my partner Winston deserves the credit. He arranged the entire evening."

Winston offered a playful bow. "A pleasure, Aimée, ma chère. As luck would have it, the museum doesn't officially open until next week—so, tonight, the mansion is entirely ours." He turned to William, gently straightening the boy's crooked bow tie. "As for the formal theme," he added with a conspiratorial wink, "that was your son's idea."

Aimée slipped her arm around William's shoulders, pulling him close with a strong squeeze. "Oh, *mon chéri*, this is incredible," she whispered. "I feel as if I'm dreaming."

Just then, she caught the faintest aroma drifting from deeper within the mansion—warm and savory, touched with butter and thyme. She inhaled again, slower this time. It was delicate, nuanced, and unmistakably French. She tilted her head, the scent pulling her forward until even the grandeur of the main hall seemed to fall away.

What was that? *Velouté?* No—there was more depth: root vegetable, truffle oil, sage just kissed by heat. The chef was building a base, she realized, her culinary mind suddenly alert. *They're working on the starter, the first step in a larger menu.*

She pulled herself back and turned to Montgomery. "Who's the dinner being prepared for? Is there another event taking place?"

The Professor chuckled. "No, it's a gourmet dinner just for us."

"Dinner?" William blurted. "That wasn't me, Mom. I didn't know we'd be having dinner, too."

"Maestro Emerson," Montgomery said, "surely you didn't imagine we'd host a formal concert in the Prescott Mansion without a proper dinner to accompany it?"

"Certainly not, Monty," added Winston, thrusting a finger into the air. "Tonight's feast comes courtesy of Chef Samuel Ramsey—newly crowned head of culinary design for the McFarland Sisters Company. Straight from

New York, no less. You may have heard of him, Aimée. His daring fusion work is all the rage."

"I've read about him," she murmured. "He's bold. Experimental."

"Yes, but for tonight, he's creating something more traditional, in honor of William's performance," Winston said. "Monty was the one who insisted on the French menu, though. In any case, my meddling has earned me a polite banishment from the kitchen."

She smiled faintly, but her attention was already drifting again, nose lifted ever so slightly. In the distance, she caught a thread of citrus. And something smoky. Not smoke exactly—a sear. A new note, bright and assertive. The next course was being born, the meal unfolding in stages.

Winston stepped forward. "Before tonight's festivities begin," he said, "Monty and I would love to give you a personal tour. And share a little history of the Prescott Mansion, if you're interested."

Aimée wrapped both arms around William, pulling him close. She whispered, "Can you believe this, Willy? It feels like we've stepped into someone else's life." William leaned into her, clutching her arms.

Winston continued, "As Will knows, Monty's grandfather, Lewis Hayden Montgomery, was the brilliant architect who designed this mansion. He and Prescott were inseparable, almost like brothers, really."

Montgomery nodded. "Yes, our families remained close for years. Winston and I spent many evenings running through these halls while our parents sipped sherry and debated art and politics."

He turned to them both. "Before our other guests arrive, Winston and I would like to give you a private tour; show you some hidden rooms, strange quirks of architecture, and a few lesser-known secrets. Winston, will you do the honors?"

"With pleasure," Winston replied. "Everyone, follow me. Now, you'll find that the mansion is a mosaic of cultures and memories. Prescott asked Lewis Montgomery to weave elements of Madeleine Monnier's touring life into its design."

They started forward, but William remained where he was. "Professor Montgomery… um, would it be okay if I explored a little on my own?"

Montgomery paused, just long enough for Aimée to waver. "Oh, Willy," she murmured, giving Winston a quick, uncertain smile. "I'm not sure. Shouldn't we stay together for the tour?"

Winston placed a reassuring hand on William's shoulder. "It's fine, Aimée. I'd want to wander too, if I were his age. Monty and I got into plenty of mischief in this old house." He winked. "Just don't disappear through any hidden doors, all right?"

Montgomery chuckled. "Go on, Will—explore. We'll catch up with you later."

His mother relented, giving him a final approving nod, allowing him to slip away down a grand hallway.

Behind him, the tour began, just close enough to hear the opening lines, "In 1910, my grandfather was finalizing plans for the Spirit of Lewis and Clark Exposition. Around that time, Prescott approached him with the idea of building a mansion for his family. The previous year, he and his wife, Madeleine Monnier Prescott, had survived a terrible car accident outside Paris…"

The words thinned, then vanished entirely as William moved deeper down the corridor. After a few turns, he came upon an imposing library that made him stop short. It reminded him of the rare book room at Shelley's— the same charged hush.

It was cool and immaculate, with dark wood paneling that carried the scent of leather and wood. A fireplace stood at one end beneath a carved mantle. William paused beside an armchair that had been staged for the exhibit—an antique lamp, stationery, and pen, an open book left mid-thought.

He walked slowly along the edge of the velvet rope that marked the boundary, eyes drifting across rows of old books lining the shelves, some leaning, others stacked neatly, all like a private archive frozen in time.

A placard near the fireplace read:

*The Prescott Library*

*Designed in the Jacobean style popular in late 19th-century England, this room once served as R.C. Prescott's private study. A visionary industrialist with a taste for refinement, Prescott curated the library to reflect his admiration for classical literature and the cultivated elegance of the British aristocratic tradition.*

He glanced both ways down the hallway, checking to see if anyone was in sight. For a breath, he hesitated but then was overcome by a strong urge. Almost before he knew it, he had slipped beneath the velvet rope.

There were hundreds of books, yet he was drawn to a specific shelf. These volumes were older, their spines cracked and faded. As he scanned the titles, one caught his eye: its spine bore a small treble and bass clefs and an Italian title stamped in worn gold leaf—*Il Quinto Elemento*.

He froze. He knew enough Italian to translate it—*The Fifth Element*.

He glanced once more toward the hallway to make sure no one was coming, then reached out and gently slid the book from the shelf. Its cover bore the faint sheen of hand-embossed lettering.

*Il Quinto Elemento di Bartolomeo Cristofori.*

William tried to process what he was holding in his hands. Cristofori—the creator of the first piano— had also written a book about the Fifth Element?

He and Lina had pored over Katarina von Paradis diary entries in the rare book room. She had known Cristofori, had even toured Europe and Asia, performing on his piano. But a published work? Had Cristofori been writing about something connected to Piano Zen?

Inside the front cover, in looping French handwriting, was a dedication.

*À ma chère amie Madeleine,*

*Cherche toujours les réponses en toi.*

*Peut-être que ce livre sera la lumière sur ton chemin.*

*— Maurice Ravel*

*Paris, 1906*

William's pulse quickened. *This must have been Madeleine's personal copy,* he thought. Ravel himself had signed it for her. Both famous musicians had held this very book.

Hands slightly trembling, he translated the inscription.

*To my dear friend Madeleine,*

*Always seek the answers within yourself.*

*Perhaps this book will be the light on your path.*

He carefully traced Ravel's signature with his finger, and a powerful impulse surged through him—to keep Cristofori's book, signed by Ravel and gifted to Madeleine. There were hundreds of volumes on the shelves; he could slip this one into his backpack and no one would ever know. But he drew a steady breath and let the temptation go.

Voices echoed from the corridor. Quickly, he returned the book to the shelf, just as he had found it.

From somewhere beyond the library, Montgomery's voice drifted in. "…to achieve the correct authenticity for each room was a daunting challenge," the Professor was saying. "Fortunately for my grandfather, the Spirit of Lewis and Clark Exposition of 1912 brought artisans from all over the world to the city of Nightingale. They were in town to build pavilions representing their home countries. He was able to hand-select many artisans to remain in Nightingale and help build the Prescott Mansion…"

The sound of the tour faded again as William stepped back beneath the rope and moved on. The hall ahead curved gently, its crown molding lined with gilded patterns from another era. A flicker of ruby, sapphire, and amber light danced across the opposite wall, as if filtered through stained glass, calling to him.

A brass-framed placard beside the doorway offered an explanation.

*The Turkish Salon*

*Inspired by Madeleine Monnier's 1905 concert tour through Istanbul, and the cultural crossroads of the Near East. This room was built to evoke the salons she visited during her travels. The colored glass, carved columns, and velvet textiles were all custom imported.*

Warm and dim, the room glowed with ruby and sapphire light diffused through ornate glass lanterns. Intricate geometric tiles climbed the walls, velvet cushions ringed a low hookah table, and a copper Turkish coffee kettle sat beside a staged bowl of figs and dates.

Along the far wall stood a small collection of Near Eastern instruments— a Persian santur, an Arab rebab, and a row of wooden flutes mounted on carved stands.

He stepped cautiously inside. On a velvet pad near the santur lay a small wooden hammer. Lifting it, he gently tapped the strings with the hammer, creating soft ringing notes.

He leaned toward the mirror, lantern light fracturing across his face. Then he froze. For an instant, it looked as though someone stood behind him in the reflection. He gasped and turned sharply, but the doorway stood empty.

William shuddered, then shook it off as Montgomery's voice floated back in. "…Prescott was captivated by her Boston performance. And she by his striking green eyes. Ah, love at first sight, as they say. It was also the first time he'd heard French Impressionistic piano music—an entirely new sound for American audiences…"

William lingered a moment longer in the Turkish room, watching the colors shimmer across the tiled walls, before stepping cautiously back into the curved hallway to the next room.

A placard beside the doorway drew his attention.

*The Japanese Tea Room*

*Inspired by Madeleine Monnier's 1908 concert tour through Kyoto and the surrounding countryside. This room reflects the meditative simplicity of the Japanese aesthetic. Tatami mats, shoji screens, and traditional tea set were imported under Prescott's direction in 1911.*

The room was illuminated differently—muted, soft, serene. Light filtered through translucent shoji screens, casting pale, geometric shadows on the tatami floor. A tea set rested on a low wooden tray near the center of the room. William stepped quietly inside, once again beyond the ropes used to keep tourists out.

He knelt on one of the mats and picked up a teacup. The glaze was layered in soft tones of blue, with subtle accents of rose and pale gold. Its shape was uneven, imperfect, but still beautiful. "*Wabi sabi,*" he whispered.

The room invited stillness. A calligraphy scroll hung in a vertical panel, inked in flowing black script. A small translation card beneath it read: *Calm the mind. Listen to the wind.*

He closed his eyes and let his attention settle—the mat beneath him, the cup in his hands, the soft rhythm of his breath.

Carefully, he returned the teacup to its tray. As he stood to leave, he noticed a sliding panel slightly ajar at the back of the room. Just an inch. He eased it closed.

Montgomery's voice floated in from a few rooms away. "…She'd sit here and read for hours. This became her sanctuary after the accident…"

William delayed briefly at the door of the Japanese Tea Room, the earthy stillness of it clinging to him. Then he stepped back into the hallway.

And that's when he heard it. Just a few notes. So faint he almost doubted them—a flutter of piano, quick and light, like wings brushing ivory. The sound faded, then returned—flickering, elusive.

He turned slowly, scanning the corridor.

*Who's playing the piano?*

At the far end, a wide staircase curved upward—more grand than he expected for a side corridor. Its banister was carved from dark wood, smooth beneath his palm as he climbed. Each footstep fell softly against the polished stairs. The faint music drifted with him, brushing the edges of his senses.

As he reached the upper landing, the notes didn't crescendo as expected. They were still faint, ghostly, but unmistakably piano music. William paused, closed his eyes, and tuned in, listening carefully.

*It sounds impressionistic. Yes—Ravel's "Noctuelles. Night Moths from Miroirs." But where is it coming from?*

At the top of the stairs, he entered the Imperial Ballroom, dazzling in scale and spanning the second floor of the east wing. Vast and pale, it rose with cream-colored archways and gilded moldings high above. Painted swallows circled across a sky-blue dome ceiling.

He walked to the center, where the polished floor mirrored the light overhead. His footsteps echoed faintly. From behind him, Winston's voice drifted in—almost as softly as the piano music. "…and, of course, the mansion incorporated cutting-edge technology for the time—recessed lighting, intercoms, even a zoned central heating system…"

The voices and steps of the trio faded again.

He followed the music through the ballroom and toward a grand staircase descending from the opposite side. The notes didn't grow louder—still thin, elusive. William rested his hand on the banister and descended quickly to the lower floor.

At the landing, the piano music vanished into the quiet trickle of water. He paused at an open doorway, where a placard explained: *The Roman Bath (1912)*

*Commissioned by R.C. Prescott as a tribute to the ancient Roman thermae, this private bath chamber combined architectural elegance with therapeutic function. Inspired by a second-century bathhouse near the Pantheon in Rome, it was designed to reflect the serenity and symmetry of Classical architecture.*

*After a devastating car accident in 1909, Madeleine Monnier sustained injuries that caused lasting physical discomfort. Prescott hoped that a dedicated space for hydrotherapy and restorative bathing might ease her pain and provide a sanctuary for healing. The circular basin, imported marble, and lion-head fountain evoke the symbolism of Roman traditions in which water was considered a sacred conduit for both physical and spiritual renewal.*

It was warmer than the rest of the house—quiet, peaceful. The marble floors gleamed, veined with blues and golds. Arched alcoves framed the space, and a circular bathing basin stood at the center like a temple well. A lion's-head fountain trickled steadily into the water, its surface glassy and smooth. A velvet rope stretched across the threshold, but William stepped over it as before without hesitation.

He approached the basin. Kneeling, he tapped the surface lightly with his fingertips, mimicking the "touching the pond" technique Miss Rosa had taught him in Piano Zen—gentle, mindful. The water was warm. Clean. Ripples quivered beneath the trickling fountain, but his touch added its own rhythm, spreading outward in small concentric waves that reflected off the lion's head.

Just then, it returned. The music again—quiet, elusive—as if answering his touch. So faint he thought he imagined it: a flutter of right-hand notes, nervous, flickering, quick. He stood. The sound pulled him onward, down another side corridor.

Winston's voice carried softly through the hallways, though William couldn't tell from which floor. "… additionally, because Madeleine's injuries affected her mobility, Monty's grandfather installed an elevator. These were uncommon in private residences at the time, but they allowed Madeleine more autonomy..."

A moment later came the metal clang of doors as the tour entered the elevator, followed by the hum of the mechanism as it descended.

William continued down the hallway. His pace slowed. A tingling sensation crept over him. A placard beside the next room read: *Madeleine Monnier's Private Quarters*

# Chapter Fifty-One

## *Reflections*

After wandering through the mansion's grand parlors, salons, and ballrooms, he had nearly forgotten the room he most longed to see. Now it waited for him—quiet, seemingly untouched by time. Even the ornate brass frame that held the placard set the room apart from all the others.

*Madeleine Monnier's Private Quarters*

*Preserved as they appeared in 1912, these rooms once served as Madeleine's personal refuge in the final years of her life. Her final performance gown and personal artifacts remain displayed here with the permission of the Prescott Estate.*

Inside the room, the balcony doors had been left slightly ajar, just enough for evening air to slip through. The cool breeze stirred the sheer curtains into motion, their slow turns moving like an improvised dance.

A dressing screen stood in one corner, its silk panels embroidered with a blue swan in mid-flight, its wings outstretched against a backdrop of silver-threaded reeds and water.

A mirrored vanity near the window held an array of vintage perfume bottles, hand-blown glass catching the room's soft light—each one a tiny sculpture swirling with pink, aquamarine, and gold.

To the side of the dressing screen, a low-lit alcove displayed two framed photographs. The first picture showed a restored 1908 Delaunay-Belleville Victoria. Its sweeping fenders and graceful curves gleamed with navy-blue enamel, brass headlights polished to a mirror shine. Spoked wheels and white rubber tires completed the look of early 20th-century opulence.

A museum label beneath it read: *Delaunay-Belleville Victoria, 1908*
*Model replica similar to the one owned by R.C. Prescott—considered one of the most luxurious automobiles of its time.*

Beside it, a second photo, grainy and black-and-white, showed a similar model crumpled at the roadside, its curved body tipped sideways into a shallow ditch. Broken spokes, a snapped carriage lamp, and several blurred figures standing in the foreground.

William leaned closer. He had never seen this picture before. The damage was startling—violent.

The placard beneath read: *Automobile Accident, 1909*
*Photograph courtesy of the Prescott Archives*
*This image captures the aftermath of a near-fatal accident involving R.C. Prescott and the celebrated French pianist, Madeleine Monnier. The incident occurred just outside Paris when Prescott's Delaunay-Belleville struck a rut while swerving at high speed around a carriage, overturning. Prescott suffered only minor injuries. Monnier sustained a serious concussion and severe trauma to her shoulder and arm—an event that ultimately ended her concert career.*

On the far side of the room, near the open balcony doors, a narrow writing desk sat with an upholstered chair tucked neatly beneath it. A small, freestanding mirror rested on its surface—ornate and distinctly Art Nouveau, with curling brass tendrils that resembled vines. Beside it sat a silver inkwell and neat stack of pressed stationery, a fountain pen lay diagonally across the top sheet.

A small placard read: *Madeleine Monnier's Writing Desk*
*Personal letters and journals were often written here in the final years of her life.*

Near the corner of the desk stood a single bottle of perfume—frosted lilac glass with a silver cap, and delicate French lettering. A matching card beneath it read: *Guerlain — Jardins sous la Pluie*
*Inspired by Claude Debussy's piano piece of the same name.*
*Madeleine Monnier's favored perfume.*
*Notes: violet, iris, neroli, heliotrope, musk.*
*Created in 1906 by the French house Guerlain.*
*Modern reproductions available in the museum gift shop.*

William picked up the bottle, a silk ribbon tied around its neck and sealed with a delicate wax stamp pressed into a silver medallion. He glanced toward the doorway, hesitating, then loosened the knot with care. The seal slipped free; the wax cracked softly in his palm. He lifted the cap and inhaled. The scent was soft—powdery and clean, faintly floral with a hint of citrus.

He closed his eyes, letting the fragrance bloom, then touched his fingertip to the bottle's opening and dabbed a small trace just above his upper lip. He reached for Madeleine's small desk mirror next. Lifting it by its ornate frame, he angled it toward himself and studied his reflection for a moment before returning it to its place beside the perfume bottle.

At the far end, behind a slender velvet rope, stood her concert gown from her last performance. Deep violet silk, embroidered with beads that sparkled like dew, draped across a faceless mannequin. Up close, it appeared smaller than he expected—delicate, almost slight. For someone whose music had filled great halls, whose legacy felt immense, Madeleine herself must have been remarkably petite.

He hesitated again but only for a heartbeat. Then he stepped over the rope, reached out, and touched the silk sleeve, lingering on the feel of it between his fingers.

Across the room from the writing desk stood her bed—ornate wood, ivory sheets, perfectly made. He stepped closer and lowered himself gently onto the edge. Beside the bed rested a small porcelain vase, its blue-gray glaze mottled with subtle variations in tone. Golden kintsugi seams traced across its surface.

He stared for a moment, then recognition dawned. It was Miss Rosa's vase. No—not hers. Rosa had once said it had belonged to Madeleine. He recognized the shape, the distinctive repair, and its history. Prescott used to place a fresh flower in it each morning, he remembered Rosa saying—so it would be the first thing Madeleine saw when she awoke.

Rosa must have returned it to the museum.

A single white orchid had been placed in the vase. Its petals curled like porcelain, fragile and luminous. William leaned closer and caught its faint, jasmine-like scent. For a moment, he imagined the vase as it once was— unbroken, flawless. And yet somehow, unaware of its true nature, a beauty had awakened only through the reassembling of its fractured parts.

Then the piano music returned—more present. No longer drifting overhead from the upper floors, the sound now gathered below. Maybe someone was playing the Érard grand?

Driven by a determination to finally solve the mystery, he left Monnier's room.

# Chapter Fifty-Two

## *Miroirs*

William raced down the staircase and reached a pair of double doors. He swung them open, revealing an expansive, oval-shaped music room. Dazzling light from the chandeliers fell across the space, catching the polished Érard grand at the far end in a soft glow.

There were no red velvet ropes this time. The piano lid was propped open, casting a shadow across the hardwood floor. Chairs had been arranged for the upcoming recital. He approached Monnier's piano cautiously. He didn't touch the keys. Instead, he placed a hand on the curve of the instrument and slid his fingers gently along the polished wood, tracing its shape as he moved around it.

Near the piano, a blown-up black-and-white photograph was displayed on a freestanding easel. William moved closer. He knew this picture— the same one he'd seen nearly a year ago in the Rodin book in Cecil Winwood's studio.

The caption read: *Concert pianist Madeleine Monnier with Camille Claudel – Paris, circa 1903.*

*The piano shown in the photograph is Monnier's personal Érard, now restored and on display in this room. Claudel, famed sculptor and protégé of Auguste Rodin, was also the artist behind the Lady of Light statue, gifted to the city of Nightingale in 1922.*

A wall of tall mirrors stood opposite the large windows of the music room. He stopped in front of them. *Miroirs*, he whispered. His own reflection stared back—a little ghostly and pale in the bright light. To his surprise, the ethereal music had stopped.

Had someone been playing and slipped away?

Or had he only imagined it?

Then—footsteps.

Winston's voice echoed from the hallway outside, growing closer, "As you can see, the mansion represents a contradiction of visions. The outer and inner design of the mansion looked backward for architectural inspiration, from the French Renaissance to Imperial Rome, while simultaneously looking forward to the future by incorporating all the latest technological innovations into a private home..."

The double doors opened with a touch of ceremonial flourish as the trio flowed into the room mid-conversation.

Winston stepped ahead and halted. "Well," he said, raising both hands, "Voilà. La pièce de résistance—the music room, inspired by the salons of Paris at the height of the Belle Époque."

Aimée followed and gasped. "Mon Dieu... c'est magnifique," she breathed, tightening her hold on Montgomery's arm.

They moved further into the room, still linked arm in arm. "La salle de musique," Montgomery said softly, "la pièce la plus précieuse de toute la maison." Aimée rested her head briefly on his shoulder, giving his arm a gentle squeeze.

Then her eyes found William by the piano. "There you are, Willy," she said with a small laugh. "We thought you might have gotten lost."

Winston drifted along the perimeter, narrating as he walked. "You can see it in the elegance of the moldings, the plasterwork, the oval-shaped floor plan, friezes, capped cornices. And that carved mantel? Limestone, just like the ones found in Parisian townhouses."

He gestured upward. "These chandeliers are genuine Baccarat crystal. Prescott had them shipped from France in 1911—same artisan lineage that furnished Versailles."

"Si beau," Aimee said. The chandeliers glittered overhead, refracting light across the curved walls and parquet floor like a thousand tiny stars.

Winston's voice dropped. "And that..." he nodded toward the grand piano where William still stood, "is Madeleine Monnier's Érard concert grand."

"Fully restored by expert French craftsmen," Winston continued. "The Louis XIV-style pedal lyre, the carving along the casework—everything is period accurate. It's rare to see an Érard this well-preserved outside of France."

"Érard pioneered the metal frame—more power, more resonance," Montgomery added. "Ravel preferred them. So did Saint-Saëns and Debussy. It was the French pianist's piano."

Aimée crossed to William and slipped an arm around his shoulders. "Oh, Willy… you'll be playing your recital on Madeleine Monnier's piano." Her voice softened, almost to a whisper. "I wish your father could see this. *C'est tout simplement magique.*"

At that moment, a young attendant appeared in the doorway, charcoal waistcoat crisp, tone formal. He bowed. "Pardon the interruption, Mr. McFarland. The second limousine has arrived."

# Chapter Fifty-Three

## *The Quiet Flame*

Moments later, the doors to the music room opened again. Hadiya entered, followed by Rosa and Lina Bauch.

William bounded forward, wrapping Hadiya in a hug. "I'm so glad you could come."

"Are you kidding?" Hadiya said with a grin. "I've been looking forward to this all week. Everyone in town is buzzing about the renovation. My friends can't believe I get a private tour."

William hugged Lina next. "You have to see the Prescott library—it's incredible."

"*Ach so?*" Lina said. "*Ja,* I'd love to see it."

At last, he turned to Rosa and embraced her. They held on for a long moment before she drew back, keeping his hands in hers.

"What you've accomplished this past year, William... I'm so proud of you. And to think—you'll be the first to play a concert on this piano since Monnier did in Paris. It was nearly forgotten, you know. Left in storage for decades in Europe. I never dreamed that I would live to see it restored."

"Bonsoir, mesdames," Winston said. "You're just in time for a private tour. The mansion officially opens next week, but tonight, you have the honor of a sneak preview. Afterward, we'll reconvene in the dining room for a multi-course gourmet dinner, and then a piano concert by William Emerson."

Warm laughter rippled through the group as greetings overlapped in the music room.

"Winston," Montgomery said, "would you mind leading our guests? I'd like a brief word with Aimée and William."

"Of course, Monty," Winston replied. "Ladies, follow me. The Prescott Library awaits—a jewel box of Jacobean design."

As the group followed him out, Montgomery turned to William. "I imagine you'll want to warm up your fingers before the concert, yes?"

William nodded, his pulse quickening. At last—he would get to touch Monnier's piano, to feel its action beneath his fingers, to discover how it responded to him.

"Excellent," Montgomery said. "Stay here and get acquainted with it. Aimée, come with me, *S'il vous plaît*. There's someone I would very much like you to meet."

Aimée arched a questioning brow but followed.

As they stepped into the corridor, Montgomery moved with surprising ease, his cane tapping lightly along the marble. "Well, I thought while everyone else was busy, you might enjoy meeting Chef Samuel Ramsey."

"Oh…" Aimée blinked, caught off guard. "Really? I just read about him—an article in the Dine-Out section of the Nightingale Observer."

"Oui," Montgomery said, pleased. "A rising star in Manhattan. Ran a tiny restaurant in the Village, hardly more than a dozen tables, always a three-month wait. Built a devoted following with his fusion style—refined technique, bold flavors, and just enough improvisation to keep one guessing. In his younger years, he traveled widely, absorbing regional cuisines the way some musicians absorb folk songs."

She tucked a curl behind her ear. "And now he's here, running the new La Luz Café?"

Montgomery chuckled. "If you know Winston, you know the moment he heard Samuel was relocating to Nightingale, he snatched him up the minute he landed. Well, all that aside, I think you'll find Samuel's culinary style *très créatif*." He grinned and offered his arm to Aimée.

The aromas she'd caught earlier had deepened now. What had begun with butter and herbs was unfolding into brightness—citrus and something floral, dill perhaps, paired with beet-cured salmon and crème fraîche. By the time they passed a long hallway, the air had thickened with braised meat, anise, and thyme over a sweeter reduction. *Sherry*, she thought, her pulse quickening. Navarin d'Agneau, reimagined. And then white asparagus, charred instead of steamed, brushed with citrus oil and finished with fleur de sel.

A purely French menu—precise, traditional, unmistakable. Not at all what she expected from a New York fusion chef.

Montgomery and Aimée walked arm in arm through the back corridor toward the kitchen. The polished oak trim gave way to clean white walls and a wide, newly tiled floor gleaming under soft pendant lights. The air shifted—warmer now, alive with butter, citrus, and fresh thyme. Copper pans hung from ceiling racks, catching the light, and rows of labeled glass jars lined the shelves above a long, marble prep counter.

The kitchen was busier than she expected but fluid, almost musical. A pair of junior cooks moved in practiced rhythm along the far station, while a pastry chef caramelized crème brûlées with a quick, confident flick of a torch. At the main line, the sous-chef leaned over a tray of plated starters, adjusting each one with quiet concentration.

In the middle of it all stood a man in a white chef's coat, sleeves rolled and brow set in concentration. He wasn't what she expected. Younger—mid-thirties, perhaps—with tousled, sandy-blond hair and a coat lightly dusted with flour. Tall and lean, he moved like a jazz musician: quick, instinctive, following the flow of the kitchen without seeming aware of the stage he held.

Even before the introduction, Aimée sensed it—something in the way he tasted, adjusted, tasted again. Improvisational by nature. A fusion chef with a New York pedigree. And yet tonight's menu was unmistakably French. It was like asking a jazz pianist to play a Mozart sonata.

Montgomery cleared his throat. "Chef Ramsey?"

Samuel looked up, startled. When he saw them, he gave a dramatic exhale.

Montgomery gestured between them. "This is Aimée Emerson."

Recognition flickered across Samuel's face, then something like relief. He wiped his hands on a towel and crossed the space to greet her. "Oh—yes! Hi. Thank God. Anthony mentioned you might be here tonight. He told me all about your background and that I shouldn't hesitate to ask for help if I needed it." He gave a half-laugh. "And with this whole French-inspired menu… well, I'm a little out of my element." He ran a hand through his hair. "Sorry—I know this is last-minute. But I'm in a bit of a bind, and your timing couldn't be better."

Aimée blinked. "I'm sorry… what?"

Samuel nodded toward the prep station. "Would you mind stepping over for a moment? I just need a quick taste—a second opinion."

She glanced at Montgomery, who sported a gentle smile, then back at the chef, who wore the faintest trace of uncertainty beneath his focus.

"Oui… of course," she said softly. "What's the issue?"

Samuel reached for something hanging on a nearby hook. "I, uh—brought this just in case," he said, offering her a neatly folded chef's jacket embroidered with the McFarland Sisters logo.

He hesitated, then added, "Mr. Montgomery mentioned you might be willing to step in if things got tight tonight. I hope that's not too forward."

Aimée raised a brow but accepted the jacket, the fabric crisp and freshly pressed. "No… ah, not at all," she murmured, already slipping off her heels and tucking them beneath the counter.

Samuel nodded toward a small bench near the pantry where a pair of white kitchen clogs waited beside a folded toque. "I wasn't sure about your size, but… close enough?"

A soft laugh escaped her. She pulled a hair tie from her purse, swept her hair into a loose bun, and slid into the clogs. Then she shrugged on the jacket, buttoning the front and rolling the sleeves with a familiar, practiced motion.

"All right," she said, smoothing the collar. "Chef Ramsey, show me what we're working with."

He led her toward a saucepan on the rear burner. "Navarin d'Agneau. I used a sherry reduction instead of white wine, added a touch of anise—but it's not landing. It feels… unmoored."

She leaned in and inhaled deeply: lamb, sherry, a whisper of anise. She dipped a spoon, tasted, and closed her eyes.

"It's off-balance," she said before she could stop herself.

Samuel sighed. "I knew it."

"It's not bad," she added quickly. "But you've got umami and sweetness pulling in opposite directions. What's missing is the anchor—the bridge."

He waited, eyes fixed on her.

"Orange blossom honey," she said. "Just a drizzle. And fresh tarragon. Right at the end."

Samuel lit up. "That's it."

He moved to retrieve the ingredients, then paused, turning back to her. "Would you mind… staying? Just a few more tweaks?"

She glanced toward the doorway and noticed that Montgomery was gone. A small laugh escaped her. "*D'accord*. Why not?"

The next few minutes unfolded in a blur—taste, adjust, stir, refine. The sous-chef gave her a respectful nod as she moved through the kitchen with practiced ease. She and Samuel exchanged quick glances as their work settled into an unexpectedly natural rhythm.

He gestured to a row of white asparagus laid out on the prep table. "Would you mind helping finish these? It's all about timing now."

"Of course," she said, slipping in beside him.

As they trimmed the stalks, brushed them with lemon oil, and sprinkled them with fleur de sel, their conversation softened.

"So," Aimée said, not quite looking up, "you're new to Nightingale?"

Samuel smiled as he brushed oil on the spears. "Brand new. Moved out here two weeks ago—still living out of boxes." He paused, choosing his words, "Manhattan was... more than I could sustain. The restaurant scene is electric—but relentless. Long hours, tight margins. The constant pressure to prove yourself." He gave a small shake of his head. "And I was mostly cooking solo. Not much of a team."

He offered a wry smile. "And then there's my daughter. She's eight now. Bright, curious—loves to draw, loves to collect rocks. Lately she's been asking about real nature. Not just Central Park but hiking and camping, all that stuff. She's been begging me to take her."

He gave a sheepish laugh. "Truth is, I don't know the first thing about camping."

He gestured out the kitchen window where the peak of Mt. Drake caught the last rays of the evening sun. "But out here... well, it seems like everybody hikes and camps. So, I figured if I was ever going to try it with my daughter... this was the place."

"You wanted something different for her," Aimée said.

He nodded. "And to give myself a little breathing room, too. Somewhere quieter. More balanced. I'd seen photos of the Pacific Northwest—tall pines, mountains, the ocean. And when I started reading about Nightingale's culinary scene..." He shrugged. "It just felt right."

Aimée glanced over, more curious. "What's your daughter's name?"

"Jacqueline," he said, gently placing the asparagus on the grill. "She's always exploring—curious about everything. And she's got this little backpack that rattles everywhere she goes—filled with rocks and pinecones."

Aimée smiled. "Jacqueline," she repeated with a soft lilt. "A beautiful name. Very French."

"She's named after my dad—Jack. He passed away just before she was born. They never got to meet. Naming her Jacqueline... it felt like a way to keep something of him with us."

For a moment, neither spoke—just the gentle rhythm of brushes, tongs, and the hiss of oil on the grill. A polite cough behind them broke the spell—a junior cook lowering the flame on an overlooked burner.

Samuel turned, blinking. "Right. Sorry."

Aimée asked, "So, you didn't have a job lined up before the move to Nightingale?"

Samuel laughed under his breath. "Not exactly. I met with Winston McFarland. He can be very… persuasive. He offered me the head chef position at the La Luz Café."

Their hands moved in quiet choreography—seasoning, turning, plating. And for a moment, the heat and clatter of the kitchen faded into the background.

# Chapter Fifty-Four

## *Dinner is Served*

William finished his warm-up on Monnier's Érard piano. Though it lacked the sheer power of the Bösendorfer Imperial Grand, it responded with a subtlety that surprised him. Whatever inflection he imagined, the instrument seemed to yield to it—fluid, natural, alive beneath his fingers. He didn't want to overdo things. He eased off, recalling Rosa's advice: warm up slowly, stay loose, save your energy for the performance.

He rose from the bench. Wondering where his mother and Professor Montgomery had gone, he followed a spill of light down the hallway into the dining room.

The space welcomed him with a soft, honeyed glow. Amber-tinted sconces curled like vines along the walls, casting shadows that danced across carved wood and ornamental plaster. Everything about the space seemed alive—curves instead of corners, blossoms instead of brackets.

His mother sat with a glass of red wine in hand, cheeks still touched with color, a faint smudge of flour near her temple. Her hair was loosely pinned, her necklace a little off-center. She nudged one of her heels back into place beneath the table and glanced up.

"Ah, *te voilà*, Willy," she said with a smile. "So, what did you think of the piano?"

William slid into the seat beside her. "It's unlike anything I've ever played. Whatever I felt, it gave back. Almost like it understood me."

Aimée set her glass down, her expression softening. "That sounds wonderful, *mon chéri*. I can't wait to hear you play."

He paused, eyeing her curiously. "Where did you go?"

"Oh, just… to the kitchen," she said, glancing away. "To speak with Sam. I mean—Chef Ramsey."

William tilted his head. "*Maman*, why is your face red?"

She gave a soft laugh. "Well, I was… ah…" as if suddenly remembering, she reached up and pulled the tie from her hair, letting it fall loosely around her shoulders, "helping in the kitchen."

She checked her reflection in a small mirror from her purse and dabbed at the faint dusting of flour near her temple.

"Helping in the kitchen?" William echoed. "How'd that happen?"

"It appears Dr. Montgomery volunteered my services to the chef," she said dryly, taking a pointed sip of wine. "I may have helped a little with the entrée."

William grinned. "You helped the chef prepare the food? That's awesome, Mom."

Aimée rose from her chair and wandered slowly around the room, fingertips brushing the carved back of a chair. The dining room shimmered with Belle Époque elegance—etched glass, curved walnut chairs, soft floral motifs in the sconces and ceiling moldings.

William watched her, curious.

Her gaze drifted from corner to corner, her expression softening. "He must have really loved her," she murmured.

William tilted his head. "What do you mean?"

"This room," she said, sweeping her hand toward the walls. "A man like Prescott would normally choose something grand and formal—Jacobean, like the library. Or Elizabethan. Even Beaux-Arts. Those styles suggest power, tradition." She paused. "But this… this is Art Nouveau. It's poetic and emotional. It feels personal. It doesn't try to impress you. It invites you in." She hesitated. "It feels… feminine."

William frowned, puzzled.

"Don't you see, Willy? Madeleine couldn't travel to Paris anymore. So he brought a little of *La Ville Lumière* to her."

Soon, the rest of the guests arrived in a buzz of conversation. Lina and Professor Montgomery entered first, their German spilling back and forth about the Austrian-inspired ballroom.

Winston followed close behind, leaning toward Rosa, already mid-story, "...during the renovation, they found a trunk of Welte-Mignon piano rolls—perfectly preserved. Performances by Madeleine Monnier herself."

Rosa's eyes widened. She placed a hand on his arm. "Are you sure they're authentic? I didn't think she made any recordings."

Winston nodded. "Without a doubt. Welte began recording artists in Paris in 1905. Debussy, Saint-Saëns, Ravel… and yes, Monnier. Imagine hearing her again, exactly as she played."

Hadiya came bounding in, all energy and light, slipping her arm around Professor Montgomery with a warm squeeze.

The dining room came alive. Laughter mingled with the clink of glasses, the warm hum of voices rising and falling.

A chime rang out from the far end of the room, a soft bell struck by one of the uniformed servers. Conversations tapered, and all heads turned as Winston stepped forward.

"Friends," he said, raising his glass slightly, "the kitchen informs me that dinner is ready."

Light laughter rippled around the room as servers began gliding into place, holding trays with polished precision.

"Please, find your seats," Winston added, gesturing toward the long, linen-draped table. "Before we begin," he continued, lifting his glass, "I'd like to introduce the man behind tonight's beautiful meal—Chef Samuel Ramsey."

A ripple of applause followed as Samuel stepped forward from the far end of the room. He looked freshly changed, though a dusting of flour still clung faintly to his sleeve. He smiled modestly and gave a slight nod.

"*Bonsoir*, everyone. Thank you for letting me share this meal with you. Tonight's menu draws on classic French flavors, interpreted through the lens of our Pacific Northwest ingredients—and with a little last-minute help from Aimée Emerson," he added, offering a quick, grateful nod toward William's mother. Samuel continued. "We begin the evening with a wild mushroom velouté, layered with sage and a hint of truffle. The first course is beet-cured salmon with crème fraîche and dill pollen—a light, bright contrast to the richness that follows." He gestured subtly toward the kitchen. "Our entrée tonight is a navarin d'agneau, slowly braised in sherry and finished with orange blossom honey and fresh tarragon. It's served with pomme purée and grilled white asparagus brushed in lemon oil and fleur de sel."

The guests murmured their approval.

"For our vegetarian guests," he added, turning toward Hadiya with a warm nod, "we've prepared a saffron-spiced vegetable tagine with fig and almond couscous—a recipe I developed for my daughter. I'm honored to share it with you."

The table stirred again—voices rising with eagerness.

"And for dessert," he said with a smile, "you'll have a choice between a citrus crème brûlée and a dark chocolate gâteau with sea salt caramel and raspberry coulis. Or," he added, with a brief glance toward Aimée, "you may wish to try them both."

A soft ripple of laughter moved around the table, and Aimée felt her cheeks warm.

Samuel gave one final nod. "Cooking is, at its heart, about connection. So, it means a great deal to share this space—and this meal—with all of you. Thank you for being here."

As Samuel moved around the table, shaking hands and offering quiet hellos, he paused briefly beside Aimée. They exchanged a few words, just long enough for William to catch a softness in her expression. He couldn't make out what they were saying, but he noticed the way his mother smiled. It wasn't the polite kind she offered strangers, but a real one.

Throughout dinner, William kept stealing glances at his mother. She laughed easily, leaned into conversations, and even sparred playfully with Chef Ramsey over finishing salts and citrus infusions. Her eyes lit up, not just at the dishes but at the exchange of ideas, the shared language of chefs.

Around the table, the conversation flowed like fine wine. Rosa, Montgomery, and Winston traded stories of old Nightingale. Some were funny, touching, a few with just enough scandal to keep things lively. Hadiya offered tales from her food cart, including the night a raccoon absconded with an entire bag of baklava. Lina remarked that Shelley's Rare Book Room reminded her of a Viennese library from her youth, only with less peeling paint and far friendlier ghosts.

As the sun finally set behind the hills of Imperial Heights, the Art Nouveau dining room remained alive, silver flashing under candlelight, conversations rising and falling in warm cadence—all things delicate and dreamlike.

# Chapter Fifty-five

## *From the Heart*

After dinner, Winston stood and declared, "Ladies and gentlemen, *le moment tant attendu* of our *soirée* now awaits you. Monty will escort everyone into the music room for tonight's concert."

A gentle, excited murmur ran through the guests as chairs slid back and people rose, following the curved corridor toward the salon.

But before William could slip out with all of them, Winston intercepted him. "Maestro—no, no, no. You can't enter with the audience. Definitely not," he said, throwing up a playful hand. "Let me show you the performer's entrance. It's on the far side of the music room. Follow me."

"*Bonne chance, mon chéri*," his mother said, giving him a quick hug. "I'm so excited for you."

With that, she drifted off to join the others.

William didn't answer—a surge of panic blindsided him, rising fast, uncontrollable. Planning the recital, keeping the secret from his mother, had been fun. Practicing for it was joyful, even exciting. But now the reality pressed down—the historic mansion, the tuxedo, the formal dinner, the expectant crowd, and Monnier's piano. A wave of anxiety broke over him.

In a daze, he trailed after Winston down a back hallway, his chest tightening.

*What was I thinking? I can't play a piano recital. Not tonight. I'm not ready. This is crazy.*

They reached a small vestibule outside the music room—a threshold between two worlds, lit only by a faint glow seeping through the cracks of the double doors.

"I'll give the guests a moment to settle in," Winston said. "Then I'll flutter the lights—that's the cue for everyone to take their seats. When the house lights fade to black, take a breath. That's your signal. I'll bring up the track lights on the piano, and that's when you enter."

He placed a hand on William's back. "It's been years since anyone has performed in this room. I've been looking forward to hearing you play tonight, Maestro. Break a leg."

And then… he was gone.

William stood alone in the darkness of the vestibule.

The muffled conversation seeped through the cracks in the door, along with a thin sliver of light.

His thoughts turned chaotic.

*I can't do this. This was a mistake. I've never played a recital before. I don't even remember how the first song begins…*

His breath came fast and shallow. He felt nauseous.

*If I throw up, they can't make me perform. Maybe food poisoning. No one can expect you to play if you're sick…*

He could hear the guests settling in—laughter, voices, chairs scraping gently on the parquet.

And then… the lights dimmed.

*No. No. I can't do this.*

His heart pounded like Ukumari hammering a djembe, his thoughts racing like Densho on a sugar rush.

Then he remembered, *My thinking stones. Yes!*

The three basalt stones—hand-selected at Beacon Rock for their shape and calming feel. He always kept one in his pocket for nerves and focus. But tonight—just for luck—he'd packed all three.

At least he thought he had…

He thrust his hand into his tuxedo pocket. Empty. Nothing.

*Noooo—mon Dieu… what have I done?*

He could picture the stones clearly—still sitting on the dresser, forgotten in his rush to get ready for the recital. Panic threatened to consume him.

And then Winston turned off the music room lights—utter darkness.

The silence was deafening.

He froze at the threshold, as if opening those doors meant leaping into an abyss.

And then… from the dark stillness… he sensed a voice.

*You don't need the stones, Sparky.*

William gasped. He spun around—but the voice hadn't come from anywhere. It had arrived like a thought, yet not his own.

*You don't need the stones…* the voice repeated.

It was clear. Steady. Somehow… familiar.

Into the void, in a desperate hush, he whispered, *"Dad?"*

William pressed his hand to his chest and felt the familiar shape of his father's Master Samaritan ring. He pulled the chain and pendant from beneath his shirt, clasping it tight.

At that moment, light burst through the crack between the vestibule's double doors. The track lighting had come on, catching his eyes.

Drawn by the light, he stepped forward, pushing through the doors—into the illumination and the sound of rising applause.

He could only make out the outlines of bodies in their seats. He bowed with more composure than he felt, then made his way to the piano bench as the applause subsided. Placing his hands in his lap, fingertips lightly touching, he closed his eyes briefly. In his mind, he ran through the Four Elements one last time.

*Earth—feet on the floor, sit bones on the bench, fingertips touching.*

*Air—soften the mind, feel expanded.*

*Water—follow the breath, tune into the flow.*

*Fire—open the heart, feel the tingling inner energy within.*

He opened his eyes, set his hands gently on the keys, and began with "Life is But a Dream." A comfortable opener—simple but expressive. As he settled into the familiar tune, with its flowing left-hand accompaniment, his anxiety eased.

Madeleine's Érard piano felt astonishingly responsive beneath his fingers. With mind and body in balance, he allowed himself to go deeper, shaping each phrase, coloring each note. Piece by piece, his confidence grew, the music guiding his expression as his fingers moved freely over the keys.

When it was time for "Ode to Joy," Miss Rosa handed out the special Piano Zen lyrics. As William played the familiar tune, the audience began to sing:

*Sing to joy and gladness now and*

*Ever more to freedom's song.*

*Open up our hearts and minds*

*Into a world where all belong.*
*Blue the sky and green the forest*
*All our children can run free,*
*And through music bring together.*
*All who sing this melody.*

Then came the final piece. "Inner Sojourn." Madeleine Monnier's composition. William took a deep breath. He would not force the Flow—not now. He simply opened himself, letting go of effort and expectation. He played intuitively, from the heart, his fingers moving without conscious command.

In that heightened awareness, he reached deeper—past technique, past thought. What was Monnier trying to tell him through her music? Before any words could surface in his mind, he felt the meaning move through him. He rode that wave all the way to the final note of "Inner Sojourn," letting it linger, fading into silence.

And then… the room erupted in warm applause.

In a slight daze, William rose, steadied himself on the corner of the Érard piano, and made a couple of awkward bows.

He could see silhouettes in the doorway—a small cluster of kitchen and serving staff applauding. He could even make out Chef Ramsey, the tallest among them.

Winston was the first to leap from his seat and shake William's hand. Miss Rosa, Hadiya, and Lina Bauch each embraced him in turn.

And then his mother.

They held each other for a long moment. She drew him in, then squeezed him once more, whispering softly in his ear, "This hug is from your father."

# Chapter Fifty-Six

## *The Return*

At last, the evening settled back into its gentle rhythms—champagne passed around, Montgomery thanking the staff and Chef Ramsey. A few brief toasts followed. As the night drew to a close, Winston and Montgomery escorted the guests to the door, where two limousines waited beneath the porte cochere.

William exchanged quick hugs with Winston, Professor Montgomery, and the others before joining his mother at the waiting limousine. Winston placed a hand on Anthony's shoulder, the two men standing together in the doorway of the Prescott Mansion, watching their guests depart.

Before William and his mother got into their limo, Miss Rosa called out to them, "Do you mind if I ride with you to the Gate Lodge?"

"*Mais bien sûr*, Rosa." Aimée touched her arm. "Come with us."

Once they were settled inside the limo, Rosa turned serious. "William, I need to show you something at the Gate Lodge. I wanted to mention it earlier, but with the concert and everything, I figured it could wait until afterward."

"Sure," William said, though he couldn't tell whether the news would be good or bad.

Rosa asked the chauffeur to stop outside the Gate Lodge, just beyond the tall iron gates of the mansion. As the three of them approached the door, she turned with a solemn expression.

"I got a call Friday night. Completely out of the blue. I had to take a last-minute flight to San Francisco. It's been quite a whirlwind. I'm still processing it all."

She turned the bolt and opened the door. The moment they stepped inside, Misha came bounding over to greet them.

"Hi, Misha!" William exclaimed, kneeling to pet her.

Misha meowed excitedly—more intensely than usual. As she placed her paws on his shoulders, she blew a soft puff of air into his ear. William laughed, scratching behind her ears.

Then he froze. Something had moved in the corner of his eye.

Another cat was cautiously entering the room—another Himalayan, slightly darker in color.

William's mouth fell open. He turned to Rosa. "Is that… Sasha?"

Rosa nodded, tears welling in her eyes.

"Oh my gosh," William said in a hushed voice. "Mom, that's Sasha. Misha's sister. She's been missing for two years.

"Come here… come here, Sasha," William said, clicking his tongue softly. "Come here, girl."

Sasha hesitated.

Then Misha trotted over and nuzzled her sister. The two cats rubbed heads, transferring scent. Slowly, Sasha crept forward, sniffed William's outstretched hand, then brushed her cheek against it. He stroked her gently. Her tail rose, and she purred loudly. The two sisters began to circle him as he did his best to pet them both.

"He told me about your missing cat," Aimée said. "*Mon dieu.* Is that where you found her—in San Francisco?"

Misha and Sasha flopped onto their sides, presenting their bellies for William to rub.

Rosa lowered herself onto the arm of a nearby chair, watching the cats with glistening eyes. "It's still a mystery. My best guess? Sasha wandered deep into the Prescott Forest—maybe met a hiker or wandered into a neighborhood. Someone must have picked her up and taken her home. Maybe a tourist from San Francisco or someone who later moved there."

"Sasha never liked collars," Rosa continued. "Always slipped them off. So, I had the vet put in a microchip. I suspect she escaped again down in San Francisco—maybe got scared in the city. A good Samaritan must have found her and taken her to a vet, who scanned her chip. That's how they reached me."

She looked down at the two cats, rolling and purring in tandem. "You should've seen them at the reunion. Snuggling. Grooming each other. It was the sweetest thing I've ever witnessed."

William picked up Sasha and held her. She nestled into his arms and began to make soft, growling coos as he gently rocked her.

"Misha's a lover," Rosa chuckled, "but Sasha's a full-on lap cat. You could pet her all day." She gave William a wink. "Sorry to be dramatic about it all. I just wanted the sister reunion to be a surprise."

"It feels like a miracle," William said. "I can't believe it."

He set Sasha back on the floor.

Rosa glanced out the window. "It's getting late. I don't want to keep your driver waiting." She approached the door, pausing to see whether Sasha might try to bolt, but the cat simply sat grooming herself, calm and content.

She turned back to William with a warm smile. "Lovely evening. Wonderful concert. I'm looking forward to our next Piano Zen lesson."

"Me too," William said.

After one last cheek scratch for Misha, he joined his mother, and they stepped through the door of the Gate Lodge toward the waiting limo, carrying the evening's excitement with them into the stillness of the night.

# Chapter Fifty-Seven

## *The Ravine*

That night at home, before getting into bed, William passed by his desk and noticed the three basalt thinking stones from Beacon Rock—still sitting quietly in a row.

School waited in the morning, along with two important quizzes, but his thoughts couldn't hold their shape anymore. He lay in bed, the room softening around him as the day's excitement finally settled.

Within moments, exhaustion pulled him under. The dreamworld, as it always did, came calling, and William drifted into sleep.

When he opened his eyes again, he was lying on soft grass. He sat up slowly, blinking through a warm haze that wavered above a marble walkway in an expansive courtyard. His first instinct was to reach for his backpack, to check the Piano Zen book. But the backpack wasn't there.

The dorje resting against his chest had begun to glow—a soft inner light through his shirt, like a candle behind frosted glass.

He drew in a quiet breath. "Parthenopolis."

He knew this place—the Court of the Cosmos. He had stood here before, amid the fountains, the arches, and the translucent domed temples. He felt the city's quiet vibration, as if it were tuning him like an instrument.

"William Longfellow Emerson, so happy to see you again."

William turned. Master Wu Wei stood a few paces away.

"I was on my way to the Praetorium," Wu Wei said. "Would you like to walk with me?"

The name settled quickly in his memory—the Praetorium. He'd been there before.

William nodded.

"Good," Wu Wei said. "Come. There is something I wish to show you."

William rose and followed him beneath a soaring archway. They crossed a wide esplanade in silence. Towering spires rose through drifting clouds; a distant glass dome shimmered with faint color.

After a while, Wu Wei spoke. "Strange, isn't it—how real this all feels? As if you're awake, not dreaming."

William glanced at him. "Wait—what do you mean?"

"Well, tell me," Wu Wei asked. "Where do you think you are, right now?"

"Parthenopolis, of course," William said. The words felt steady at first, then wavered.

"Are you sure? How certain are you?"

A faint jolt moved through him. He stopped walking, breath tightening as he tried to focus. The Court of the Cosmos... the colonnades... the temples of Parthenopolis. All of it felt solid, unmistakably real. He looked down at his hands, turning them over, feeling the weight of himself in this place.

He looked back into Master Wu Wei's eyes. As he did, the City of Light began to blur, fading. He took a small step back and stumbled over a stone bench behind him. At once, the world gave way, and he tumbled backward into a vast emptiness—falling as though he had slipped from the sheer cliffs of Mount Parthena.

His fall seemed endless as he plunged through layers of dream realms, some familiar, some unknown. The farther he dropped, the darker it became. His descent quickened, spinning out of control, hurling him toward a blackness below, and he reached out his hands in a futile attempt to slow himself.

He closed his eyes, bracing for impact.

In the next instant—only silence.

When he opened them again, he was suspended in a cavernous space—dark, damp, with only the faintest glimmer of light. He was still floating, but the heaviness of the space seemed to press in on him. Slowly, his vision adjusted. Shapes emerged from the darkness, resolving into a room.

A bed.

A figure lying asleep.

William drifted closer, observing the body with curiosity. He couldn't see the face, yet somehow, he knew this person completely—their history, their joys, their fears—everything rising inside him at once, intimate and overwhelming.

Then a force emanated from the sleeping form, a gravitational pull drawing him toward it. His weightlessness began to falter. The closer he drifted, the cloudier his mind became, the heavier, almost clay-like, he felt. The energy of his body began to contract, compressing inward. As it did, memories of Master Wu Wei, the colors and sounds of Parthenopolis, began to slip away.

Instinctively, he reached for the Dream Dorje at his chest.

The next instant, William was sitting on a wooden bench overlooking a forested valley. Before him, rolling hills folded into the distance. He drew a sharp breath. The air was cool and still, the sky a pale quilt of clouds—except for one slender ray of sunlight breaking through.

The place felt familiar, though the memory hovered just out of reach.

He rose slowly. A deep ravine opened below, veiled in fog and tangled branches. Something in the chasm breathed—a wind rising from the hidden depths, curling around him like a whisper.

A narrow trail led downward. Beside it stood an old wooden sign, the lettering weathered but legible: *La Vallée des Cloches.* Curiosity tugged at him, luring him toward the path that descended into the narrow canyon below.

The path was perilous—steep, slick, cut into tight switchbacks that forced him to move slowly, hand brushing damp stone. Any misstep felt as though it could send him slipping into the shadowed depths. Fog thickened as he descended, swallowing the trail, cooling his skin. The world dimmed to shades of white and gray. For a time, the path vanished into haze, each step appearing only as he took it. Then, gradually, the mist eased. Shadows stirred, gathering into shapes.

Great pillars materialized around him—not stone but trunks, massive and as straight as the columns of an ancient temple. Redwoods. A whole cathedral of them, rising from the ravine floor, their crowns lost high above in a canopy that turned the lone ray of sunlight into drifting gold dust.

A gong sounded in the distance. Low and resonant. As if some unseen bell tower had struck a single note.

The forest responded.

Birdsong erupted overhead—hundreds of voices waking at once, fluttering from nest to nest, a sudden chorus spiraling through the vaulted canopy. William closed his eyes and let the sound wash over him.

When their song finally faded away, he opened them again and noticed a faint glow beyond one of the largest tree trunks ahead.

He moved around its enormous girth—the bark ridged and tinted a cinnamon-red hue. On the other side, a staircase emerged: an intricate wooden structure winding upward through the giant trees like a helix. The glow seemed to come from a large platform at the end of the staircase.

Compelled by the mystery, he began to climb. Each step rose into deeper quiet, the forest floor slipping farther away beneath him. When he reached the upper platform, he understood the source of the glow.

Master Wu Wei sat upon a large bench, his form suffused with a soft, pearl-white radiance. He gazed out across the treescape.

"Greetings, Dream Traveler," he said, still facing forward. "The view from here is quite stunning. Please—sit with me."

William stepped closer and lowered himself onto the bench.

The redwood forest unfurled before them in a sweeping panorama—ancient trunks rising like guardians, wisps of fog and drifting light weaving between them.

For a long time, neither spoke.

A bell struck in the distance, its resonance threading through the ravine like a trembling of the earth. William stepped to the railing. "I wonder where that sound is coming from," he murmured. "I've heard it before. Is there a church nearby?"

"No," Wu Wei replied. "That sound is not of this place. Its source lies far from here… in the deeper realms of the dream worlds."

The bell rang again—clearer this time—and the Dream Dorje against William's chest stirred in response.

"Does it have something to do with the Fifth Element?" William asked. "Is that where it's coming from?"

Wu Wei didn't answer.

William lifted the dorje.

This time it glowed with a sky-blue fire, and as he held it, the light seemed to ignite his hand with the same-colored flame. It moved through him—up his arm, across his chest—until he and the dorje pulsed in rhythm with the same radiance, as though body and talisman were no longer separate but vibrating in one shared harmony. It drew him inward until the world around him dissolved. Time loosened. Even the platform beneath his feet fell away.

When he finally raised his eyes, Master Wu Wei was gone.

So was the platform.

So was the ravine.

# Chapter Fifty-Eight

## *The Threshold*

Night had fallen—not gradually but all at once, as though a curtain of darkness had been drawn. William stood on a long, open shoreline that curved beyond sight in both directions. Moonlight lay across the world in silver bands, revealing the hush of waves. But this ocean moved as if it were alive—more energy than water, a vast, humming sea of light.

Along the shoreline rested a multitude of boats, each one faintly luminous, shimmering in every hue imaginable—and shades that seemed beyond the range of earthly color.

He heard the sound again from the ravine.

It was closer now, warmer—more rich in tone. It was as if all the music of the world had gathered itself into a single, flawless chord. The sound rolled across the cosmic sea, carried along like the wind, lifting soft waves along the shore. The boats rocked gently in response.

This celestial tone seemed to be calling to him, expressing itself inside him in a way that words could never reach.

He felt drawn to its source. The origin lay somewhere on the horizon, beyond sight, across the cosmic sea before him. Perhaps one of these boats could take him there. Even as the thought formed, a small vessel brightened—like a beacon—casting a flare in the same sky-blue hue that shimmered around his body.

As he approached, he noticed something strange about the motion of the waves. Each crest rolled toward the shore, carrying the celestial sound with it—yet a second rhythm moved in the opposite direction, a returning wave traveling back toward the unseen source. The two currents—outward and returning—interlaced like breathing.

William placed a hand on the illuminated boat. He drew it into the water, angling its bow toward the horizon. Then, like a surfer waiting for the right swell, he steadied himself. A returning wave rose beneath him. He pushed off.

The vessel lifted, gliding forward as the wave gathered strength. Then it carried him—smoothly, silently—farther and farther from the shore, bearing him toward the source.

The dream worlds he had known appeared, not as solid places but as drifting veils. The dark hush of the Whispering Woods, the Palace of Ubar, the Awakening Orchid, all appeared as reflections across the rippling water. Each scene flickered past like a page turned too quickly to grasp.

The wave climbed higher. Parthenopolis glimmered far below, its luminous domes and soaring towers reduced to tiny lanterns floating on a mirrored sea.

Then, even those vanished.

The returning wave lifted him toward the farthest edges of the dream worlds—past the place where mountains ended and wonder began. The boat rose higher until even the horizon dropped away and he found himself borne gently yet impossibly far, into the boundless night sky.

He drifted in silence, the cosmic sea carrying him toward swirling masses of light. Galaxies—vast, innumerable—turned slowly in the dark of space. They stretched beyond comprehension, farther than any mind from the physical world could conceive. Like the boats on the shoreline, each galaxy radiated its own unique color.

William's vessel adjusted course without his guiding it, angling toward one galaxy among the many. Its spiral shimmered entirely in the same sky-blue that lived within him.

As he neared, the stars of that radiant wheel sharpened into something strange. Each point of light flattened, revealing itself as a luminous panel—drifting—thousands upon thousands fanning out like petals, circling around a brilliant central sun of pure white he couldn't look at directly.

These weren't stars at all.

They were records—living, breathing archives.

Like the sleeping figure he had hovered above, each panel felt familiar, intimately so. Each containing the full record of a life—its incalculable number of thoughts, feelings, words, and actions.

Every panel glowed with the same sky-blue hue.

He drew his vessel closer.

The nearest panel brightened, revealing a scene, a life compressed into a single flash.

A Phoenician sailor leaned over the railing of a wooden sailing ship, salt wind stirring his dark hair as an amethyst sunset spilled across the Mediterranean.

Another panel drifted near.

A Roman engineer, sleeves rolled back, worked with solemn precision as, using massive pulleys, he guided stones into place along a rising aqueduct—an artery of water meant to feed a distant, thirsty city.

A flare of blue caught his peripheral vision.

A tribal woman wrapped in wolf-fur hurried along a snowy ridge, an infant pressed to her chest. Behind her, the earth trembled beneath the thunder of mounted warriors—Huns sweeping down through the frozen forests like a living storm.

Another screen peeled away from the spiral, gliding closer.

A man in a world far older still—older than Rome, older than Babylon and Egypt—carved immense blocks of stone with nothing but the power of the black obsidian. With every gesture, the blocks reshaped themselves and then floated with precision into place as though obeying his intention. An enormous temple rose around the man, its angles crisp, its purpose unknowable.

Another screen came alive.

A woman sat beneath a half-open shōji window, her black hair gathered into a simple knot. Her kosode was patterned with soft florals, and her obi caught the light as she leaned forward. A brush hovered above a drawing coming to life on rice paper. William knew the scene taking shape—the cliff, the father and son, the persimmon tree above them. Then, with a single, quiet stroke, the artist added a soft orange to the fruit on the branch.

Panels continued to drift by—tens of thousands of them—each one familiar in the same impossible way. He sensed their lives not as strangers but as voices humming from a single chord.

Then, from somewhere within that chord, one note shone brighter. It seemed to draw William's vessel to it.

A woman in a violet silk gown sat before an Érard concert grand, the performance hall full to bursting. Her posture was serene, luminous—her fingers commanding the music with effortless grace.

A name surfaced.

Madeleine Monnier.

William's breath quickened.

Then another screen beckoned him forward, as if summoned—an echo of the same bright note, but older.

A girl in lavender silk, silver embroidery catching the candlelight, leaned over a small, beautifully crafted piano—its shape slender, more delicate than the Érard. Her eyes were closed in rapture, each note she played sparkling, as though the keys themselves were stars.

Her face turned slightly, radiant and serene. William knew her.

Katarina von Paradis.

The name rose through him like a forgotten melody, startling in its clarity. He watched her fingers move—fluid, sure, overflowing with a devotion he understood. Something in the music tugged at him.

Then a spark of recognition flared—not just for Katarina but for the instrument and its maker, Cristofori the mystic.

The moment the thought formed, the panels with images around him folded inward, collapsing into streaks of light. The cosmic sea tilted beneath him. A pull awakened—drawing him downward. Darkness and starlight spiraled past. His vision blurred; sound and color merged as the wave of remembrance carried him like a tide.

In an instant, the motion ceased.

William opened his eyes.

He was sitting on a marble bench. And rising before him—mysterious and unmistakable—stood the Praetorium.

# Chapter Fifty-Nine

## *The Praetorium*

As often happened in the dream world, William remembered little of how he had arrived—only that he was here and that something within him recognized this place.

He rose from the marble bench and faced the massive structure before him. It resembled the Pantheon of Rome, yet not the weathered monument he knew from books. These columns gleamed with veins of deep red and honey-gold. Their painted capitals shimmered with lapis and warm amber. Long banners of crimson and blue rippled between them in a slow, graceful rhythm.

Above, the pediment blazed with color—gods, musicians, and animals carved in relief, each figure still alive with blues and greens and deep ochre. Even the bronze doors shone as if newly cast, their surfaces shifting with movement in the changing light.

*This is different,* William thought. *Not like the faded Roman one... this feels alive.*

He wasn't sure how he had ended up seated before it, or why the air felt thick with memory. But some part of him sensed that whatever he had come to find, it was waiting for him inside.

He let his gaze drift briefly across the plaza. Other buildings rose in the distance—arched walkways, domes, and towers shaped from marble and sun-washed stone—each vibrant with movement as figures drifted between them like currents of light. The whole city seemed to breathe, luminous and interconnected. And yet, even in its splendor, nothing drew him the way the Praetorium did. Its presence eclipsed the rest, quiet and commanding.

William stepped toward the entrance. Before he could reach the doors, the massive bronze panels swung inward of their own accord.

Inside, a vast rotunda opened around him. Sunlight streamed through the oculus at the dome's center, casting a silver beam onto the polished floor.

The interior shimmered with color. The walls were sheathed in panels of porphyry and green serpentine, veined like rivers. The coffered dome above glowed with painted stars, each recessed panel edged in gold so the whole ceiling seemed to shimmer. Bronze statues stood in the niches, polished to a soft radiance, and mosaics rippled across the floor in geometric patterns.

Then William noticed them—marble benches spaced around the perimeter, each with a softly glowing screen hovering above it. Now and then, someone appeared on a bench, as if materializing out of thin air. Some rose and wandered the rotunda, dazzled by its grandeur, vanishing into distant corridors. Others stayed seated, wholly absorbed in the screens before them, and when they were finished, they simply faded away.

William stepped closer and settled onto one of the benches. The screen before him was mounted on a simple pedestal. When he touched it, the whole panel brightened, pulsing softly with light.

A three-dimensional cube rose from the center—clear and crystalline, turning slowly as if suspended in air. He brushed one of its panels and it opened like a journal, unfolding into a tiered structure of years and days. William narrowed his focus on the year 1730 and touched it.

At once, hundreds of points of light burst into view, scattering like fireflies before settling into tidy rows of entries by unknown authors. Each page revealed sketches of music—fragments, motifs, and sometimes entire melodies without accompaniment. William scrolled slowly until one entry caught his attention.

He touched a small musical-note icon. A melody began—soft, distant, almost imaginary. William looked around; there was no speaker nearby. Then he understood: the sound was unfolding inside him. As he focused, it sharpened with perfect clarity, as though he were hearing through an inner ear he had forgotten he possessed.

He recognized it at once: "Minuet in G"—a melody he had always believed was by Bach. Yet, here, no composer's name appeared. Only the melody itself, offered without origin, waiting for someone to carry it onward.

He flipped a few pages.

There it was again—the same melody, but this time carried by a broken-chord accompaniment for the left hand, a style made famous by composer Domenico Alberti.

A small jolt of recognition ran through him.

It was the exact version found in his Piano Zen lesson book.

William continued scrolling through the years until another familiar melody caught his attention. He let the music play inside his head—"Ode to Joy."

When he tapped the entry, multiple drafts unfolded before him: fragments, variations, half-formed ideas. Someone had returned to the theme again and again—altering rhythms, shifting intervals, refining the line until it felt inevitable. Some versions wandered so far they seemed to be entirely different melodies searching for their true shape.

William looked up. Master Wu Wei was approaching across the rotunda, lifting a hand in greeting.

"William Longfellow Emerson. Hello. I see you have been exploring the Praetorium's book of records."

William nodded. "It's amazing. I could stay here for hours."

Wu Wei chuckled softly. "Yes, I believe you could. But I suspect you arrived with another purpose this time."

William hesitated. "Oh… I guess. I remember reaching the Praetorium and walking inside, but I don't remember what I was looking for."

"Are you certain you do not remember, Dream Traveler?"

William glanced around the rotunda. Yes—there *was* something. He felt it now, faint but insistent. But what?

His gaze drifted toward the center of the chamber beneath the oculus. Something was there. He could sense it, though it hovered at the edge of his perception.

William relaxed his mind and softened his gaze. Slowly, a shape came into focus. A polished white piano stood beneath the silver beam of light from the oculus.

William knew it instantly.

Cristofori's Dream Piano.

# Chapter Sixty

## *Dream Piano*

William stood frozen, breathless.

This was it—the first piano. The wellspring of them all. The instrument the Element Masters had spoken of in hushed reverence. Forged in the dream worlds, unbound by strings, metal, or felt hammers. A piano that responded not only to touch but to the heart.

Wu Wei stepped back, extending a hand toward the bench. "Go on, William. It is waiting for you."

William approached slowly. He noticed that the keys were reversed—dark where they should have been light, light where they should have been dark—as if the instrument were a mirror of every piano he had ever known.

He sat at the bench and rested his fingers on the surface. Then, gently, he pressed Middle C. The note rang out—pure, crystalline. A wash of blue light rippled outward from the piano, spreading through the rotunda. When he lifted his finger, the color faded.

He tried another, then another. Each note unfurled its own hue, sending waves of light dancing across the dome. He played a few melodic fragments, then let his hands fall into rich, ringing chords. The tone was resonant— warm and alive. It felt less like he was playing the piano and more like channeling something deeper, some hidden current of expression.

Drawn by the sound and the spectacle, several Dream Walkers stopped in their tracks. Even some Dream Travelers lifted their hands from their screens, turning to listen.

He played on, and the rotunda responded—waves of light and sound blooming outward, as though the music were shaping the very air. Joy rose in him, bright and effortless. Soon, he was improvising freely, spinning new melodies into the space. Colors arched overhead, painting the dome into a living fresco.

Wu Wei stepped closer.

"Cristofori was a Soul Traveler, William. He created this piano beyond the limits of time and space, embedding a Pythagorean Code into its design so it could serve as a bridge between the worlds above and below."

His voice softened.

"Would you like to see… the Code?"

William answered with a slow nod.

Wu Wei gestured for him to rise. "Stand with me, William."

William rose from the bench and moved next to Wu Wei.

"Now," he said, "hold your Dream Dorje. And look again—past the instrument's shape, into the architecture of light that makes its sound possible."

William closed his fingers around the dorje.

The air around the piano shifted. The white lacquered case began to quiver, a faint hum rising in pitch as though the instrument itself were awakening.

All at once, the piano turned translucent. Not transparent like glass but outlined in living geometry. The outer case dissolved into golden spirals, arcs, and soft blue ratios floating in the air. Strings hovered freely like threads of silver tone, vibrating faintly.

Within the body of the piano, a ghostly lattice appeared—an architecture that had always been present but never seen. Sacred ratios—3:2, 4:3, 5:4—flickered across the harp frame and along the keys, as though inscribed in starlight.

And then William understood: the entire instrument—strings, bridges, keys, hammers—was not merely mechanical but mathematical and multidimensional. A cosmic diagram housed within a harmonic engine. The golden mean wound through its frame. The Fibonacci curve swept through its string layout. The intervals between notes were not only physical—they were relationships of space, energy, and emotion.

Every line of the piano's design pulsed with precision.

Wu Wei's voice came beside him, low and reverent. "*This* is what Cristofori embedded. Not just a mechanism but a code. A key to harmonize matter and spirit. The Four Elements unlock its physical form. But only the Fifth Element, what we call Ether—the breath between worlds—can fully animate it.

"As you have just witnessed," Wu Wei said, "here in the dream world, the Code can be seen. In the lower worlds, it remains hidden."

Slowly, the luminous geometry folded inward. The ratios dimmed. The case re-formed. The piano stood once more in its familiar shape—white lacquer and gold inlay, still beautiful but no longer transcendent.

William stood there, transfixed. The vision felt dreamlike, yet he sensed the ratios and celestial architecture had etched themselves inside him—as if the Code now lived within him.

# Chapter Sixty-One

## *Reunion*

Wu Wei's voice came gently, almost playfully, pulling him back. "There are some friends who would love to hear you play."

"Friends?" William blinked, startled.

Wu Wei lifted a hand toward one of the archways. From the far end of the rotunda came Densho, Ukumari, Quetzal, Ning Jing, and Amara.

William's heart leapt. He didn't wait—he ran to meet them.

"Densho!" he cried as the white-tufted marmoset leapt into his arms. Ukumari bounded forward and nuzzled into his side, nearly knocking them over.

"William," Amara said, embracing him. "We've missed you."

Ning Jing laughed and reached out to steady them as Quetzal circled overhead, singing a bright, lilting melody.

As they exchanged hugs and greetings, their voices overlapped in cheerful chatter.

"Ukumari and I composed a piano duet called *Paws and Claws,*" Densho said proudly, giving Ukumari a playful nod. "We want to play it for you sometime—once we've practiced a bit more, of course."

"No surprise there," Ukumari chuckled. "Densho can't relax. He gets too excited and always rushes the tempo." The bear rolled his eyes dramatically, making the others laugh. "But with a little more practice," he said, nodding, "we'll be ready to perform it for you!"

"I'd love to hear it sometime. Maybe I can help you write the music down," William said.

Amara came forward. "William, our Piano Zen lesson together inspired me," she said, beaming. "I've started teaching beginner piano lessons at the Palace of Ubar—mostly little ones, but a few grown-ups, too. One of them is eighty-four years old and insists on starting every lesson with a bow, like the Elements Masters."

Everyone laughed.

Ning Jing stepped closer. "I brought you something, William—a new tea blend I created just for you. Calming, grounding and good for clarity." She reached into her satchel and drew out a small tin; its lid engraved with a lotus.

William opened the tin and inhaled deeply. "It smells amazing. Thank you."

William looked around for a place to set the tin box—only then realizing he had nowhere to put it.

Master Wu Wei approached, holding out William's backpack. "Perhaps you were looking for this," he said with a warm smile.

William's eyes lit up. "I was! Thank you." He slipped the lotus tin carefully inside.

They gathered in a tight cluster, exchanging stories and laughter.

From the opposite side of the rotunda, Element Masters Shinichi, Zaria Rumi, and Lan Su entered. William turned to greet them as they approached, each offering a graceful bow of welcome.

"Everyone wished to come to Parthenopolis," Wu Wei said, "to hear you play the Dream Piano."

Wu Wei gestured toward the center of the rotunda. At once, a ring of benches materialized around the piano. The guests moved toward them and took their seats as a stillness settled over the hall. Densho hopped lightly onto Amara's shoulder.

William glanced at Master Wu Wei, who gave a slow nod. He then sat on the piano bench and removed the Piano Zen lesson book from his backpack—opening it to "Inner Sojourn." Placing his hands on the keys, he drew a slow breath—then began to play Madeleine Monnier's composition.

The first chords rang out. The rotunda blossomed with color—amethyst, then rose, then teal. He moved to the next measure. Another burst of light unfurled through the hall. With each passing note came more color—soft, otherworldly. As he played, he felt himself gliding along a ribbon of pure musical expression.

Like dreaming while awake.

His fingers flowed across the keys with ease, more gracefully than ever before. There was no self-doubt. No second-guessing. Only love—pouring from his innermost being into every note.

When the final chord faded, he looked up. Everyone's eyes remained closed, their expressions peaceful, radiant— except for Densho.

The white-tufted marmoset couldn't contain himself. He leapt onto William's shoulder and hugged him tightly. Ukumari bounded over next, wrapping him in a big bear hug. Amara followed, embracing him as well. Overhead, Quetzal tweeted a melody of approval, her feathers flickering with color. The Element Masters stood, placed their hands over their hearts, and bowed.

At last, the time for farewells arrived.

Wu Wei, Shinichi, Zaria Rumi, and Lan Su departed, their robes trailing faint eddies of light.

While the rest of his Whispering Woods friends mingled, William remained near the center, his gaze drawn once more to Cristofori's piano.

Just then—a breeze caressed his face. It moved with intention, brushing the hair from his brow, then curling around him like a sigh.

He felt her presence at once.

Nasim.

She said nothing aloud, yet her message unfurled, playing in his mind like the soft music of the Whispering Woods.

*Lovely music. I savored every note. You are more than you know. Goodbye for now, dear one. Let my wind give lift to your sails whenever you wish to return.*

Her breeze rose gently, gaining strength as it spiraled upward through the dome.

William stood motionless, his heart full, his face lifted toward the light of the oculus.

"Goodbye, Nasim," he whispered.

# Chapter Sixty-Two

## *The Orange Tent*

A loud clatter jolted William awake.

He sat up in bed, blinking against the soft morning light, momentarily disoriented.

The picture frame with a photo of him and his dad on a hiking trip lay face down on the wood floor. A gust of wind had swept through an open window, toppling the frame and scattering a stack of school papers across the room.

He swung his legs over the edge of the bed, still shaking off sleep. Then—like a switch flipping—a surge of adrenaline shot through him. It was Wednesday: school, a presentation, quizzes.

He wasn't prepared.

He reached for the fallen frame and paused, holding it in his hands. The photo drew him in—the camping trip when he was a toddler, riding in the backpack, his dad's easy smile.

He gently set the frame back on his desk.

His mind snapped back into motion, scanning for everything he needed to bring to school. Papers lay strewn across the floor—his presentation notes among them. He dropped to his knees and rifled through the mess, heart pounding as he tried to pull himself together with little time left before school.

But partway through, he stopped and sat back on his heels. His thoughts drifted to the night before—the concert at the Prescott Mansion. The music room with its tall windows, mirrors, and sparkling chandeliers, and Madeleine Monnier's Érard grand piano.

Then something else surfaced, rising from the deeper recesses of his memory. Last night… while he slept. What was that all about? A wild dream he'd been having just before he woke—floating back now in fragments, somewhat hazy.

*I have to get this down*, he thought. *This is too good to lose.*

He jumped to his feet and crossed the room to where his backpack lay on the floor. He unzipped it and pulled out the small, leather-bound journal his mother had given him before his first Piano Zen lesson. She had even had the cover embossed: Dream Journal

He opened it and began scribbling—fast, almost frantic—trying to capture the details before they scattered like dandelion seeds on the wind:

*There was this strange city… I think I was in Rome. But the city wasn't ruined. It looked shiny and new.*

*I seemed to be playing a concert—in a huge round building. Looked like… the Pantheon.*

*Playing on a white piano—not like Monnier's—but one that looked like it belonged to Mozart.*

*Only… it didn't look old. It glowed like moonlight. The keys felt alive beneath my fingers.*

He paused, closed his eyes, and tried hard to remember. Then he noticed a subtle scent lingering in the air—Madeleine Monnier's perfume, Jardin sous la Pluie. Yes… he'd dabbed a bit beneath his nose in her bedroom at the mansion last night.

Somehow, it was still there. The faint fragrance sharpened his focus, as though inviting the dream to return. He leaned into it, and more details began to surface:

*There was a small audience. People in robes… kind of scary looking, but I wasn't afraid.*

*There were animals too, sitting in chairs. Weird, I know—but I've seen them before.*

*That monkey again. Always that talking monkey. Friendly little guy. And the bear—the one who always wears a vest. Like the guy in Professor Montgomery's band who plays the djembe.*

*After the concert, the monkey jumped up… on my shoulder? I think he's a… marmoset. Not sure how I know that.*

*And then—*

*When I played the piano… I saw lights. They filled the hall. Colors were dancing everywhere. Maybe it was a magic piano, like the one Sparky had in the story.*

The images were fading, dissolving as fast as he could scribble. He paused, scanning the strange fragments and scenes scrawled in haste.

None of it made much sense.

He let out a short laugh and gave a little shrug. "Wow… that was one crazy dream."

From downstairs, his mother's voice called up, "Willy, I have your breakfast ready! You better get moving before it gets too late. It's a school day—*allez, s'il te plaît!*"

"Coming, Mom!"

He closed the dream journal and slid it into his desk drawer. Then, snapping fully back to reality, he dropped to the floor and gathered his school papers, scooping up his presentation notes and shoving them into his backpack.

He bounded down the stairs, backpack thumping against his shoulder.

As he passed through the hallway, something caught his eye—a row of camping gear neatly laid out along the wall: hiking packs, sleeping bags, a portable stove.

Some of it looked brand new.

At the far end, leaning against a bundle of gear, was the orange tent.

"Mom, what's all this?" he asked, stepping into the kitchen.

Aimée turned around from the counter, setting a breakfast bowl on the table with a bright smile. "I had an idea, Willy. How about a little camping trip this weekend—with Sam Ramsey and his daughter, Jacqueline?"

William blinked.

"Camping? Us? With… Chef Ramsey?" He gave a half-laugh. "Uh… sure, I guess. Wait—he has a daughter?"

Aimée nodded, placing a spoon beside his bowl.

"She's eight years old. Never been camping before, and she's been begging her dad to take her."

William grinned. "Sure, that sounds fun. Can we hike to the waterfalls in the Rogue River Gorge?"

"That's exactly what I was thinking," she said. "Maybe we can even show them the old growth forest. You don't find anything like that in New York."

William raised an eyebrow. "Um… you sure you know how to find it, Mom?"

"We'll see," she said with a soft laugh, brushing a strand of hair from her eyes. "*Tu sais*, Willy, you can't plan everything. Sometimes life requires you to improvise a little."

William slid into his chair, still smirking at her remark. Then he glanced down at the breakfast bowl in front of him—eyebrows lifting.

"Mom, this is… different. It didn't come out of a box. What is it?"

"Oh, a homemade muesli," she said, smoothing her apron. "It's got baked oats, quinoa flakes, millet puffs, honey, almonds, walnuts…"

She looked up, as if reading from an invisible recipe overhead. "*Qu'est-ce que j'ai oublié…?* Ah—*oui*! Coconut flakes, dried apricots, cinnamon… *et des cerises séchées.*"

She dusted her hands on her apron with a little flourish. "And I stirred in homemade yogurt—*avec une touche de vanille*—and topped it with fresh Nightingale marionberries."

William scooped a spoonful, tasted it, and his eyes went wide.

"This tastes amazing, Mom!"

She smiled and reached up, slipping the band from her ponytail. Her hair tumbled loose around her shoulders.

"Watching you hone your piano skills the last few weeks gave me a nudge to find my cooking mojo again. I went to the Nightingale Farmer's Market last weekend and met some interesting organic growers."

Her lips quirked in amusement. "I may have given one of them an entire lecture on the virtues of *amandes grillées*. Though I'm not sure he was quite as passionate about almonds as I am."

A flash of recognition crossed William's face. He remembered his mom talking with Chef Ramsey at the mansion—about food, about building a team… and now this breakfast.

"Are you thinking about working at La Luz Café?"

Aimée paused, letting the question hang in the air before a playful light came to her eyes. "Well… he did say he needed to build a team. And, as you can see," she said, gesturing toward the bowl with a laugh. "I do make a pretty mean muesli."

William grinned. "*Maman, ce serait fantastique.*"

A gust of wind swept through the open kitchen window.

"*Mon dieu*, it's been breezy all morning," she said, moving to close it. But she paused, her hand resting on the sill.

She stood at the window, the wind tousling her hair. Outside, trees swayed gently in the morning light. Beyond the treetops, the distant peak of Mt. Drake rose clear against the sky.

"*Les vents du changement, mon petit,*" she murmured, almost to herself.

William looked up, still munching on a spoonful of muesli. "What did you say, Mom?"

She smiled faintly. "Oh, just something my grandmère used to say when I was a little girl."

Turning back to the sink, she rinsed a fresh batch of marionberries, the water swirling over their deep purple hues as she hummed along.

"Winds of change, *mon petit*. Winds of change."

# Chapter Sixty-Three

## *Epilogue*

William stood in the living room of his new apartment, surrounded by unopened boxes, aware that much still lay ahead. He would need this larger space now, especially to accommodate Rosa's grand piano. He had been shocked when she insisted he take it. In the end, he had agreed—grateful, though hesitant to accept such a gift.

William had never owned his own piano before, having always practiced on a rental upright. Rosa felt that if he was going to open his own Piano Zen studio in Nightingale, he should have a better instrument to teach with. Along with the piano, she gave him the old bench carved with demoiselle cranes—the one he had sat upon for so many years at his lessons—and her Tibetan bowl.

He sensed that the gift of the piano and the Tibetan bowl were Rosa's way of saying thank you for the years he had spent helping bring the online Piano Zen program into being. It had always been her dream to make the teachings available to people around the world, and she entrusted William to carry that vision forward. Only recently had they celebrated together the official launch of the program.

It was also William's long-held hope to finally have the space—and the piano—to open his first Piano Zen studio. More than fourteen years had passed since he first began lessons with Miss Rosa, and now his focus was on helping beginning students learn to play, guided by the same patience she had once shown him. Already, word had begun to spread, and inquiries from prospective students were finding their way to him.

There was still work to do before he could welcome anyone in, and the apartment around him reminded him of that. But things were already in motion.

One of the boxes held his small collection of albums—recordings he had made over the years, reflecting a love not only of classical music but of many other styles as well. He had begun recording while studying at Pacific University in Nightingale.

William earned his graduate degree in piano performance there but chose to remain in Nightingale afterward, close to family and friends. The world of competitions had never appealed to him, nor the idea of leaving to teach at a distant conservatory.

Instead, he had built a modest life as a working musician. For several years, he ran a small concert series at Professor Montgomery's Music School for the Blind, held in an intimate Edwardian-era hall with ornate moldings, a balcony, and tall windows lining one wall. He welcomed a wide range of music and frequently invited friends to perform alongside him, shaping evenings that felt less like recitals and more like shared gatherings.

As he sifted through the remaining boxes, one caught his attention. It was the kind of box you could tell had been sealed for years—carted from apartment to apartment, always meant to be opened someday. The only word written on the outside was Childhood.

He found a pair of scissors and cut through the shipping tape. Inside were things from that earlier time: an Art Nouveau frame holding a photograph of him and his father on a camping trip; a worn copy of *Walden* Miss Rosa once gave him on their hike along the Wildwood Trail; and his first Piano Zen lesson book.

He sat down and flipped through the pages he hadn't seen in years—"Ode to Joy," "Minuet in G," "Inner Sojourn." In the margins were notes from Miss Rosa, and small drawings of the characters he had once imagined as companions: the little monkey, the bear in a vest playing a drum, the resplendent quetzal bird.

Though he had completed all the Piano Zen levels long ago, those characters lived only in that first book. He had made sure to include them in the new online program. They had been his companions then, and now he could share them with other beginning pianists around the world.

Beneath the lesson book, William discovered a leather-covered journal. At first, he didn't recognize it. He turned it over in his hands. Embossed on the cover were the words *Dream Journal.*

As he opened it, something blue slipped free and fell to the floor. He picked it up, puzzled. It was an origami swan, folded from blue paper. He studied it, searching for a memory that refused—at first—to surface. Then he noticed a name written along one wing.

Ariya.

William glanced upward, as if the answer might be waiting there. And then quietly, unexpectedly—he remembered.

When he was a child, before he ever took piano lessons with Miss Rosa, there had been a girl at Shelley's bookstore. She had teased him about *The Little Prince.* She'd folded the swan and pressed it into his hand, spelling her name carefully along its wing.

William placed the journal on his kitchen table and flipped through the entries. He remembered Miss Rosa encouraging him to write down his dreams, the frantic scribblings he had made as a child, trying his best to capture what he had experienced.

The pages were filled with uneven handwriting and scattered thoughts. The monkey and the bear appeared often, along with crude sketches of other figures—a man in an aikido uniform, a woman in a hijab, a bald man with a long ponytail.

He smiled to himself. It was fun to read now, though it made little sense. Just the remnants of an overactive imagination, he decided.

The rest of the boxes would have to wait. For now, he needed to prepare his music.

Each Christmas, William was hired to play background music at the Prescott Mansion museum as tourists wandered through the rooms, taking in the holiday decorations and lights. It was always a treat to play on Madeleine Monnier's grand piano, and the evening paid well.

He put on his tuxedo, tucking the same light blue silk handkerchief into his breast pocket, as usual. With his music satchel in hand, he headed up into the hills of Imperial Heights.

As he arrived, it was clear the crowd would be larger than usual. The air was mild. The mansion glowed with light, and a dusting of snow traced the branches of the surrounding tall pines. Colored uplighting illuminated the spires, making the scene resemble one of the postcards sold in the museum gift shop.

Fortunately, William had a reserved parking spot near the back entrance for staff and performers. Traffic up the hill was heavier than usual, and he arrived a few minutes late. Rather than push through the crowds, he slipped inside and made his way up the hidden back staircase to the music room.

He settled in and began playing a light mix of jazz arrangements of holiday favorites. Visitors drifted through as he played, and he placed a small dish on the piano holding his business cards, quietly promoting his new Piano Zen studio.

William looked forward to these evenings each year. He never tired of the mansion, often wandering through its rooms during his breaks, pausing by Madeleine's bedroom.

His mother and stepfather usually came to hear him play, and this year, his stepsister Jacqueline joined them as well. She was studying geology and had returned home from college for the holidays.

William loved watching the expressions of visitors from out of town, all reacting in much the same way as they entered the elegant music room—its chandeliers reflected endlessly in the surrounding mirrors.

As usual, a few guests stopped to speak with him as they passed by. This year felt different. He finally had his Piano Zen business cards ready and would soon open his local teaching studio. With the recent launch of the online program, it felt good to see the pieces beginning to connect.

Throughout the evening, William noticed a young woman who didn't move through the mansion with the usual flow. She lingered, watching him. Her long red hair fell loosely along the sides of a knitted Irish sweater.

It wasn't unusual for people to gather near the piano, listening for a while, sometimes applauding a particularly lively holiday tune. But this felt different. The woman seemed familiar, though he couldn't place her face. She watched him closely, and when his eyes met hers, he was the one who looked away.

When William finished his set and rose to take a break, she was gone. The space where she had been standing was already filled by others drifting past. He found himself wishing she had stayed, wishing she might have come over and spoken to him—but she had vanished into the steady flow of tourists.

During his break, William wandered into the gift shop. He chose a bottle of Jardins sous la pluie for his mother, a hiking guide to the Rouge River Gorge for his stepsister, and a book on French cuisine, organized by region, for his stepdad.

When he returned to play his final set of the evening, the woman with the long red hair was there again. She watched him with a seriousness that made him feel suddenly self-conscious. As he finished an improvisation on *The Holly and the Ivy*, she finally stepped forward.

William resisted the urge to stare, looking away as she drew closer.

She picked up one of his business cards. "William Longfellow Emerson, huh?" Up close, he couldn't help noticing her emerald-green eyes. "I know you from somewhere," she said. "But I can't place it."

"Oh—um… maybe you've seen me play around town," William said. "I play a lot of gigs in Nightingale."

"No… that's not it," she murmured. "I just moved here."

"For work?"

"Yes. I was hired by the McFarland Sisters Restoration Company," she said. "I'm an architect. When the opening came up, I jumped on it."

"So, this is your first time in Nightingale?"

"Second," she said. "I came once as a kid, on vacation with my family. I wanted to see the Prescott Mansion. I've been fascinated with this place ever since I first saw it in a magazine." She laughed softly. "This probably sounds strange, but I would often dream I was the owner, walking through the hallways."

William smiled. "You don't have to explain. I've always had a strange fascination of my own—with Madeleine Monnier."

"Oh—right," she said. "You mean Prescott's wife?"

"Yes. Madeleine Monnier-Prescott. This is her piano."

She hesitated. "Sorry. I know I've been staring at you. Pretty creepy, I know. I'm just trying to figure out why you seem so familiar."

"What's your name?" William asked.

"Ariya. But it's not spelled like it is in music.…"

"Wait," William interrupted. "Do you mean A-R-I-Y-A?"

She blinked. "Yeah. How do you know that?"

William shook his head. "I can't believe this."

"What?"

"We met once before," he said. "At Shelley's bookstore. We were kids."

"Shelley's…" Ariya echoed. "Right. The big bookstore in the middle of town. I remember that. I had begged my parents to take me there. They had great architecture books." She frowned slightly. "You remember that? That was years ago."

"This is really strange, I know," William said. "I just moved into a new apartment, and in an old box, there was an origami blue swan you made for me. It fell out of my journal. You had written your name along the wing."

Ariya paused, tapping her chin. "That sounds like something I would have done back then." She smiled. "I must have thought you were cute."

She glanced at his business card. "Piano lessons, huh?" She chuckled. "I'm not sure about lessons, but how about coffee instead? I don't know anyone here yet. You could show me around town."

"Yeah," William said, smiling. "I'd love to."

"Well, it's a date then," she said. "I should probably get going. See you soon, William."

She turned to leave, then spun back around. "*The Little Prince*—right?"

"I'm sorry?" William said.

"That was the book you were holding at Shelley's," she said. Then she smiled. "Oh—now I remember you." She smiled. "I did think you were pretty cute."

The next day, William kept himself busy organizing the remaining boxes. Many were filled with music, which he placed on the bookshelf beside Rosa's piano. Nearby sat a freshly printed stack of Piano Zen lesson books, ready for his new students.

He looked around and exhaled. The studio finally felt ready.

The doorbell rang. When he opened the door, he saw a woman wearing a turquoise-blue silk sari. Her dark brown hair was tied back in a neat ponytail, and delicate gold earrings shaped like lotus blossoms caught the light. She didn't seem dressed at all for the chilly weather.

"William—hello!" she said, pulling him into a warm hug.

Startled, he returned it awkwardly.

She stepped back, studying his face. Something softened in her expression.

"Ah," she said gently. "You don't remember me, do you?"

"Excuse me?"

She gave a small, knowing smile. "Master Wu Wei said you might not remember me in this realm. I'm Amara. Your friend from the dream worlds." She paused, letting that settle.

William blinked hard. "Uh… are you here for… um, Piano Zen lessons?" he asked.

Amara laughed. "No. I teach my own students at the Palace of Ubar. I'm only here to deliver this to you."

She held out a small, dark-wooden box, its surface worn smooth with age.

William hesitated, utterly confused, then reached out and took it.

"I can't stay long," Amara said. "It's difficult to maintain a physical form in this realm, especially for a Dream Traveler. The vibrations are extremely coarse here."

William glanced down at the box, shaking his head.

"I don't understand," he said.

When he looked up again, Amara was gone.

William stepped out onto the front walkway and looked around. But there was no sign of the woman in the turquoise sari.

He stood there for a long moment—scanning the apartment complex. The brisk temperature crept in. He shivered and went back inside, closing the door behind him.

He placed the small wooden box on the kitchen table. Whatever had just happened was too strange to make sense of. For a moment, he wondered if he was dreaming—if he might wake up in his bed.

He pinched himself. Hard.

Then he sat there, staring at the box.

Curiosity finally got the better of him, and he carefully lifted the lid. Inside lay a tightly rolled piece of parchment, tied with a thin gold string. He unknotted it and unfurled the paper.

*Place this Dream Dorje around your neck. It will help you navigate the dream worlds. In time, it will stir your memory—to remember.*

*Wu Wei — Master of the Fire Element*

William stared at the strange note. Who was Wu Wei? And what was a Dream Dorje?

He peered back into the box and noticed a folded piece of purple velvet. Carefully unwrapping it, he uncovered a small metal object of silver and gold. It didn't reflect the light; it pulsed, as if alive.

He recognized the shape. It resembled the dorje from Rosa's old piano studio. But this one was smaller, suspended from a chain—a pendant meant to be worn.

William lifted it gently, watching as it cast tiny prisms of light across his skin. A faint harmonic chime seemed to resonate from within, so soft it was almost imperceptible.

He removed the chain around his neck bearing his father's Master Samaritan ring and set it beside the box. Then, with a quiet sense of surrender, he slipped the Dream Dorje over his head and let it rest against his chest.

The dream journal lay on the kitchen table. As if drawn by some unseen force, he opened it, turned to the first page, and read the first entry.

The next thing he knew, he was sitting on a wooden bench at the edge of the Smiling Pond, in the Whispering Woods of the Tall Pines.

…and he remembered.

# Author's Note

Piano Zen began as a teaching philosophy long before it became a story. In time, I discovered that the character of William was the truest voice through which these ideas wished to be shared. The novel you've just finished is complete in itself, but for readers who are curious, the Piano Zen teachings do exist in the real world, guided—much like in the story—by music, mindfulness, and listening.

You can find more at: www.pianozen.com

Wherever your own journey leads, thank you for walking part of it here.

# Meet Thomas

**T**homas Rheingans, an accomplished pianist, composer, and educator, is the visionary creator of the Piano Zen method. With a graduate degree in piano performance from the University of Illinois and over 25 years of experience, Thomas has dedicated his life to exploring music's transformative power.

As a concert pianist, Thomas has performed across the United States, captivating audiences with his expressive style. His compositions have enriched plays, musical theater, and independent films, showcasing his versatility.

Thomas's teaching career spans several colleges, where he taught classical piano, jazz, and music theory. However, it was in his private studio that he developed the revolutionary Piano Zen method, blending Eastern mindfulness practices with Western piano techniques.

The Piano Zen method is the result of Thomas's 20-year journey, inspired by mindfulness and Eastern practices of mind and body balance such as yoga, tai chi, and meditation. This holistic approach nurtures both the mind and spirit, transforming the way students engage with music through a deeper, more meditative connection.

His novel, *Piano Zen*, brings the magical world of music and self-discovery to life for readers of all ages. Through his online Piano Zen courses, speaking engagements, and written works, Thomas continues to inspire pianists worldwide.

When not at the piano, Thomas enjoys hiking throughout the Pacific Northwest and meditating. At home, he shares a house filled with music, laughter, and harmony with his wife Amy—who loves experimenting with plant-based recipes—their children Jacqueline and Samuel, and their beloved pets: two dogs, Terra and Nova, and two cats, Ginger and Gemini.